MW01231834

To Heather —
Best Regards & Thanx
for the weekly
"shock and ice!"

Barry

A Soldier's Question

A Soldier's Question

Barry A. Lauer

ISBN-13: 978-1466363601
ISBN-10: 1466363606

Printed in the United States of America

Dedication

To Janet and Lindsey

Contents

Acknowledgements

You don't begin something like this just to test your creative writing and typing skills. In addition to being half-ways interesting, the subject matter has to be reasonably available, viewed and even experienced either personally or at the feet of good storytellers and, most of all I believe, felt inside your soul. Otherwise, the finished work is simply a measure of the writer's God-given ability to put reasonably coherent thoughts down on paper or into a computer file.

In a terrific stroke of Divine Providence, especially in not having to rely on any particular God-given ability, or in spite of the unfortunate lack of it, I have been given terrific subject matter along with both spoken, first-hand knowledge and historical, written information from newspapers, battlefield accounts, and more importantly, personal letters. If I have learned nothing from this writing endeavor, I can certainly realize how much our lives have been diminished due to the "lost art" of letter-writing.

Most of all, the same blood pulses through my veins as it did the members of my Family whose stories I try to open up on the following pages. Somehow, I think that adds a bit of magic to their stories for me; specifically, I can honestly begin to say, "Yes, I understand what and how you felt."

I'm an Engineer, a Metallurgist to be precise, not a professional writer. But I was also a soldier, just like the men described next, and just like countless military men from the dusty past. As a result, although the weaponry and circumstances have changed dramatically, from individually-thrown stones to mechanically- or even electronically- energized, awesomely-powerful high-velocity projectiles, I have likely thought many of the same thoughts and asked the same answer-less questions.

I also feel privileged to relate these Family stories and lucky too, mainly because the historical research stars became magically focused, properly aligned, and near-instantly available in my lifetime.

My actual co-conspirator in this written work is my wife, Janet, family historian, genealogical sleuth, and organizational genius extraordinaire. The ability to assemble the following stories and reasonably tie them together in at least a semi-coherent package has been facilitated by her researching perseverance and dogged determination. Much of the background information that I lacked even through personal conversations with the individual soldiers in my Family was discovered through her patient digging.

Perhaps the writings that follow could have been put down in a generally historical form, mostly in an, "I remember…" manner. But I'm certain that it would have generated a body of work nowhere near as poignant or personal without Janet's uncovering of the many facts and seemingly-at-the-time small details that truly bring their subjects into focus as real people, and not just paper characters in a dusty, yellowed history book.

For example, the letters from my great-great-Grandfather, Samuel Berkey, would likely never have been noticed if Janet had not contacted military records personnel in Washington, DC. There, the very special letters written by Samuel to his parents shortly before his death were brought to light. Without Janet, these letters would likely have eternally rested in a dusky record vault, lost in the both wonderfully and frustratingly mysterious government bureaucracy. I say, wonderful, because who knows what other pieces of first-hand history might still lie unnoticed, buried somewhere, waiting for some patient family-detective to ferret them out?

Regarding digging into family genealogies, this is not for someone faint of heart or sensitive to what may turn up; in other words, don't ask questions to which you don't really want to know all of the answers. Families really are exactly what they are – the individual has no choice as to when or into whose family they are born. The ads on television indicating that you or your ancestors may be or were born next to historical celebrities or the possibility of having an esteemed ancestor are not untrue; however, as with the highway of life, there are many side- and cross-roads. In fact, like the junkyard you see from the nicely-maintained Interstate, you may find things that aren't quite so pretty once you happen to take one of the exit ramps.

For example, at one point in her investigating into her own Family roots, Janet found an ancestor of Swiss aristocracy from the 15th Century. I immediately took to referring to her as, "The Duchess." Several weeks later, however, she also found mid-19th Century relatives by the name of Donner, as in "The Pass" fame/infamy. By the way, I had to use Spell-Check to remember if there was one or two "n's" in cannibalism.

"I know which side of the family THEY come from!" I told her. "That's not funny!" came her clipped reply. Still, the fact remains that when you dig into your Family history, some of the roots of the Tree may seek out the manure pile rather than "the good earth."

But you can also find the very human, even tragic side of things as well. Research into my Mom's side of the Family, the Kimmels, indicate a relatively close kinship to Admiral Husband Kimmel, the unfortunate commander of the Pearl Harbor Naval Base at the time of the December 7, 1941 Japanese attack. History today tends to treat Admiral Kimmel much more graciously than it did in the first ten or twenty years after the incident. In fact, information today reveals plenty of blame to go around at many levels of the Government and Military. Still, it happened "on his watch". Regardless, the devastating personal impact on Kimmel and his immediate family remain wrapped in meager written information, all after-the-fact. Today, his family members still work to clear his good name.

Finally, regarding "you can't pick your ancestors" or in the "just plain strange" category, I also have a devout Family member who lived in the 18th Century, Johann Philip Kimmel. Although born in Darmstadt, Germany in 1724, he immigrated to America in 1755, and proceeded to live a rather full and I gather interesting life in Colonial America, passing on in 1796. According to historical records, Philip was a clergyman ("Presiding Elder in the Stony Creek Church of the Brethren"), "co-operator of pottery", tax collector (recognized by the NSDAR (Daughters of the American Revolution) as a "Patriot" for his esteemed services in collecting taxes for the Continental Congress), and tavern-keeper, including owning two whiskey stills. The latter occupation apparently led to considerable grief in his life.

In 1788 Philip reportedly succumbed (at least temporarily) to pressure from his fellow church members, voluntarily giving up his two stills. It seems, however, that the distillery business was, shall we say, still in his blood, because he was found to be part of the Whiskey Rebellion of 1794 in Pennsylvania, the dispute eventually put down when George Washington sent Federal troops to bring the insurrection to a conclusion. Again, reportedly, Philip was fined "for owning stills" and, in an indication that his Church was somewhat skeptical of the sincerity of his second act of repentance, proceeded to excommunicate him. There is no record of whether the Church's suspicions were once more justified prior to Philip meeting his Maker two years later.

In short, regarding your ancestors, you have what you have, the exact opposite of the military recruiting slogan of the 1950's – "Choice, not chance." The really neat part about that, assuming you have a strong enough stomach, is you do get a chance to discover a whole patch-work quilt of human drama, emotion, triumph, defeat, and many times outright weirdness. It may not be Hollywood stuff, but it certainly can be interesting, entertaining – and very often deeply personal!

I'm happy to be passing the Family mantle on to my Daughter, my Pride, Lindsey, who dutifully has read (and re-read) portions of this manuscript and shown interest both in people she never knew and military concepts concerning which she admittedly had no clue. I suppose she feels some of the same blood in her own young-woman's veins.

I also owe a debt of gratitude to Phil Saracin, a writer of action novels concerning the heroic Sean and Darcy and their diabolical arch-nemesis to America, Nurideen, for his constant encouragement to complete this work. Phil's friendly technical advice and the occasional kick-in-the-butt have been instrumental in getting this written work accomplished.

To all of the members of my Family – past and present – I'm proud to be one you! And to the Family veterans who have answered America's call to arms for the past 150-plus years, I would echo Samuel Francis Smith's words, written in 1831: "Our Fathers' God, to Thee, Author of Liberty…Long may our Land be bright, with Freedom's Holy Light…"

To past Pastors and Chaplains: you'll probably never know who all actually listened.

And as a final comment, while being a fairly devout Methodist, no, I'm not sure I would have given up my whiskey stills either. After all, sometimes you just have to stand on principle.

Introduction – The Question

Standing in line at the Ft. Lewis, Washington U. S. Army Supply
Center in July of 1971 with dark green-everything flying in my
direction – wool socks, fatigue shirts and trousers – along with
black combat boots and white T-shirts and boxer shorts, the not-so-
melodious strains of *"You're In the Army Now…"* kept repeating
itself inside my head. The tune was still re-playing itself over and
over that afternoon as I stenciled "L" followed by the last four
digits of my Social Security number on every article of clothing
and personal equipment, and I do mean everything. The other day
I was rooting through a bedroom dresser drawer and happened to
find a plain-white handkerchief neatly folded lying in the back
corner. Sure enough, I saw the "L___" neatly inked along one
edge. I smiled slightly, and then said to no one in particular,
"Gosh, was that really 40 years ago?"

That first evening at Ft. Lewis as I stood in formation for Retreat in
my fresh Army-green fatigue uniform with the "U. S. Army" patch
on the left breast fatigue shirt pocket and the name "LAUER" in a
matching subdued-green patch on the right shirt pocket, and raised
my right hand in salute, it began to hit me: "Today, I'm a soldier.
Or at least, someday I really will be."

The specific rocket-sled ride that had propelled me from civilian to
military status in what seemed to be a single flash in time had
begun in Pittsburgh, PA three days earlier as I had boarded an
Allegheny Airlines twin-engine "Viscount Rolls-Royce Jet-Prop"
to Chicago where my first Boeing 707 ride eventually deposited
me in Seattle, WA. There, a uniformed soldier dressed in starched
green fatigues and a "Smokey the Bear" hat who I would soon
come to know quite intimately as a "Drill Sergeant", or more
informally "the devil incarnate", was standing, holding a sign with
our home units listed. As we Ohio-based men clustered together,

sort of following the basic safety-in-numbers herd instinct, I first noticed a trace of an ominous smile on the Drill Sergeant's face. Beneath the shallow grin I could almost feel the unspoken words, "I am not your friend!"

"Quit being paranoid," I told myself, "He's not 'an instrument of the devil.'" By the way, this was one of my initial lessons in both the potentially high value of and extreme risk in ignoring first impressions.

After boarding the dark-green Army bus (never to be mistaken for a Greyhound "Scenicruiser", by the way) we found ourselves rolling through the seedier side of the city of Seattle. In his initial on-bus statement, the Drill Sergeant announced, "Those people out there are what we call, civilians. They are the lowest form of human life on the planet, save one still-more-inferior species…and THAT'S YOU! YOU are "trainees", nothing more! Insignificant, slimy worms of humanity! You should be saluting those civilians out there!" I was watching an obviously down-on-his-luck gentleman root through a battered dumpster as we rode by, thinking to myself, "Okay…"

The Drill Sergeant continued, "You do NOT salute me – ever! You do not call me, 'Sir' – ever! You are not in any way, shape, or form worthy to do any of those things, let alone speak unless spoken to! The only thing you are called to do is to do what I say, when I say it, and at the instant I say it. Follow those rules, and your Basic Training experience at Ft. Lewis will possibly be half-ways tolerable. Ignore my rules, and your stay here will be very unhappy, of that I can promise you." As we trundled through the gates at Ft. Lewis, I admit that I was less than impressed with the U. S. Army's "welcome wagon" as well as the "Wagon-master". And that was perhaps the first time "The Question" had barged into my consciousness.

I spent the next 5 months trying to condition, learn, and otherwise prepare to become a combat soldier in the United States Army. Basic and then Advanced Individual Training – Infantry, were designed to do that quickly but in a reasonably effective manner.

Then, for the next 7 years, I learned how to live as a soldier, training in peace-time but always prepared for war. I had questions that first day at Ft. Lewis; I still had questions the day I gave and took my last active-duty salute. I came to the conclusion that soldiers always have questions, including the biggest, most profound, and unquestionably the most un-answerable one – "Why me?"

Looking back 40 years now, I suppose that my response now would simply be, "Why not? What made you think you were so unique?" After all, anyone who has accepted (voluntarily or not) the duty of "a soldier" has joined a very unique but well-populated and ancient fraternity. Membership in this group (perhaps the first true *Animal House*?) began, I suppose, with the first stone-spear tip and flint-knife disagreements between Stone-Age clans and eventually included other bigger, more organized groups with names such as Egyptian, Persian, Greek, and Roman. The soldiers' implements used for combat may have changed over the past 3 millennium or so but the purpose has not – to take "the fight" to an enemy in victory. The physical means to accomplish this purpose, however, has remained the same: the soldier.

With the exception of those particular souls "born to bear arms" – the professional soldiers bred for combat through status or culture such as the Spartans, along with kings and other exalted classes - most human beings who have ended up bearing arms had no real intention of ever doing so, at least in the beginning. The eternal, "common", quite often citizen-soldier, has usually gone from a life of almost mindless day-to-day existence dealing with usually innocuous events involving scratching for a living in an attempt to avoid starvation, to moments of stark reality and abject terror at "the tip of the spear".

Sometimes those moments are final ones. I was once told, "Gentlemen, if called to action we will be the tip of the spear! Remember, however, being ahead of the spear-tip really sucks." As a college-graduate I found it necessary to ask, "Okay, sir, and how do we remain the former and not end up at the latter?" His response was, "That's what the men at the Alamo or in Custer's regiment wanted to know, I'll wager. The fact is, you train well, you lead well, and you pray hard; same formula as has been taught and practiced in some form for thousands of years." I replied, "Okay, sir." That, after all, was about as lucid an explanation as I would ever get.

Of course I wasn't really "okay" with that answer. It smacked too much of, well, pure chance. I'm an Engineer and I like things to spit out logical answers in response to logical inputs. Sure, I had read the accounts of the Battle of Midway, where seemingly random events such as Japanese Vice-Admiral Nagumo's air-strike arm being caught on-deck of their aircraft carriers during re-arming, the Japanese fleet air-umbrella being pulled down to wave-top level as they completed the slaughter the heroic, self-sacrificing American torpedo-bomber crews, coupled with the magnificently coordinated arrival of the higher-flying Navy fighters and dive bombers – completely fortuitous and ultimately decisive but all events were actually and remarkably unplanned.

And, I figured, if engineering-like precision in planning and execution didn't necessarily lead directly to success and victory, then I could hypothetically find myself well ahead of the spear-tip at some point in time despite careful, even exquisite attention to detail. The only semi-comforting thought, I concluded, was that I likely would have a great deal of historical company. And all of us would have ultimately asked the same question, "Why me?"

What, I wondered, would be running through my own mind if faced with the realization that my immediate or near-term survival was seriously and momentarily at risk? And how would I feel when the means of this stark, abundantly real extermination threat was directly at hand, staring me straight in the face. Even more confusing, how would I come to grips with the fact that often the threat is seemingly random, totally unplanned? In essence, Life and events appear to defy the rules; they simply don't "play fair."

Granted, the subject of whether Life is fair or not is an entirely separate philosophical subject. Neither the strongest force nor "the good" always win; and we human beings don't like that one bit.

We all seem to have the concept of a universal rulebook where for every specific input there's a certain result. There's nothing capricious about anything, so we feel. Then, it seems, Life flat-out cheats and we're left thumbing through the rulebook looking to see what tiny "however," clause we have missed. Eventually, we realize that for some reason, whatever we've just experienced is clearly not covered in the rulebook, or anywhere else in the realm of logic. Sometimes it just seems as if two invisible, uncaring military gods rounded a corner, stopped, glared, and then agreed, "Here is a good place to do battle. Now is a good time to fight."

Of course, the common combat soldier has experienced all of these not-in-control feelings and emotions. Whatever the form this date (or location) with mortality has decided to take, it has usually shown itself to be uniformly and decidedly unfair along with unspeakably horrific, and indescribably tragic. Even worse, surviving soldiers down through history have had to live and attempt to deal with the memory of these devastating thoughts and emotions day after day, far beyond what ordinary "civilized people" would ever dream of having to consider or endure. Often, there is guilt at simply having survived where others did not and many times the living have envied the complete rest and peace of the deceased.

Over the past 40 years, I've spoken with a number of friends and family who have fought as combat soldiers in the Armed Forces of the United States of America. The common thread I've found, I believe, is the question, "Why me?"; or, more specifically, "Why and how did I get myself into this avalanche of events which have lead me straight into this valley, plain, sea, expanse of space, fortress, redoubt, trench, …" or whatever battlefield location in which the soldier has encountered an armed enemy who is equally determined to extinguish his life. Inevitably I've found that thoughts of home and family have flashed momentarily into mental view along with emotions and desires rubbed raw and then swallowed up by the rush of the imminent hailstorm of violence rapidly forming directly ahead (or all around). But when the actual time for face-to-face combat comes, the really good soldier has followed the urging of my martial arts Sensei: "When it is time to do battle, the mind must be clear and with a single intent – fight!"

A soldier – at least a volunteer (however you want to define the term) compared to a slave or a conscript – has at least in the beginning made the conscious decision that the risk of losing his life is somehow worth being a part of an organized and armed military force. I won't begin to argue that motives such as greed, revenge, abject and prejudicial hatred, and even an immature quest for adventure have sometimes been the catalysts to a citizen forsaking the plow and becoming a soldier. Nor would I argue that there are not human beings who actually enjoy killing other human beings. Simply put, as a species we often leave a lot to be desired. I'm afraid that Plato was right when he remarked, "Only the dead have seen the end of war."

But getting into these kinds of philosophical debates on human behavior is somewhat like watching the evening news: after the first half-dozen features you're convinced that people are scum-bags, that you wouldn't blame God one bit for sending a 50-mile wide meteor on a dead-on collision course with earth, and you find yourself scrambling to find the weekly TV listings to locate what channel *The Andy Griffith Show*" is on.

Somehow, though, as an alternative to Andy, Barney, Goober, Opie, and Aunt Bea, I'd like to propose conjuring up enough faith in humanity and in whatever could be described simply and plainly as "honor" in the common, individual soldier to believe that more than a few times – starting with the picking up of the previously-mentioned stone-tipped spear and crude flint knife down through history to the wielding of modern weaponry – a citizen-now-soldier has willingly offered service simply and exquisitely because it was the right thing to do. Whether it was to stand against monstrous cruelty, tyrannical injustice, or purely because their Country was in danger and desperately needed their service, soldiers have found themselves hurtling down the lightning-quick slope of destiny towards pending or certain death simply because they believed in their heart of hearts that it was both the right as well as the necessary thing to do.

At that point, there are no easy, readily satisfying answers to the "Why?" questions and, most importantly, "Why me?" Instead, I'd offer the possibility that somehow fear-fueled dread becomes magically mingled with what General Douglas MacArthur simply but profoundly stated as "…Duty, Honor, Country…", his "expression of the ethics of the American soldier." In fact, in May of 1962 when he gave this, his farewell speech to the cadets at West Point, MacArthur added, "**Unhappily, I possess neither that eloquence of diction, that poetry of imagination, nor that brilliance of metaphor to tell you all that they mean.**" I think, however, he made a pretty fair stab at it when he said:

"**Duty, Honor, Country: Those three hallowed words reverently dictate what you ought to be, what you can be, what you will be. They are your rallying points: to build courage when courage seems to fail; to regain faith when there seems to be little cause for faith; to create hope when hope becomes forlorn.**"

At that point, emotional campaign slogans, lofty philosophical arguments, or learned, flowery pronouncements have become irrelevant. The reality is simply that the soldier is present – now – in place and in the uniform of his homeland as is the enemy and both combatants are now locked in a lethal, un-holy partnership with mortal danger. At that particular juncture of time and space nothing else matters to the soldier other than "Duty, Honor, Country…" Indeed, I believe that for the American soldier, nothing else CAN matter.

In the spirit of these my own personal thoughts, the following are short but fact-based descriptions of the experiences of real-life individual soldiers – members of my own Family - set in historical American military actions from the Civil War to Korea, all drawn from their written letters, spoken remembrances (okay, with one minor exception as I explain below), and also the musings of other

Family members. Each of these brave soldiers is gone now, their individual caskets having been draped in the Flag of their Country beneath which they had fought and, in some cases, died. Any additional, potentially clarifying thoughts have been buried with their earthly remains; I'm left with what I remember, what I wrote down, my interpretation of what they told me (sometimes, simply what I saw in their eyes) and any personal information that I have researched from newspaper columns and stories along with Janet's (my Wife) diligent family genealogy efforts.

This is not meant to be nor would I suggest that it is a strictly historical work. I'm admittedly a history buff but clearly not a historian. I've tried to insure that the settings, actions, and their corresponding dates are accurate and complete.

But the following are stories about people – my Family, my direct kin. The military events that my ancestors found themselves swallowed up in are, of course, far more important in the overall scheme of history than any single combatant. However, for me personally, the story of the individual soldier has been my goal and focus. Hopefully, my overall endeavor will at least meet the criterion stated in the words of Jesus regarding the efforts of the woman who had anointed his feet prior to his death: "She (he) did what she (he) could." (Mark 14:8a, NIV)

In each of these scenarios to follow, along with recalling the soldiers' personal experiences and feelings to me, I've tried to both explore and empathize with the feelings of these individual soldiers who have shared my blood, all staring down the barrel of possible or even probable Death. Together with the battlefield-emotions they shared with me, I've also tried to put myself in their places, attempting to consider what random thoughts and gut-level fears were churning inside each one. But I also wanted to try to juxtaposition each of their emotions directly into my own real, known-but-to-me thoughts as a raw recruit soldier facing the distinct possibly of being sent to fight in the jungles of Southeast Asia in a place called Viet Nam.

As a freshly-minted college engineering graduate in December of 1970, I had quickly (early-February, 1971) found myself in a line at the Pittsburgh Federal Building for a pre-induction Army physical. Less than two months later I was raising my hand and saying:

I, Barry A. Lauer, do solemnly swear that I will support and defend the Constitution of the United States against all enemies, foreign and domestic; that I will bear true faith and allegiance to the same; and that I will obey the orders of the President of the United States and the orders of the officers appointed over me, according to regulations and the Uniform Code of Military Justice. So help me God.

Immediately afterwards, I found myself serving as a "buck private" in C Company, 145th Infantry Division of the U. S. Army - Ohio National Guard. On July 6, 1971, I began my journey through Infantry Basic Combat Training in Ft. Lewis, WA and then Advanced Individual Training – Infantry at Ft. Polk ("Tigerland USA"), LA. The training curriculum was termed "SEATA" (short for Southeast Asia Training), a not-so-subtle reminder that the war in Viet Nam was still being waged, that the conflict was indeed still a hot jungle battleground, and that National Guard troops had effectively served in every major conflict throughout the Nation's history. As my Uncle Bill always reminded me, National Guard troops of the 29th Infantry Division had been in the first assault wave at Omaha Beach on D-Day, June 6, 1944. By the way, I could see through the subtlety of the SEATA acronym; after all, I WAS a college graduate.

The early days of AIT (Advanced Individual Training), full of training in jungle combat, booby-trap avoidance, and other clearly "Asian" subjects ("Boc-Boc cong wah" means "Kill all Communists!" if I remember correctly, and "Dong lai" means "Don't move!") began to bring home the blunt reality of my situation as a soldier in the United States Army. Perhaps too it was the day that we were herded into a shallow trench to hear the sounds of machine gun fire and rounds cracking overhead along with the distinct and unique sound of "the weapon of choice of your enemy, Charlie (aka Charles, Chuck) – the AK-47!" This was probably the first time that I found myself mouthing "the eternal soldier's lament", namely, "Holy ___! WHAT have I gotten myself into?! Why me?" It would not, by any stretch of the imagination, be the last time that this question bounced around my U. S. Army Infantryman's brain.

But first, these short sections that follow also find my Family ancestors - decidedly American volunteers - asking themselves this same question (probably without the expletives, as they were all Christian gentlemen, albeit sometime in the future for a few of them), at least as much as I could deduce from their letters or in my own feeble efforts to crawl around within their soldierly brains through casual conversation. For the Gettysburg story, I've drawn heavily on letters penned by my Great-Great-Great Uncle, James Madison Hebe, and my Great-Great-Grandfather, Samuel Berkey, to their respective parents in an effort to try to describe the sentiment and pure reality of the times.

The "enemy soldier" character of Corporal Virgil McCoy, CSA, is admittedly fictional. I debated concerning his inclusion in the otherwise factual and personal Family saga of James Madison and Samuel, both Union soldiers. Having visited the Gettysburg battlefield site several times since the late 1950's, however, I felt that I couldn't really tell my ancestors' stories without contemplating "the view", if you will, from the Confederate side of the field downhill from Cemetery Ridge on that fateful third day. Standing there even 100+ years later, one can't help but be struck with the hopelessness that those gallant Confederate soldiers must have felt staring across that field and up that long sloping hill, realizing that the eventual casualty count and human carnage would be horrific. Yet, on the orders to move forward, they commenced their march into the proverbial jaws of hell and death as well as into the pages of American military history and, if you will, glory.

As you walk the path across the wheat field and uphill towards "The Angle" on the Gettysburg battlefield, you can only imagine the hell-on-earth maelstrom of shot and fire that converged over that limited stretch of ground. And when you stand at the wall on top of Cemetery Ridge, you can almost see the oncoming tide of gray along with the huge chunks of their formations disappearing among the smoke and general havoc being wreaked by the Union heavy artillery firing almost point-blank.

Although Samuel Berkey survived Gettysburg, he was killed at the Battle of Cedar Creek later in 1864 and the letters provided to the War Department after his death by his parents as proof of their dependence, written (perhaps for him by a fellow-soldier, as Samuel was essentially illiterate) up to two weeks prior to his death are both amazingly informative of the times while also uniquely heart-rending. The haunting words and thoughts expressed particularly in a letter two weeks before he was killed while trying to rally his comrades to face Confederate General Jubal Early's initial Confederate onslaught, express the agonizing "Why?" question in plain, albeit unscholarly, but equally profound and breathtakingly beautiful sentiments. They also speak in starkly candid terms of his premonition of death.

The World War I section is based upon the brief recollections and experiences (brief only in that he didn't talk much about them) of my Grandfather, Corporal James R. Kimmel, Company K, 318th Infantry, during the Meuse-Argonne campaign. He was a "Doughboy Over There" in the France of 1918 where, upon the signing of the Armistice, mankind became convinced that the end of this "War to end all Wars" would somehow translate into everlasting world peace. Clearly my grandfather thought so at that time.

Unfortunately everyone underestimated the impact of the grievous war reparations demanded of Germany by the victorious and equally vengeful Allies, the terrible economic collapse of the proud German nation, and the appearance of a perceived savior who proclaimed that Germany's problems were "someone else's fault." Mixed into this volatile atmosphere in the 1930's was the rise of fascist nationalism along with the apparent demonic bent in human nature that finds it necessary to routinely proclaim, "Down Venus, up Mars!" (reportedly of Roman origination, the phrase, not the concept).

James R. Kimmel also brought home to me personally the fact that the horrors of war leave permanent scars regardless of the toughness or resilience of any individual human's character. In particular, the spontaneity of the memories he sometimes expressed, seemingly unconnected with anything that was transpiring at the present time, was as jarring to me as the actual comments themselves.

The World War II story is expressed through the again brief recollections of my Father's brother, Sergeant Merle B. ("Bill") Lauer at what we Americans call "The Battle of the Bulge". As a member of the 506th Parachute Infantry Regiment, 101st Airborne (he was an original "Toccoa" graduate) and a veteran of such brutal actions such as the D-Day Invasion and Operation Market Garden (or Marketgarten) which he claimed was by far the worst mission of his combat experience, he survived – although wounded, then decorated - the German trap which had promised complete annihilation of the "Screaming Eagles" at Bastogne. I've tried to capture the events preceding and after Bastogne including the story of the Dutch couple that heroically hid him from capture by the Gestapo and then the gut-wrenching unknown of "Missing in Action" experienced by his parents as they desperately waited to hear if "Missing in Action" would ultimately lead to a more somber and final pronouncement. The question of "Why?" was, in this case, not limited to the involved soldier alone.

The Korean War portion is based upon the remembrances of my Mother's brother, Sergeant James W. Kimmel, whose Ranger unit found themselves battling the Communist human wave assaults on the frozen, windswept plains near Korea's Chosin Reservoir. The gross disregard expressed by the Chinese for International conventions let alone general humanity was difficult for him to understand in 1950. Unfortunately, 1950 was by no means the last time for the world to witness man's inhumanity to his fellow man, nor to experience one nation's treachery against another. I suppose that I came away from James W. Kimmel's story with a certain amount of disgust for the Mao-led Chinese and also a sort of Reagan-like weaponry-limits mindset of "Trust, but verify" in regard to future dealings with a Communist regime. In other words, I fervently hope for the best in humanity and the honor of nations but I never, ever assume or expect that humanity or honor as a human characteristic will triumph, at least not until Jesus Christ returns.

My uncle's frost-bitten fingers and toes, legacies from that desolate, frigid hell in Korea, plagued him for the rest of his life along with the chilling memories of the early days of what has been called "The Forgotten War."

All three of my direct, then-living ancestors rarely spoke about their combat experiences. Usually, if the general subject came up, they would talk about the funny things that happened in day-to-day Army life. Grandpa Jim once told me that their pup-tents would occasionally be frozen in rigid shape overnight even when the tent-poles were removed. He'd laugh and tell me that, if in a hurry, they would simply set fire to the straw that they had used for bedding to thaw the tents. They jokingly referred to it at the time as "the Doughboys' Scorched Earth Policy."

But when and if the words did come out concerning the combat in France, Germany, or Korea, they poured forth unexpectedly, almost as a momentary explosion of emotion and memory, expressed graphically and often in anguished tones, then quickly shut off like a garden hose spigot. I never knew when or what would trigger their responses and, oddly enough, it wouldn't be such obvious things as world events and newscasts or some other seemingly geographically-related occurrence. Those moments of illumination would literally happen out of the blue, uninitiated and understood only by those baptized into that fraternity of combat. But, as MacArthur also stated, "…the soldier, above all other people, prays for peace, for he must suffer and bear the deepest wounds and scars of war."

After I had returned from my initial training in the U. S. Army, waiting to see how my military destiny would unfold, these three soldiers seemed a bit more willing to share some of their long-hidden feelings with me. It was almost as if I had somehow passed through some sort of profound initiation rite and had been pronounced "worthy as a soldier". And, as such, I was somehow apparently deemed "worthy" of hearing the private thoughts expressed by combat soldiers, even though I had not yet faced a mortal enemy in anger.

As a young boy in the 1950's I was caught up in the Walt Disney *"Davy Crockett"* craze, wearing my coon-skin cap to school and singing the few words I knew to *"Davy Crockett – King of the Wild Frontier"*. As a result, I also became fascinated with the story of The Alamo. In fact, the first book I ever read on the subject showed Davy standing on the parapets of the old adobe mission and defiantly swinging "Old Betsy" like a mighty war-club as the swarming Mexican soldiers poured over the battered walls. The tattered lone-star flag fluttered in the background. I was enthralled.

Over the next 50 years, I've found myself unashamedly and unrepentantly in awe over that old 1836 battle, regardless of the additional historical information that has evolved over the years. For example, was Crockett killed, captured, and/or surrendered first? What about the tale as told from the Mexican soldier perspective? What about Jim Bowie and William Barrett Travis? Apparently both men suffered from not unusual but serious human weaknesses and failings.

The attempts by historians to bring past figures down from bigger-than-life to an average level of human perspectives is disappointing but probably natural; after all, we're an eternally skeptical species, I think. We always want to discover "the angle"; what was "the hook" that made people travel into harm's way aside from "Duty, Honor, Country?" We cherish our legends but today we're not satisfied with thinking that someone might simply do something because they felt it was the right and proper thing to do at the time. I admit that I find myself falling into that pattern of thinking, probably because as I've grown older I've seen heroes fall, succumbing to the same human failures and indignities to which the rest of mortal mankind have proven vulnerable. In the end, we all look for and expect to discover "the hook." As a sad consequence, we've evidently outgrown our legends.

And yet…back in March of 1836, 182 to 257 soldiers – Texans (or Texicans, if you desire), Tennesseans, and whoever – chose to stay bottled-up inside a crumbling mud mission for 13 days, well beyond any hope of reinforcement. Day after day they watched as the Mexican army swelled to over 5000 troops while enduring nerve-shattering artillery barrages day and night.

Whether you believe or doubt the "crossing the line" story, the supposed choice offered by Colonel William B. Travis as he drew a crude line in the sand with his sword defining their personal Rubicon - to stay and fight or attempt a break-out and possibly escape - is not the point. The undeniable fact is that virtually every man remained in the Alamo and died fighting as the Mexicans assaulted and overwhelmed the Alamo's vastly-outnumbered defenders at dawn on that 13th day. At the very least, the most cynical among us would admit that every defender died, period. Yet, one hundred and fifty-plus years later, Travis' last written words still stir even a cynic's heart: "I am determined to sustain myself as long as possible and die like a soldier who never forgets what is due to his own honor and that of his country. VICTORY OR DEATH!"

As a boy I wondered why those men would do that? What inner belief or ideal drove them to stay, and not run and save their own skins when they had the chance? As a new Army recruit I found myself occasionally asking the same question, this time as a soldier myself, serving in a period in our Country's history when being in the military was very definitely not a popular thing to do. In effect, I was asking myself, "If they don't care, why should I?"

I remember asking myself what difference would it make if one man simply decided to chuck it all and just bug out, disappear, go home? Would my single effort (or lack of it) possibly do anything to change the wild and seemingly unstoppable course of human history? Would NOT "crossing the line" really matter? The answer to those questions was always, "None. No. Not a thing."

The "Why, me?" question will never have a complete, final answer, of that I'm sure. As I wrote this book my own view of "A Soldier's Question" changed. In the beginning, I think that I was content to pose the question and let it dangle, if you will, leaving it up to the reader to contemplate and propose his or her own possible answers. I eventually found that stance untenable, though, almost as if trying to be an impartial referee instead of what I personally ended up being – an active participant. Truly, it's impossible to understand even the reason for the question, without having been standing there, right hand up, and ending up saying, "…So help me God."

Although I suppose that definitive answers to these "Why me?" questions still escape my feeble mental abilities to come to grips with let alone comprehend, I think I've finally understood this one solitary thing: if not me, then it would have had to have been someone else. When I put my right hand up and took the military oath, I don't remember any part of it being in parenthesis for me to run by the legal-council of my choice. Nor was there a qualifier such as, "unless things get really, really tough, scary, and personally threatening, in which case I will feel free to immediately and at any time beat-feet and let someone or everyone else take whatever heat is to come." Instead, along with the other men in that room at that time, I simply ended my oath by saying, "So help me God."

As a result, I somehow and in some way feel privileged to at least be allowed to stand at the back of the Classroom of History, observing in silence the replays of my ancestors' individual times and events, now mostly lost in the supposedly enlightened but often mercilessly harsh, cynical glare of 21st Century.

A Soldier's Question – July 3, 1863 – Gettysburg, Pennsylvania

The continuing concussion of Colonel Edward Porter Alexander's heavy guns battered his eardrums, even though he knew that the Yanks on the receiving end up there on Cemetery Ridge were getting the worst part of the incessant cannon barrage being laid down by Lt. General James Longstreet's corps artillery chief. Cpl. Virgil Simpson McCoy was, however, preoccupied as he sat huddled with the rest of the 53rd Virginia regulars just inside the tree-line on the southeast side of Seminary Ridge. After all, as a veteran of frigid Fredericksburg the past December and then Chancellorsville, where the gallant but also unlucky Stonewall Jackson had fallen just a month or so ago, he knew that even the pounding of over 100 heavy field guns could only do so much to reduce the formidable Federal position at the top of the hill roughly a mile away. No, not really that far, he had been told; only about 1000 yards. "Only" a thousand yards… His chin stiffened at the thought: one thousand yards across open ground into the teeth of the Yankee fire. For the tenth time in the last five minutes, he once again stared at the umbrella-shaped clump of trees, mentally marking the spot that General Lee had called "the objective" of the coming assault. Just a clump of trees, he mused, but they might as well be on the far side of the moon.

"Oh, General Jackson," he said to himself, "Lord knows we could surely use a 'stonewall' of any kind right about now." McCoy sighed, thinking of how much the Confederate forces missed their legendary Virginia Military Institute professor/corps commander. As darkness had fallen on that final May 5 day of victory at Chancellorsville, General Jackson had chosen to conduct an ill-advised reconnoiter of the still-unstable front lines. In perhaps the Providential happenstance with which history often turns, General Thomas J. "Stonewall" Jackson had ridden into his own jittery picket lines where a hail of frantic musket fire had cut him down. He had lingered for several days, troops fervently praying along with the rest of the entire Confederacy. When he finally succumbed to his wounds, the entire South had shuddered, almost as if feeling the chill of a spring breeze when storm clouds first gather and darken the sun. In a little more than a month, however, when the storm had broken just over the border of Maryland and into Pennsylvania, the whole Confederacy began to fully recognize the magnitude of the loss.

True to any army that has ever existed, rumors act as "secondary chow." A soldier lives off of rumors just as surely as salted-beef and biscuits. The Confederate army at Gettysburg was no exception. By now, everyone knew that General Henry Heth had blundered badly just two days before on the opening day of battle at this small Pennsylvania cross-roads town, although some said that both Brigadier Generals James Pettigrew and James Archer had erred as well. A more determined push, it was said, would have overwhelmed Brigadier General John Buford's beleaguered cavalry regiment – a bit of a unique outfit, armed with repeating rifles and trained to fight as highly-mobile infantry - and the high ground would have been the South's for the taking. If there had ever been exactly the right moment for "Old Stonewall", the initial struggle with Buford's cavalry would have been it.

Jackson personally would have been perched on the high ground as the evening dusk settled in and the savage second day of fighting would very likely have been largely unnecessary. Major General John Fulton Reynolds' (at first, the "senior commander" on the field; he was killed in action later that first day) and then Major General George G. Meade's reinforcements would have been forced to take up defensive positions between the Confederate forces and Washington D. C. Then, if they would have decided to turn and fight, General Lee (God bless him!) would have been able to pretty much choose the ground for battle. Rumor had it that, indeed, the War might have been already won at that point.

But, instead of aggressively exhorting his Virginians onward and upward, gaining the high ground, General Thomas J. "Stonewall" Jackson lay eternally buried in Lexington, Virginia. Lacking his charismatic leadership, the Confederates had hesitated, then moved indecisively on that first day, still short of the high ground to the east of Gettysburg. In the space of those few undecided moments, the seconds that sometimes mark the fate of nations, the Union reinforcements had arrived en masse to effectively block any hope of further upward movement. Reportedly, after Rebel troops had attempted to mount a belatedly piecemeal, uncoordinated assault, one soldier in Archer's command had shouted, dejectedly, "Hell, that ain't no milishy; that's the Army of the Potomac!" And now, on July 3, 1863, here they all sat – the Confederates still looking up at the high ground controlled by the Yankees, and that God-cursed clump of trees.

Virgil McCoy shook his head and tapped his jaw a bit too sharply with neck of his canteen. He splashed some luke-warm water against his eyes, trying to will the sight of that stand of trees out of his line of vision. But there they stood, taunting, almost defying the men in gray huddled at the edge of the opposing tree-line to come forward, if they dared, and grapple with the men in blue beneath their protective shade. He shook his head again; still, he fully understood that the only way to dislodge the Yanks was for him and his Confederate companions to fight their way east across the intervening field which he knew would be a chasm of death, across that sturdy, rough-hewn fence just short of the Emmitsburg Road, then wheel northeast up the final hill and into the teeth of the Union positions. He knew that this meant braving flanking cannon, musket fire from both sides, and that the big guns would be spewing their deadly brew of canister and grapeshot like a white-hot metal scythe through the Rebel ranks of flesh, bone, and musket.

In truth, Virgil McCoy had not figured that things would end up this way a week earlier. In fact, when the Army had crossed into Pennsylvania and Southern sympathizers (although not as many as had once been hoped for) had cheered their ragged gray-coated ranks, he had ignored a soldier's proverbial fatalism and had allowed himself the faint hope that maybe, just maybe this devil-bred, hideous, monstrous war was ready to be finished for good. Strange, he thought, how a single week's worth of time can change a man's viewpoint. Before, they had felt themselves invincible, like a rushing tidal bore in a Virginia estuary, unstoppable, sweeping everything in its path. Now, after two days of hot battle, not defeated but far short of being victorious, the matter had come down to this place, this time, and an imminent, desperate battle.

Gazing across the field for at least the twentieth time towards the sloping hillside at what now appeared as the other side of the world, Virgil's soldierly instincts once again instantly sized up the situation. By now he knew that even if Longstreet's First Corps. (virtually all Virginians under Maj. General George Pickett) along with Lt. General A. P. Hill's Third Corps. (his divisions commanded by General Pettigrew and Maj. General Isaac R. Trimble, along with a mixture of troops from North Carolina, Mississippi, Alabama, and Tennessee) were somehow incredibly heaven-protected and wildly fortunate, maneuvered rapidly across that meadow of death, battled valiantly up that awfully wide-open hill, and then successfully stormed the Yankee positions at that infernal wall, the casualty count would be absolutely dreadful.

As he fingered his lucky rabbit's-foot in his right trouser pocket he had to wonder if there was anywhere near enough luck left in it to get him through the upcoming battle. True, he had only suffered a grazing slice in his left side from the shrapnel of an enemy canister round at that wild melee of a battle at Chancellorsville; actually, it had only cracked a single rib, glancing off of his rough leather ammunition pouch first. Since then, his buddies had simply referred to him as "Lucky McCoy". Yeah, he half-wondered, boy you sure are lucky now! After all, the "lucky" veterans that had survived previous battles were now just lucky enough to end up here, today, in this what-was-its-name Pennsylvania town. Heck, he mused, even the town would probably be referred to as "Lucky"; chances were pretty good, though, that people would ultimately remember its name in the future. "I wonder if they'll remember me, 'Lucky McCoy!'" he half-chuckled. Than again, maybe luck wasn't all it was made out to be, he thought. After all, even "unlucky" Thomas J. "Stonewall" Jackson had found final peace in the aftermath of Chancellorsville, bless his eternal soul.

And now here he was, crouched in the light cover of scrub-brush on a slight rise known as Seminary Ridge in this sleepy

Pennsylvania town called Gettysburg. He had heard it said that "Luck is a lady!" Corporal McCoy smiled at the thought; more like a savage, cruel, vindictive tramp, he thought. What had the ancient Greeks called their goddess of vengeance – Nemesis? Even through the haze of smoke hanging low in the late-morning July humidity he could catch the unmistakable glint of bayonet steel on the tips of the Yankee infantrymen's muskets as they crouched behind the low stone wall at the soon-to-be-launched attack's focal point at the peak of Cemetery Ridge – The Angle. He could almost imagine the image of a robe-clad Greek goddess standing behind that line of Yankees, laughing with all of the mirth of hell. Yeah, Virgil McCoy, you ARE one lucky fellow, and bloody Lady Luck waits for you on top of that hill!

He pulled off his tattered campaign hat, the gray almost bleached to a dirty off-white, the shine of the narrow front brim long since removed, and wiped his forehead on his already sweat-and-grime-stained sleeve. For a brief moment or two he tried to imagine that Major Alexander's cannon barrage was battering the Union troops up on that ridge senseless. After all, he mused, who could reasonably stand in the face of all of that red-hot metal, flying viciously in death-dealing fragments with no thought of class, rank, or age.

But, then again, he had seen this many times before. Somehow it had seemed that enough of the enemy would still be able to climb out of the shallow dug-out depressions they had crafted (and then tried to pour themselves into, cursing for not having dug deeper), immediately pick up their muskets, and fight like blazes. Good troops could and would do that. No, he knew, those Yanks might be dazed and battered but they were also hardened veterans too. When they would catch the first glimpse of General Pickett's troops dressing in lines as crisp as could be expected for a half-shod assortment of Southern men, and the Stars and Bars being unfurled, those Federals would quickly gather their senses as their blood-lust along with their self-preservation instincts pounded into their veins. Then, Virgil knew, there would be hell to pay on their giving end.

McCoy continued to wipe the sweat, by now dripping like a small hair-rooted spring, as it trickled off his nose. He could feel the cool tickle of it flowing down the channel of his spine, dampening the rear of his britches. For a moment he felt embarrassed; then he almost smiled. Heck, even if he HAD wetted himself, no one would ever know. As he continued to stare at the gray-stone wall in the distance, he debated not only urinating but also getting up, turning, and high-tailing like a terrified jackrabbit. That, at least, is what a sane animal would do, faced with the drama likely to be unfolded over the field out yonder. How in God's wondrous mercy and infinite yet incomprehensible plan did he, Virgil S. McCoy, son of Benjamin X. and Rebecca J. McCoy, end up here, at this very ultimately unlucky point in time? All of his 23 years of earthly existence logic were failing to make any sense out of things. This wasn't in any way part of the plan he had meticulously crafted for his life, certainly not to include a desperate charge through a blazing-hot iron cannon-and musketry-shot hell.

The day seemed to grow hotter with each passing concussion-filled minute and by high-noon his gray cotton-flannel shirt was now completely sopping wet. He looked at the water-soaked sleeve-cuffs, suddenly remembering how Annabelle had sewn the garment last Christmas, proudly mounting his newly-awarded Corporal stripes on each arm. Although he knew such thoughts weren't going to do him a lick of good, he couldn't help but mutter, "What I wouldn't give to be back in our Shenandoah home over the other side of Winchester, sitting on the farmhouse porch swing, rocking back in forth, arm around Annabelle in the early-evening stillness." He had married the girl the day after her eighteenth birthday, right before Beauregard's guns had fired on Ft. Sumter over two years before, and her daddy, a powerfully religious Methodist man, had been visibly relieved to have one less mouth to feed out of the brood of thirteen siblings.

With the help of his two brothers and some funds saved from two years of back-breaking rail-spike driving on the Winchester and Potomac railroad, the young married couple had managed to put in a modest corn crop that first year and also build a tolerably spacious 6-room farmhouse with a small barn on the southwest slope just below the house. From their second floor bedroom window they could watch the sunrise and from the steps of the front porch, track the last vestiges of the setting sun at evening tide. And, although the farm work was almost as physically brutal as his time on the railroad, the hours long and seven days a week, and their family sadly locked at two, the McCoy's had been happy overall. In fact, Annabelle had balked at Virgil even considering going off to join the Confederate Army. Why, she had reasoned, would they need another farmer when they could pull from the reputed "vast field of the finest flower of the Confederacy", or at least that was the phrase she had heard to describe the initial scores of patriotic Southern volunteers. Why would they need her very own dearly – no, powerfully-loved Virgil to serve and fight For the Cause? Deep down, there was only one cause that mattered to her, that being the thought of a brood of youngsters to be raised and a peaceful life to be lived with her man. And, while she had never openly voiced that opinion, Virgil knew exactly what she felt.

As he replayed the conversations over and over again in his mind, Virgil remembered his proud but gentle reply. "Because I'm a son of the State of Virginia, because my home has been invaded, because if everyone decided that 'the other fellow' could do the duty then the Army would have no soldiers, but mostly, because it is the right, decent, and honorable thing to do." Virgil McCoy half-smiled again. "I wonder if you'd give the same proud dad-burned speech now, ya' durn fool?" he said out loud.

"You say something, Virg?" the scarecrow-thin private leaning against the even-thinner poplar tree just to McCoy's left said, looking half-startled. Virgil looked at the young man – no, he couldn't have been more than a 15 year-old boy – and with the kindest smile he could muster said, "No, boy; just talkin' at myself, that's all." He tried his best to remember the lad's name (as he had tried to do several times before without success) but the boy had arrived only two days earlier with a group from Maj. General Henry Heth's chewed up old division which had been soundly bloodied in battle on the first day and, true to the nature of a veteran infantryman, it was usually best not to take the time (and expend the emotion) to get to know the "new-fellow", even his name. Holding the hand of someone you didn't know at all while he was gasping his last agonized earthly breaths as the result of some hideous wound, was somehow less devastating than the same with a fellow veteran with whom you had shared your meager rations and three-stick fire for many long, humid-hot or frigid-cold nights.

But now, all of these musing seemed to be disappearing like the vapors from a rear-echelon laundry steam pot, crowded out by the over-riding vision of that blasted field just in front of their position, the sloping hill, and that ominous stone wall with the flag of the United States of America – once his own – still flapping defiantly even as the shells from the Confederate guns burst all around. He remembered the savage carnage his own Army had dealt the Union troops as they had valiantly tried to advance across the open slopes at Fredericksburg the previous December while the Confederates had huddled behind another stone wall, popping up to hurl murderous death at the unprotected Yankee infantrymen in their death-advance. Stone walls, it was beginning to appear, were good for infantrymen to be hiding behind, not advancing upon. Even a corporal could see that, he grunted.

Virgil took a few shallow breaths and shook his heady slowly while he recalled the early, heady days of The War for Southern Independence, as he liked to call it. Back then everyone was spouting the same rhetoric regarding "States Rights" and the threat of "Yankee Hegemony". Plus, everyone was sure that a "proper Southerner" could whip three – no four – Yankees in a fight. He too had been caught up in the initial intoxication of the apparent glories of armed combat. It only took one battle to sober him up completely. His wife, however, had never shown any thrill for any of it. He had to admit that even the sight of Virgil in his then-new Confederate gray hadn't filled Annabelle with anything but sadness mixed with fear. Then again, he thought, she had always been the one who seemed to be wise beyond years.

But now, two-plus years later, the Confederate Army was finding – just as so many armies had discovered down through history once they were well into a war – that the enemy, even those Yankees, could be just as determined, just as courageous, and just as ferocious as any Southerner. True, especially earlier in the War, the Federal military leadership may have left a great deal to be desired, particularly where political patronage had routinely trumped military training and experience. Then again, the South had suffered from the same curse, that is, the mistaken belief that a good upper-crust politician would usually make for a good leader of fighting men. Regardless, the old soldier's adage remained true for any age – "When Privates make mistakes, Privates get killed. When Generals make mistakes, Privates still get killed." Corporals too.

Virgil had witnessed that truism first-hand, as shrewd, educated political minds had sent many a foot-soldier into the slaughter-pens at Second Manassas (or Bull Run, as the Yankees called the battle) in August of 1862, Antietam in September, Fredericksburg in December and on and on. Funny, he thought, not very many of those shrewd political minds ever took the time to come up to the front and stand with the Privates (or Corporals). If they did, maybe the term "acceptable casualties" would have a more profound or at least mildly significant meaning to them. No, he mentally decided, even ticks in a soldier's bedding were a good bit more tolerable than a politician trying to lead fighting men.

When it was all said and done, a soldier ultimately wanted someone trained AND experienced as a combat soldier leading them; someone "possessed of the art of war." Of course that divine gift by itself never guaranteed a favorable outcome; however, it sure seemed to work out that way most of the time. After all, he figured, about the worst a political enemy can do is get the best of you in an election debate. A war enemy can kill you utterly and completely dead, regardless of the potential volume of brilliant rhetoric on your part. Heck, they were saying that some Yankee General out west – Ulysses S. Grant – was nothing but a failed, drunken storekeeper. And probably a politician too!

Virgil half-smiled again, thinking, "One helluva fighting failed, drunken storekeeper, though." He also knew that Grant had reportedly fought admirably in the Mexican War back in 1846 as a recently graduated "West Pointer." And, The U. S. Military Academy at West Point, New York, had definitely turned out quality military leaders, Southern and Yankee. In particular, General Robert E. Lee (God bless him!) had not only graduated from there but had superintended the College and Classes of Cadets.

No, he said to himself, there were now many good fighting men on both sides; the incompetents, the frail, the "talkers" had been weeded out, or killed, often the victims of their own lack of battle savvy. The new breed of military leaders were uniformly improved, probably because they had once been all on the same side, trained thoroughly in the art of war, then baptized under fire in the Mexican conflict. And, like artists, while some were obviously more divinely gifted, like "Marse Robert", they had all received the finest available military training of the age. And some of them, like Maj. General Winfield S. Hancock who was commanding the Union Army of the Potomac's II Corps. across that field and behind that stone wall, were reputedly master "artists." Hancock would never panic or collapse his battle line; neither would the troops under his command be expected to break and run at the first hint of the onslaught, no way.

So why, Virgil asked himself again, was anyone and, in particular, General Lee, ordering troops out on what was obviously going to be a field of slaughter? He had not been alone in that thought. As he had commanded a squad of pickets guarding the left flank of the 53rdVirginia bivouac area the night before, he had overheard the semi-hushed conversation between Longstreet and Brig. General Lewis A. "Lothario" Armistead, commander of the 14th, 9th, 57th, 38th, and 53rd Regiments, as the senior commander had passionately but quietly savaged the next day's battle plan with his trusted friend and brigade commander. Virgil had played back their conversation about a dozen times in the past three hours, each time finding himself awestruck over their obvious caring for the troops in their respective commands along with their fears concerning the impending action.

"Lo'," General James "Old Pete" Longstreet had said in an agonized voice, "You know what's in store for the men once they start across that field. The long-range shot, then canister artillery rounds, and then as they reach the Emmitsburg Road, murderous combined weapons fire from three sides…I just don't believe human beings can fight their way through all of that inhuman exploding iron and steel. I told General Lee that straight out. In fact I said to him directly, 'General Lee, no fifteen thousand men ever arrayed for battle can take that position.' I swear I did"

"And did the General have any response to that, Pete?" Armistead asked, knowing that an answer would come anyway.

Longstreet had poked at the dwindling campfire absently and then, after drawing a long, deep breath said, "Yes sir, he said, 'The enemy is there and I am going to strike him.' And I knew then that the matter had been decided."

"But Pete," General Armistead had answered, trying to sound somewhat confident, "If we CAN take those heights, push the Yankees back off of the ridge and divide their line even for a few minutes while J.E.B. Stuart (Maj. General J. E. B. Stuart, Lee's cavalry division commander) attacks Meade's rear up along the Baltimore Pike, we may just be able to end this nightmare war tomorrow. There would be virtually nothing between our Army and Washington. All of this carnage could be finally ended, ended do you hear me say?"

General Longstreet had remained silent for almost a minute before replying, "That's one helluva bunch of mighty big 'ifs', Lo', including that small detail concerning 'taking the heights'." He had taken a few more draws on his buffalo-head pipe, then added, "The worst part is that once we're committed, there's nothing I can do back here but watch and pray. I can't bring more troops up on line without getting the whole Army tangled up in each other and meanwhile the Yankees will keep pouring in fire and death from that stone wall along with the two flanks. I'm sure worried about us getting up there, but I'm damn-near frantic concerning how we stay there if we DO get there."

Unlike other military commanders whose tactics never seemed to change with evolving weapon technologies, Longstreet had learned quickly to develop new patterns of thinking. Although he and many of the other commanders – North and South – had received their combat baptisms in the Mexican War of 1846 as part of the 13,000-man Federal Army, Longstreet was one of the few to recognize that musket developments in the early-1850's had given the defense important advantages; namely, the invention of a French Army captain by the name of Claude E. Minie, specifically, a way to load a rifled-musket with a bullet just as easily as an older smoothbore weapon. The .58 caliber "Minie Ball" ammunition was ingeniously hollowed at one end. That, and the fact that it was small enough to be dropped down the rifle barrel made it easy and fast loading, yet when fired, the projectile expanded enough to engage the barrel's rifling. The result was an increase in effective range from roughly 150 yards to almost 500 yards, a tremendous advantage to entrenched defenders who were, if well positioned, able to begin firing at much greater distances to break up massed infantry formations. And, Longstreet knew, the Model 1855 Springfield rifled-musket was now standard Union issue.

"One whale of a gamble, for sure," General Armistead had admitted. "But Pete, it's also one heckuva potential jackpot if we can pull it off. THE ultimate jackpot! Think of it, being able to go home, our own Government free to direct our States the way we want. But most of all, to be able to end all of this slaughter once and for all. Pete, I think it's worth the gamble. I surely do."

Longstreet had slowly, absently stirred the fire again with the stub of the crooked pine branch. "But if we don't pull it off, we could also lose it all. If we falter even a little, the Yankees can counter-attack and cut our own front in two and here we'd be, deep in enemy territory with a decimated and divided army. And I was always taught that you don't gamble with what you can't afford to lose." He had slowly stirred the fire again before adding, "Aw hell, Lo', but that's Meade up there commanding the Yankees. If they stop us I doubt they'd try to press the advantage, not unless old 'Winnie' could convince him otherwise, and that would still take time." Armistead thought gloomily about General Winfield Scott Hancock and his dear, charming wife Elmira, whose unspoken affection had been more precious than life. Here they were, Hancock, a fellow West Point-trained military leader, a classmate and good friend to many of the Confederate officers on this very ground, but now facing each other across that long, sloping field, deadly foes.

"No, Lo', the Yankees have the high ground and we shouldn't choose to fight 'em here. I begged General Lee to let me push further south and force Meade to follow in order to keep between me and Washington. I told him, 'Let me catch Meade strung out, his artillery and wagons on the march, tired, and possibly tangled up along the roads, maybe good and muddied if God provides the rain. Then we can wheel the full division around, catch him in between and out in the open, and force him to fight where we choose to fight. I don't like this ground, General Lee, I don't like Meade, and I especially don't like ol' Winnie commanding the high ground.'"

Armistead had slowly nodded his head, saying, "You may be right, Pete, maybe right. But think a minute; General Lee can't really break off this battle now, not without ruining and wasting the splendid morale of our troops. They got their blood-lust up now; these Virginians are just spoiling for a fight. No, I think this battle tomorrow has got to happen. I think that the stars are aligned, the heavens poised, and our moment is about to come into being. What did ol' King Agis II of Sparta say back around 450 BC? 'The Spartans are not wont to ask HOW MANY the enemy are, but WHERE they are.'"

General Longstreet had smiled vaguely, nodded barely, and simply said, "You and old King Agis keep your head and your wits about you tomorrow, Lo'. I'd feel a real profound and personal loss in not being able to bounce my thoughts off of someone with such a thoroughly competent and thoughtful demeanor." General Armistead had half-laughed, nodded, and then proceeded to join in stirring a half-burned pine branch into the fire-stew in front of the two men.

Virgil drew himself back to attention and stared out across the field again, watching the already-three-quarters trampled and broken wheat stocks shift slightly in the brief hint of an early-July breeze. No, he thought after a few minutes, General Armistead was right. The Army is here, the enemy is here as well, and the time to settle the issue is right now, right here. No more playing cat-and-mouse games maneuvering through tiny Virginia, Maryland, and Pennsylvania hamlets, watching your comrades drop away, crumpled in agony, usually in two's and three's in sudden, sporadic firefights like ripe crab-apples shaken by late-afternoon summer thunderstorms. Today, the matter would be resolved; either the Confederacy would finally by force of combat make the Union acknowledge Southern independence or, like the final series of straining waves at high tide, the South would begin falling back, perhaps surging a few more times, but never beyond the high-water mark located in this small Pennsylvania town that happened to be at the confluence of several vital roads. No, today was indeed the day, the Fates were aligned, the die was cast, and nothing or nobody was going to change the coming blue-gray collision of destinies

Suddenly the blaring of bugle calls sounded above the now obviously-diminishing cannon fire. "Git 'em on their feet, Corporal," Lieutenant Stoner called almost matter-of-factly. "Bring 'em on-line and dress 'em on General Trimble's 16th North Carolinians to the left. You've got our left flank."

A good soldier has the ability to move instantly and confidently even without giving the matter serious thought and Corporal Virgil Simpson McCoy was indeed a good soldier. He was already gathering his cartridge pouches and securing the worn leather straps even as he moved out of the tree-line to the edge of the field. His own voice rousting the men of G Company sounded detached, distant, as if he were standing alongside himself observing the proceedings. Looking to his left he could see more long gray-coated lines striding confidently out into the open, moving quickly to form surprisingly impressive straight ranks. My God, he thought, I'm genuinely proud of these soldiers. A third of 'em doesn't even have shoes, let alone a soldier's boots, but they sure can still dress a smart line!

"Bearer, uncase the colors!" barked Stoner. Almost immediately the tattered G-Company guide-on and often-patched, gallantly tattered "Stars and Bars" were unsheathed and pushed defiantly skyward. Virgil shot a glance over his shoulder and quietly said to himself, "I've never seen the colors look so glorious." Yet, he clutched his heavy musket in shaking hands, all the while staring up the slope at the far end of the field like a farmer watching the ominous black clouds of an oncoming storm. He shuddered involuntarily despite the heat and humidity. I hope, he mused, the Yankees feel the same way, as they watch us forming up.

Suddenly and almost magically, the hour-long crash of cannon-fire ceased and he swore the only replacement sound was the savage beating of his own heart. No one spoke; even the birds seemed hushed and silent and the only sound he could now hear was the occasional flapping of the colors in the breeze.

Moments later and at a half-run, General Armistead moved to the head of his command, pivoting to attention facing the troops. He drew his sword and held it high directly in front of his face, hilt almost against his nose. "Men, for your homes, for your wives, for your sweethearts, for Virginia…forward…march!"

Sergeant Virgil McCoy readied his well-worn British-made P1858 file musket across his body and stepped forward. All he could see now was the Flag and, in the distance, that stone wall atop Cemetery Ridge. With surprisingly now-steady hands he moved ahead, the only other thought in his mind being of Annabelle seated on the porch swing many miles to the southwest. Strange, he thought, I wonder what she will be cooking for dinner tonight?

■■

His blue Union uniform was already soaked through with sweat, so the obvious situation highlighted by the cessation of artillery fire and flurry of activity down the hill and across the long stretch of open field didn't add much more to Private Samuel D. Berkey's discomfort. The word passed down, reportedly from General Winfield Scott Hancock himself, was that the Rebs would surely try to crack the Union middle here on Cemetery Ridge. Chances are, he figured, this small but sharp 90-degree bend in the line, "The Angle" as some had called it, would be smack dab in the middle of it all, along with the roughly 250 men of the 71st Pennsylvania Regiment. As he involuntarily shielded his eyes from the early-July haze he couldn't help but wonder how he had gotten to this point, so far away from his Pennsylvania home almost 200 miles to the west.

After all, he was no "spring chicken", no youngster looking for fame and glory. Born in 1825 and married to Leah Lape since 1846, Samuel had felt he had nothing to prove, except possibly to himself.

Only 4 months earlier, he had been back in Hooversville, a small rural town up in the Laurel Mountains along a lazy stream affectionately known as Stony Creek, south of Johnstown's small but vital iron works. Subsistence farming was still the mainstay of the overall local economy and the Berkey families spread out along south-central Pennsylvania were no exception. There, in one of the many shallow valleys meandering within the Laurel Mountain portion of the Appalachians, Samuel and Leah Lape had made a home for themselves along with eight children, five girls and three sons.

The oldest son, Daniel, was ready to turn sixteen and burning to enlist in the Union Cause. Leah had been near frantic with the fear of her first-born running off to enlist, in addition to the fact that her Quaker upbringing still resisted any thought of active participation in armed conflict. Eventually, in fact, part of the reason for Samuel enlisting was an attempt to keep Daniel pacified and back on the farm supporting the Family.

"How did that work out for you, Samuel?" he found himself asking, a slightly resigned smile tracing his heavily bearded face. "Well, at least it had sounded good at the time, particularly to

Leah," he said half-out loud. But in fact, he had been a bit (or maybe a lot) put out at Leah's seemingly quick agreement to his impromptu proposal, even though afterwards she had vigorously denied wanting in any way for her husband to participate in fighting by joining the Army. "Women," he thought to himself, not realizing that he was perhaps the umpteen-millionth male to ever begin a statement with that expression, "I guess it's only natural that they want to protect their brood."

The youngest, Benjamin Franklin Berkey, barely four years old, could not understand any of what was happening; however, his toddler mind did manage to comprehend what a soldier might look like, at least from a rough tin-type picture of his father's cousin, James Madison Hebe.

When the Civil War had broken out, most everyone in their rural Pennsylvania village had felt safe and secure in the notion that their little valley by its obscurity would always be immune to a Confederate invasion. After all, the Rebels had been reported to be out-gunned and out-manned more than three-to-one. Plus, the South itself was seemingly far away, again reportedly preoccupied with fighting to protect their capital in Richmond. And, although a few citizens had answered President Lincoln's call for volunteers in 1861 like his cousin, James Madison Hebe, the war remained a far-away occurrence for most everyone in the state of Pennsylvania. Scratching a living from the earth to keep from starving had a way of keeping one's priorities straight and in focus.

True, the elder Hebe, Uncle George to Samuel, had been among the first of the local citizenry to answer President Lincoln's initial call for 75,000 men, at least in spirit. George Hebe had been born September 27, 1810 in Wittenberg, Germany, symbolic birthplace of the Protestant Reformation. This was the site of the All Saints (Castle) Church where, on October 31 in 1519, Martin Luther had nailed his 95 theses to the church door protesting the doctrine of works-based alternatives to the sole redemptive power of the Cross.

In 1819 the elder Hebe had come to the United States along with his mother, settling in the town of Pottsville, eastern-PA, Schuylkill County. Filled with the love of his new motherland, George Hebe had volunteered for the Army in 1846 when hostilities broke out between the United States and Mexico, rising to the rank of Captain, reportedly in the locally-famous, "Tioga Dragoons." As was so passionately stated by one officer in the group, "Each man was a host in himself and each had a personal ambition to satisfy." Following his honorable service to his country, George Hebe had returned to Pennsylvania, moving the family sixty miles northwest of Pottsville to the town of Liberty.

On the occasional visits over to Liberty, Samuel Berkey remembered the elder Hebe as a stern, passionate German, a rigid disciplinarian with his sixteen children, but also filled with optimism in regard to the opportunities he believed available to American citizens. He was fiercely patriotic, insisting that English be spoken in his household, despite his never quite eliminated German accent, most notable in his rolling "R's" and an inability to avoid making any word beginning with "T" sound as if it was starting with a "D." Then again, he had sounded very much like his other formerly-Teutonic neighbors.

As a "War Democrat", and shortly after the Rebels' firing on Fort Sumter, George Hebe was one of the first men in Liberty to rally around the flag of his adopted country, doing everything in his power to not only raise conscripts but also join them in their military destiny. Samuel remembered how crestfallen Uncle George had been when he had been honorably but firmly rejected for military service due to his advanced age. Samuel also remembered how equally proud he was when his son, James Madison Hebe had immediately enlisted.

But even Cousin James' path through the earlier portions of the war had seemed distant and almost foreign. Samuel had listened with more curiosity than actual interest in the beginning when James' letters began to arrive for Great-Aunt Hebe (Samuel had always called her "Mother Hebe"). He had been a Sergeant in

Company F, 5th Pennsylvania Infantry (34th Pennsylvania Volunteers) and from all accounts, a very fine soldier.

Samuel remembered his first letter home dated November 19, 1861: "Dear Father and Mother, I received your kind letter a few days ago and I was glad to hear from you. I am well at present and in good health. I am hoping that these lines find you enjoying the same blessings."

As with soldiers from any era, messages "from home" were always secretly treasured, although none would ever admit how important news from "outside" could be to someone struggling to maintain his sanity amidst continued and dreadful insanity. A letter, even containing nothing but local gossip, would be mentally devoured, then savored, transporting the reader back to a familiar, safe place, even if only slightly removed from the present hell.

By contrast, a soldier was usually very careful to avoid describing in any sort of detail what he had been experiencing. Some things were best left unspoken, or at least unrepeated in the memory of the writer. Besides, there was no need to worry those at home any more than they already were; after all, the home folks knew all too well that in war, people get killed. It wasn't necessary to remind them that one of those killed could always be their beloved son.

The initial letters were no different; a description of general camp life, his initial duties, and a request for basic necessities for the upcoming winter:

"Dear Father and Mother, I am glad to (here) that you are well and glad that you got my earlier letter, for it is getting very cold (here). I need (them) mittens this winter (if) somebody will (send them). The sample you sent in the letter (suits) very well. I was (scart) when I (lookt) at the envelope, I thought someone had (this was crossed out) was very sick because it was Directed in haste. When you send the goods, please direct them in care of Colonel Simmons (sp?), 5th Regiment.

Enclosed you will find five Dollars to pay the expense of the goods(.) (Please) send them by the Adams express for they run from Washington to our camp every day(.) You had better put them in a box, they will be safer(.) No more at present but (wright) soon so good (by)."

One letter was, obviously, concerning finances: "I haven't got much news to tell you this time, so you can't expect anything very interesting. Our regiment was paid of the nineteenth. We got all paper money in fives and tens. I would have sent you some money but some of our boys owed the sutler all that was coming to them and I lent them all I had but ten dollars which I kept for my own use." (Note – in his final letter in June, James sent $35 home; good boy.)

Another letter stated: "The weather is very bad here. It is raining every other day and then it got very cold. Today it is nice and clear but the wind blows very cold and our Company is on Camp Guard today and I am (Sargent) of the Guard. There is some prospect of us leaving (here) soon. They say the whole reserve is going to Front Royal this Spring and I wish they would take us down there. We would show the Rebels how the dog chased the fox! Me and Corporal Stoup, now he's a Kittanning boy from the 106th, we both think that the whole army is moving south as soon as the streams clear."

"P.S. I just now went the ground rounds with our Captain. It is now half-past twelve o'clock. This picture belongs to Mary Ann. (Mary Ann Hebe was, coincidentally, my Great-Grandmother.) Tell her it's from her Big Brother Jim. Tell her to take good care of it till I come home and good bye."

Another letter had commented: "On the eave of march to Lewisville. This town is noted for its Rebel inhabitants but I think having 218 troopers will have this town converted to the Union once more and our good old stars and stripes will float over the town where it was once so highly disregarded. I think it will turn out with a game of ball or I am awfully mistaken, for I have twenty rounds of cartridges in my Cartridge Box so I am prepared to meet them coming since the whole army is on the (march)."

As 1862 had moved into late-winter, however, his cousin's tone had begun to sound less optimistic: "Dear Father and Mother, I am going to tell you now that I can't come home this winter and so I think I won't come home till the war is over, that is if I don't bite the dust before it is over, so you mustn't look for me any more until peace is declared."

The last letter sent by James, dated June 21, 1862 and written from Mechanicsville, VA, not far from Richmond, had reflected his cousin's change from an eager, green recruit to a veteran trooper: "Dear Father and Mother, The weather is very hot here at present and getting hotter every day. We were on picket duty on Wednesday no further than 50 yards of the Rebels. We had to hide ourselves behind trees and stumps to keep them land sharks from picking us off. They are working day and night at their mud works in sight of us. The Rebels are building a fort right under our nose. We are going to drive them out when they get it done.

There was a deserter come over day before yesterday and we took two more prisoners. They look tuff and ragged. Our artillery killed their commissary yesterday and that made the Rebels skedaddle out of their works.

Whenever I get out of the Volunteer Service I guess I will stay out. The regulars are taken care of but we hasn't been and we must do all of the fighting and the regulars have got the praise for it.

I wrote 5 letters home and I never got one answer but I hope you will answer this for it makes me feel as if my friends were all dead."

Five days later, Sergeant James Madison Hebe was killed in action at the Battle of Mechanicsville, VA, mortally wounded by a single musket shot to the side. When the news came, a grieving Mother Hebe had taken to her room for 3 days. Then, she had bathed, dressed, and proceeded to run her household without mentioning another word of James' loss.

George Hebe too mourned his son's death quietly, in traditional German stoicism. Yet, although he survived James Madison Hebe by 20 years, George Hebe never did forget his son's sacrifice "on the altar of the Republic", as the newspapers had solemnly proclaimed. It is said that his dear son's name was on his dying breath. (As an aside, almost 150 years later, James Madison Hebe's military swords hang, proudly crossed, above the door of my study along with a period-brass bugle trimmed with gold fringe and an Army Infantry cloth swath. As you will understand later, there is a family and military kinship recognized and cherished, hopefully many generations after I am gone and nothing but a distant, dim memory.)

With James Madison Hebe's death, the Civil War had finally and officially come to Hooversville, PA as well as to Liberty and seemingly the rest of the State.

If the deaths of Pennsylvanian soldiers had failed to sound the alarm to the local citizenry, Lee's subsequent foray into Maryland and the bloody fight at Antietam the previous September of 1862 had finally brought the comforting illusion of isolation to an abrupt, teeth-jarring halt. Then, as late-June of 1863 had come, the alarming news had been received that General Jubal Early had led his raiding Confederate troops up out of the Shenandoah, swiftly across Maryland, and into Chambersburg, PA, a scant 90 miles from Berkey's home.

In quick succession, other Pennsylvania towns had also been rudely introduced to the invaders wearing Confederate gray and marching under the Stars and Bars – Carlisle, Hanover, and even the outskirts of the State capital, Harrisburg. No, the invaders had arrived for sure on home turf displaying gray uniforms instead of blue, the Stars and Bars as opposed to the Stars and Stripes, along with regimental bands playing jaunty "*Dixie*". It had been one thing to read about such things or hear about them third-person.

But now and suddenly, the war had become much closer, increasingly threatening, and far more personal.

Actually, it was Samuel's friend, Elliott Clark, who had volunteered first; but then again, Elliot always had been more of a history buff, claiming that the only way to guard personal liberties was to be willing to stand up for them, defending them through force-of-arms. His wife, Elizabeth, had been obviously distraught over his decision, seeing above all the risk of losing a husband and father to two-year old Anna. It was a bit strange, Samuel thought, how women seemed to care less about the principle (and, of course, the manly bravado) and more about practical matters, namely, how to keep food on the family's table in a reasonably consistent manner. Elliott, though, had once tried to explain his strong feelings to her.

"How can the Union be preserved if everyone stays back on their own farms?" The South had seceded, he had reasoned, and they were not about to return voluntarily. And, they most certainly were not going to willingly relinquish the practice of slavery. Although Elliot had been only at best a casual Abolitionist, typical of most rural Pennsylvania residents who had never even seen a black man except in drawings from books, he believed slavery to be morally wrong. All in all, his patriotic responsibility had been clear to him. His wife, however, despite her even deeper anti-slavery feelings, had remained unconvinced.

But today, Samuel thought, I'll bet Elliott would probably give a considerable price to be back there in Hooversville mindlessly tending crops or anything else rather than sitting in this infernal force-of-arms heat, waiting. Ironically, Elliott was over somewhere to Samuel's right about 400 yards. He wondered how Elizabeth would feel if both of them ended up being killed in the same battle. He also wondered if Elizabeth would secretly mourn deeply for him as well as for Elliott.

Almost immediately he felt ashamed of himself. Leah had never given him any cause to regret their seventeen-year marriage. True, Old Man Lape had rather grudgingly given his daughter to marry an illiterate farmer (Samuel could barely read and write and, in fact, had signed early documents with simply an "X.") The elder-Lape had hoped that Leah would marry the young Quaker pastor that had stayed with them back in the summer of '45. But, in her quiet yet firm way, she had set her heart on Samuel despite other suitors. Leah had steadfastly supported his remaining at home during the early years of the War, then despite her religious training, and out of fear for her eldest child, had dutifully agreed when Samuel had eventually decided to enlist.

Even young Benjamin Franklin Berkey had been powerfully proud of his Daddy going off to fight the Rebels. With the Family so united behind him, Samuel silently renewed his determination to survive the conflict and return to Hooversville, and there remain a devoted husband and father for the rest of his born days. Now, he thought, all I need is for the Rebs to cooperate!

Samuel had joined the Army less than a month after Elliott, who had already been rushed forward to the Union battle lines. Despite being sent to Maryland for general picket duty, they had found themselves camped along the Rappahanock opposite a Rebel camp, trading pot-shots at each other more as a game than with intended malice. But then, in late-June, things had turned suddenly serious. Rumors of a Rebel push to the north were quickly followed by orders to wheel the entire division, direction north. He and Elliott had found themselves being hurriedly placed under the command of General Meade to serve in II Corps under General Hancock at the suddenly-strategically vital crossroads at Gettysburg.

About all that Samuel knew concerning Gettysburg was that it was east of Chambersburg where he and his family had traveled each summer for peaches. Around Hooversivlle, the late mountain springtime and not unusual early frosts had always made the growing of peaches next to impossible, while apple trees seemed extremely well suited, particularly to the late-summer cool nights. However, on the eastern slopes of the mountains, and particularly from Chambersburg east, with the help of the moderating winds along the southern side of the Appalachians, peach trees seemed to thrive. Each year the family would make a four-day trip of it, over Bald Knob, down past New Baltimore, through the railroad town of Bedford, and on to Chambersburg.

He could remember the younger children pretending that they were pioneers on the Oregon Trail, bravely fighting off savage Indians, poking their heads out from under the white canvas canopy of the blue-painted farm wagon. His mother and father had seemed to enjoy the trip despite the bedlam in the wagon bed. Even the two plow horses, Jake and Bo, appeared to take to the novelty of the annual non-farm excursion. For everyone, the annual "peach-trip" to Chambersburg was almost like traveling to a nearby but foreign country. Going further east, to Gettysburg and Hanover, would have seemed like a trip to another continent. Only those very lucky as well as rich could hope to do that.

Well, Samuel thought to himself, I'm not wealthy and sure not lucky either, but I've made it to Gettysburg at last! Then he had to half-chuckle. As luck would have it (bad type, that is), he had not only made Gettysburg but also been given a front row seat to history - dead-center of the Union lines on top of an aptly named rise called Cemetery Ridge, southeast of the town.

From the beginning, General Meade had remembered that a second part of his mission was to keep himself and his Army between the Rebels and Washington. Therefore, II Corps was prepared to disengage at any time in order to protect the Capitol. But from the start of the soon-to-be three-day bloodbath, there had been a sense that history would be recorded, not on the road to Washington, that the climax to the battle would be here, on these fields and rolling hills, today, in this tiny Pennsylvania farm town.

Ironically, during the second day of battle the day before, the really heavy action had occurred a few hundred yards off to the south, around the wooded slopes of two nondescript hills, whose simple names would be forever remembered. There, the Union's 20th Maine had withstood three separate, savage assaults along their assigned front lines. The Rebs had almost turned their left flank at one point, which Samuel knew would have been a catastrophic event resulting in screaming Confederates charging from the side and rear of II Corps. And then, old Robert E. Lee would surely have sent a wall of troops forward to sandwich the Yanks square in between. The War could have been ended (and lost) the day before.

It was rumored that the 20th Maine had been commanded (and extremely ably so) by, of all things, a college professor of Rhetoric. At the precise moment that the 20th was about to be flanked and overrun, and almost completely out of ammunition, Colonel Joshua Lawrence Chamberlain had desperately ordered a wild bayonet charge down the slopes of Little Round Top. Understandably, the Confederates had been dumbfounded by such fiery audacity and before they could recover and regroup, had been driven back down the shallow slopes of the tangled wooded hill with many gray-shirted prisoners being taken. Samuel had heard the roar of the musketry but had not known how close the Union cause had come to disaster. That evening, though, he had heard his own regimental commander, Colonel Watson exclaiming, "Damndest thing I ever seen!"

As the sun had broken through the morning haze on July 3, 1863 the scuttlebutt had been that old General Longstreet might take his two Corps and make a dash for Washington. Meade would have been forced to give pursuit. But as the sun had begun to climb higher, there had been no sign of movement south in the gray lines across the field on Seminary Ridge. Even though he was a veteran of less than six months, Berkey knew that the lack of movement likely signaled the Rebs' intention to stay put and slug it out. Then, at mid-morning, offered almost as divine confirmation, the Confederate artillery under Major Porter Alexander had thundered into action. No, this was definitely a softening-up treatment in preparation for a direct on-line assault and Samuel felt as if a huge bulls-eye had been painted directly on his personal forehead.

He had barely moved for over an hour during the man-made deluge, hugging the stone wall, trying to melt his body into the cracks and crevices, alternately praying and cowering as the ground shook from the hellish onslaught of fire and metal fragments. Many of the shells were bursting well behind him and over the other side of the ridge, but some were close enough that he could feel the savage flash of heat as the charges detonated. No one can adequately describe being under artillery bombardment; fully understanding such experiences is like learning to box – there are many books describing techniques and footwork, the shifting of weight, defending from a sharp right-cross, the timing of a left-uppercut, but until you've been actually standing alone in the ring, except for your opponent, been hit at least once, hit really well, so that you can literally feel your brain bouncing off the inside of your skull, you can't appreciate the overall art and power of a thrown punch.

For Samuel, the reality of the situation manifested itself in the occasional close call, where the ground shook with such violence that he could suddenly see over top of the ragged stone wall even though still hunched over in a full crouch. With each explosion his brain seemed to shake in sympathy with the artillery concussions, caught in the pressure waves of explosive force, flying loose dirt, and lethal shards of jagged shrapnel. He had only experienced canister rounds one time before, fortunately with a sturdy stone wall intervening between his mortal flesh and the supersonic meat-grinder. He remembered those tinny "snick" noises, sounding like a deadly hail on a thin-slate roof as they had impacted that wonderfully solid stone wall. How he hated artillery barrages!

After what seemed to be two solid eternities, and almost magically, the shelling had stopped, as if the hand of an angry storm god had waved his imperially mystical hand over the battlefield. The succeeding moments of silence were almost as unbearably loud as had been the artillery salvoes. Samuel could hear the thumps of his own heartbeat pounding in his still shell-shocked ears.

But then, as he relaxed slightly out of his crouch he could see the movement. Almost like gray ants coming out of green holes, the Rebs were moving smartly out to the edge of the field, first a few platoons, then quickly entire battalions. Regiments and Corps quickly and steadily swelled. The waiting was over; this was really the time. Samuel watched as what appeared to be the entire

Confederate army formed smartly on-line, the unmistakable red and blue Stars and Bars fluttering mildly from dozens of poles, some ragged, some beautifully ornate.

In a few minutes that seemed like hours, it was almost as if nature was being caught up in the grand spectacle, providing almost imperceptible puffs of breeze in an otherwise breathless day in order to seemingly salute the gallant enemy's colors. Samuel watched the entire scene with rapt wonder, his mind trying to comprehend the vision before him. Absently, he wondered if this was how Christ felt when the devil showed him "all the earth and all their kingdoms in a moment of time". It was starkly alien, darkly menacing, awfully fearful, and yet stunningly beautiful.

Perhaps it was also the sudden clarity of sound, not the ear-shattering blasts of exploding shells or the ground-shaking concussions of the answering Federal artillery, which was equally awesome. There are those few times in a person's life when the senses operate at an ultimately-heightened level, when every rattle or clink of metal-on-metal seems like a thunderclap, even through the distance of hundreds of yards. He could almost imagine hearing the quickening breaths of the hosts aligned in front of him. Yet, it wasn't fear or mortal anxiety that flashed over him; simply, a few seconds of life at maximum intensity, the kind of rare feeling that possibly gives one a glimpse of eternity, a moment that most humans on earth never – for better or worse - experience.

Samuel Berkey was not alone in his trance. Every blue-clad eye on Cemetery Ridge was transfixed by the sight, almost like a seaside crowd watching the gathering of a tidal wave crest while still well out to sea and knowing that it was too late to flee, so why not unfold a beach chair, sit back, and simply enjoy the spectacle while you can.

It was almost like a physical kick when the platoon sergeant quietly said, "Check your weapons and cases, boys. They'll be starting out any minute." With the mindless precision of a soldier who has gone through the drill countless times, Samuel checked the seat of his cap and the lock on his bayonet. He was ready.

Now, it was simply the waiting that had to be endured, along with the last-minute questions: why me, why here, who does or will care? And along with these rapid-fire, constantly repeating final personal queries, the over-riding question: will my being here, at this precise moment in time, make a difference in any of this?

Almost like a tree being felled at the moment in which it stands perfectly balanced for one more second, quivering slightly but still towering upright over all, the Confederate lines were formed, motionless, and massive. Then, although out of hearing range, Samuel could clearly see division, then brigade, then battalion, then company commanders raise their swords in silent attention. He could imagine the shouts of, "Forward!" A moment later, he watched the sword arms drop, weapons pointed seemingly directly at his position. Samuel imagined the words, "March!" echoing across the Rebel lines and then he could see it. They were on the move, stepping out in a quick route-step like an incoming tide of killing humanity, all ready and fully willing to snuff out his puny life.

Now, though, the fear, the questioning "Why's" quickly vanished from Samuel's mind. The end of his Model 1855 Springfield musket and the tip of his gray steel bayonet were his focus now, coupled only with the swelling tide of gray moving relentlessly forward to his front. The oncoming flood of humanity was clambering over the split-rail fence, lurching onward even as the Union canister rounds carved huge bloody gaps in their ranks. Now Samuel could see the look on each oncoming Confederate soldier's face, a grimness and focus that ignored the surrounding whirlwind of hell and fire, their eyes forward, always forward. Slowly, his finger squeezed the trigger, and the world exploded in front of him in smoke and flame.

■■

Epilogue

Sergeant Virgil McCoy, CSA, survived Gettysburg and the slaughter of the battle known to history simply as Pickett's Charge. He actually managed to scramble the last few yards through hell and over the stone wall, stumbling over fallen comrades and blue-clad soldiers alike, and following just behind General Armistead. McCoy watched the gallant Armistead fall, mortally wounded, as they desperately tried to wheel the captured Union small cannons around to support their own rapidly-diminishing fire-power.

For a few seconds, the Stars and Bars had gone up, fluttering in a single breath of explosion-driven breeze, the battle decision seemingly teetering. Then, the Union reserves of the PA 72nd had moved forward to stand in the breach, and somewhere in those few seconds Virgil had been knocked to his knees by a musket butt-stroke up the side of his head. Through the smoke, noise, and daze of semi-consciousness McCoy found himself surrounded by blue uniforms, pinned to the ground, and quickly made a prisoner of war.

In the aftermath of the battle, he was quickly taken to the far side of Cemetery Ridge and herded into a makeshift stockade. Following a brief name-rank-unit interrogation session, Virgil McCoy, POW, found himself on the floor of a cattle car being hauled by an aging locomotive steam engine westward. The eventual destination was the POW facility located just west of Sandusky, Ohio (now known as Camp Perry).

There, he spent the next 18 months in confinement, learning just how cold the northern weather could be in winter time, particularly when situated on the windward side of Lake Erie. Just as a comment – I spent time at Camp Perry, as the Ohio National Guard used the facility for annual small-arms re-qualification training. The coldest November evening I think I've ever experienced was in one of the unheated concrete-floored barracks with a gale driven misting-sleet blowing in off of Lake Erie. Eventually, I had fallen asleep, only to be awakened by the odor and glow of a fire which had been unceremoniously kindled in the middle of the barracks floor by several soldiers returning from one of the local entertainment establishments in the area. Not surprisingly, alcohol was somehow involved in the minor and soon extinguished conflagration.

But even then, I could curl up in the warmth of a modern down-filled sleeping bag as opposed to a single tattered, thread-bare blanket. That Lake Erie winter must truly have been unbearable to those miserable Confederate prisoners. They say that age and latitude change a man's tolerance to cold; I firmly believe in the transforming power of both.

Virgil returned to the Shenandoah Valley in the spring of 1865 where he lived his remaining days as a simple farmer but thankfully surrounded by his children, grandchildren, and great-grandchildren. The worn, stained gray hat of this doomed Southern cavalier hung from a single metal peg in the farmhouse hallway all of his life, undisturbed even by his beloved Annabelle.

Sergeant James Madison Hebe was my Great-Great-Great-Uncle. Military records show him to have been an excellent soldier, very capable, and cool under fire. As a former non-commissioned officer myself, I feel a certain bond with James. And, as mentioned previously, his twin sabers hang crossed above the entrance to my study, a reminder of duty and devotion, from one Sergeant to another Sergeant.

Private Samuel Berkey also survived the climactic battle at Gettysburg, receiving only a minor grazing wound to his left side from a wildly-thrust bayonet which had glanced off of his cartridge case, saving his life. He later admitted that the happiest moment of his young life was when he saw that solid line of Union reserve troops from the 72nd supported by the 19th Maine and 42nd New York plowing relentlessly forward, moving the faltering Rebels back towards the stone wall like a house-broom handles small clumps of dirt.

In a twist of pure chance, location in the western part of Pennsylvania, and the random intermingling of family lines, Corporal William J. Stoup, remembered in one of James Madison Hebe's letters, was an ancestor of my wife, Janet. Stoup was born in February of 1843 in Tarentum, east of Pittsburgh, and originally enlisted at Kittanning, PA in September of 1861. He fought in many major engagements, being wounded at the Battle of Fair Oaks, VA on May 31, 1862. The explosion and following concussion of a near-miss artillery shell rendered him deaf in one ear and partially so in the other.

As a member of the Pennsylvania 106th Infantry Co. C, he rose to the rank of Sergeant, reenlisted at Roanoke, VA in January of 1864, and survived the war, being mustered out in June of 1865 at New Berne, NC.

William J. Stoup returned to the Pittsburgh area following the Civil War and worked as a coal miner before applying for an eventual disability pension in 1879. It seems that his hearing loss made it impossible for him to react to warning whistles and signals, a definite disadvantage when working in the extremely dangerous mining industry of the late-1800s. Leaving the mines also likely made a positive contribution to Stoup living to the age of 72, dying in 1915.

Samuel Berkey indeed survived Gettysburg and, in the months that followed, fought in the Wilderness campaign, and then when his enlistment expired, returned home briefly to Hooversville. In late 1863, he fathered his last child, a son, Samuel Thomas Berkey, Jr. However, regarding his military career, as the country saying goes, he went to the well once too often.

After the Wilderness campaign, he eventually lost touch with Elliott Clark, who had also survived the three-day battle at Gettysburg. In a packet of letters submitted by Samuel's parents and wife, Leah, to the War Department substantiating his familial relationship and general financial support, he had written, in surprisingly articulate form for a previously illiterate man, regarding becoming increasingly depressed over the loss of friends and comrades in arms. In one particularly heart-rending letter written two weeks before his death, Samuel wrote, "I haven't heard or seen anything of Elliott for two months now. I fear he has met his Creator. Elizabeth must be terrified."

Samuel Berkey's luck ran out at the Battle of Cedar Creek in 1864 while a member of Company I, 93rd Regiment, Pennsylvania Volunteer Infantry, just outside of Winchester, Virginia. He reportedly was attempting to wheel his company around and form a defensive line to counter General Jubal Early's hard-charging Confederates. Company I was overrun in fierce and savage hand-to-hand fighting. Although General Philip Sheridan ultimately if somewhat belatedly forced Early from the field in victory, Samuel Berkey received a mortal wound to the head. He died on October 19, 1864.

In another twist of historical and military coincidence, Colonel George S. Patton was also involved in the Battle of Cedar Creek, at the head of a brigade of the 22nd Virginia Infantry. While attending the Virginia Military Academy, he had studied under a rather stern and equally unexceptional professor of Natural and Experimental Philosophy and Instructor of Artillery, Thomas Jonathan Jackson, soon to be forever known to history by the nickname, "Stonewall."

Colonel Patton joined Samuel Berkey in death at the Battle of Cedar Creek that day. Perhaps, though, he is best remembered for the World War II legacy of his grandson, General George S. Patton III.

In 1922, my four-year old Father, Frank, accompanied by his grandfather, Benjamin Franklin Berkey, recalled the family traveling to Northern Virginia on a pilgrimage to visit Samuel Berkey's gravesite, although the decades and youthful memories had fixed the gravesite in connection with Second Manassas (or the Second Battle of Bull Run). Luckily though, with the advent of 21st Century computing power and the persevering tenacity of my wife, Janet, his final resting place was pinpointed as being in Winchester, Virginia following the Battle of Cedar Creek.

Upon visiting the area in 2003, the ever-helpful Battlefield/Park Rangers were able to lead me directly to the reported spot where he was struck down. Samuel Berkey is buried in the Winchester

National Cemetery, Winchester, Virginia, in Section 25, Site 1027, albeit with an incorrect spelling of "Burkey", along with many of his fallen Union comrades. He was a good and gallant soldier. He was also my Great-Great Grandfather.

Winchester National Cemetery, Winchester, VA, overlooking the gravesite of Samuel "Burkey"/Berkey, Co. I, 93rd Regiment, PA Volunteer Infantry, Grand Army of the Republic

Sergeant William J. Stoup, 106th PA Inf., Co. C – Grand
Army of the Republic

A Soldier's Question – Meuse-Argonne, October, 1918

As the unearthly roar and raw concussion of the German '88 artillery rounds pounded and echoed in his wide-rimmed steel helmet, while also filling the trenches with a mixture of dirt, dust, and general muck formerly lining the roughly dug-out walls, Corporal James R. Kimmel couldn't help but smile slightly. Even as he hugged the front of the trench wall, trying with all his might to present as small a cross-section possible to any stray piece of jagged shrapnel that might somehow streak its way supersonically into the somehow much too shallow trench, he couldn't help but catch the tiny glimpse of humor. No matter where he went, he could never seem to escape dirt. It was just about the same in 1918 France as it was back in rural Pennsylvania, except not as far underground,

For most of his too-quickly-upon-him adult life he had been a small-time independent coal miner, spending 10 to 12 hours each day (except for Sundays) crammed into an 18-inch high tunnel, carving out the South-Central Pennsylvania bituminous coal to feed the insatiable coke ovens and blast furnaces of the U. S. Steel and Jones & Laughlin Steel mills 80 miles northwest in Pittsburgh, "The Steel City."

His own private mine was a hard-scrabble, single main shaft following one of the many off-shoots of the major bituminous coal seams worming their way through the ancient Allegheny Mountain chain. While most other area inhabitants chose the equally hard but relatively safer vocation of farming, James Kimmel had compared the two and decided that at least with coal mining, you were not at the mercy of the fickle mountain weather, where storms and fronts off of the Great Lakes often met up with those jetting up from the south along the Ohio Valley. You could get a killing frost in June along with months-long drought and blistering heat. Or, the first fall frost could hit in early-September, followed by -30°F cold in January.

For young Kimmel, this dependence, upon anything or anyone other than himself, was unacceptable. He had decided early on that if hard work was his lot in life, then he was going to handle it with as much personal control as he could exert. Mining coal as a solitary miner was inherently dangerous, backbreaking-hard, and certainly lonely. But that was all right by him; nothing to distract or delay him from day after day extracting a living from beneath the earth's surface.

He had adjusted to just about every facet of the coal mining business except for the dirt, always the infernal dirt – mixed with the all-pervasive, ever intruding coal dust, along with inky, deathly blackness that, without the warm light of his carbide-fueled head-lamp, hid even fingers almost touching his face. But it was simply part of the life of a hard-scrabble coal miner; he knew it and accepted the fact.

 Besides, coal dust wasn't just confined to the mine; even the modest wood-slat houses situated along Stony Creek were usually coal-fired for heat, and the thin lath-and-plaster walls provided little barrier to the carbon-black invading army. It was everywhere, in the furnace flues, draperies, clothes closets, and even the daily food. Anyone who has experienced it knows the slightly gritty, inescapably oily taste. Eventually, you could get used to it but never totally ignore it. Coal essentially owned every nook and cranny of coal-mining country life. So, even the chalky French dirt was no total stranger to James Kimmel.

Now too, aside from the extreme threat of having to face his own mortality at any moment, he felt nothing but disgust for the dirty life in the trenches. At least after a day in the mines there was always plenty of clean hard-water and harsh but thorough lye soap to wash with. Even in the dead of winter and sub-zero temperatures, the big cast-iron wood stove in the farmhouse kitchen could still faithfully heat a coal-bucket full of water to a reasonably warm temperature.

He had always wondered about the stories of ancient people who reportedly bathed only when they found themselves unfortunate enough to be drenched by rainstorms. Even in the early first years of the 20th Century, regular body-washing was often thought to be unhealthy, the cause of disease including the dreaded pneumonia. Young Kimmel had always ignored those fears, reasoning that the perils hiding in dirt were probably far more fearsome than a clean body collecting "foul vapors." Although he was a mountain boy and an outdoorsman at heart, cleaning up regularly was a habit that had never left him. Of course that was probably why this trench warfare was so particularly distasteful to him. After a full week of nothing but a quick "bird-bath" courtesy of a worn-thin face-cloth and soap-less shave out of his tin hat, Kimmel felt like a walking grease-bag. Silently, he vowed that if he happened to live through the war, he would spend whatever it took to enjoy the luxury of a hot bath each and every day of his life.

It was small comfort that, reportedly, the Germans were even worse off than the Allies. In his first skirmish with the Huns, Kimmel had been mildly disappointed in the overall dress of the enemy. He had expected to see crisp lines of elite Kraut troops sporting the legendary "Pickelhaube" helmets, spikes buffed to a chrome-plated shine. Instead, all he had seen were the dark, dull-gray "kettles" worn by the German infantry. Clean uniforms and even bandages had become impossible to replenish in Germany after better than four years of World War. In fact, the oft-repeated joke circulating in the trenches concerned a German infantry squad leader and members under his command.

"Achtung!" the head-Kraut had shouted, "Today, we change underwear." A cheer went up from Hans, Fritz, and Johann. "Now, Hans, you change underwear with Fritz; Johann, you change underwear with Hans…" For some odd reason, Kimmel always ended up giggling no matter how often that joke surfaced. Just like the blasted Huns, he would laugh to himself; despite four years of conflict they were sticklers for routine, regardless of how inane it might be. Chuckling to no one in particular, Kimmel thought, "It wouldn't surprise me a bit that they DID have a written and strictly-followed procedure for underwear-changing!"

Bandages could be left incredibly foul but by gosh underwear "rotation" would be religiously enforced!

Allied troops were always spreading stories about the Huns, probably just the same as all armies have done since the Stone Age, when Dag's raggedy cavemen likely poked fun at Thor's equally scraggly band. But, just as the ancient armies also realized, their enemies could usually fight, and the Krauts could not only fight but do it exceptionally well. This was self-evident in the German flyers, whose Fokker Triplanes, led by the Red Baron, Manfred von Richthofen and a deadly group of his comrades, had driven that very point home to a great number of French, British, and American airmen. And their artillery, the vaunted '88s, was fiendishly effective, accurate, and as the American Expeditionary Force had come to find, thoroughly lethal.

Almost both reinforcing and interrupting his thinking, another shell whistled overhead. Once again, James Kimmel found himself longing for the cool stillness and subterranean "safety" of those Pennsylvania mines. Again, he had to laugh to himself – safe! On the contrary, the mines had been lethally dangerous in themselves and he had never before conceived of anything on earth more treacherous than loosely-timbered walls and cross-bracing holding back tons of rock and dirt above and around. Of course, that was before he had set foot in France of 1918.

"Yeah," Corporal Kimmel thought to himself, "But at least cooped up in the mine, no one was lobbing high explosive shells inside!" That, and the sounds, the high-pitched shriek of lightning-speed hot shrapnel, the low-frequency rumble that, although perhaps lacking in decibels, could be felt more than heard, and of course the sudden, volcanic explosion which could be deafening, but if you actually heard it usually meant that you were still alive.

Now he, like virtually every other Doughboy, would have welcomed the quiet solitude of their jobs "back home", even if in a mine, a raucous steel mill, or a dizzying textile plant. Almost any kind of labor would have been preferable to James Kimmel compared to the current nightmare and the ultimate terror of laying in the mud and filthy grime, possibly suffering from an ultimately fatal but unmercifully non-instantaneous wound. No, anything would be more agreeable than staring at one's innards roiling outwards, defying the futile efforts of grimy hands trying to hold everything in place. He shuddered, involuntarily, at the deeply-hidden fear that he had usually been able to keep locked deep inside. Then, as if willing the nightmare-demon back into its foul box, he snarled, "Oh, damn! You knew what you were signing up for!"

 In fairness, James Kimmel had not joined the Army for the perceived lure of adventure or to escape hard work. Almost a full year ago he had been called to serve his country; without a second thought or a moment's hesitation, he had answered that draft call. Mary and Wesley Kimmel had suppressed their own parental fears and put on brave faces as James had boarded the train heading for Johnstown, PA. The tears were shed after waving goodbye to the steam engine and four passenger cars disappearing along the edge of Stony Creek heading northeast. Mary whispered fervent but silent prayers, her own tears falling on the worn edges of her Prayer Bible; Wesley clenched his jaw but fought back the urge to allow tears to flow. He knew it was hard enough on Mary without him losing his own self-control and while he did not necessarily share his wife's deep religious faith, he knew that his only son would always do his best for his Country. That alone gave him something to hang his hopes on.

After all, members of both Wesley and Mary's respective families had served without reservation during the Civil War or, according to Mary, whose full name was Mary Lee McDevitt Kimmel, the "Recent Unpleasantness." Actually, Mary had mellowed some as she had aged, once insisting that "Uncle Robert" had not surrendered the Army of Northern Virginia at Appomattox in 1865 but had only suggested a conference in order to discuss possible peace initiatives. However, according to a younger, feisty Mary, his noble efforts had been "misunderstood."

As a young married man, Wesley showed remarkable restraint in keeping silent and merely smiling slightly when Mary would begin her defense of the beloved Confederate general that she claimed kinship to. After all, there were many Lee surnames in the region, stretching all the way into mid-Virginia, and the exact lineage trace was sketchy at best. But, in a demonstration of his newly-acquired marital wisdom, and despite his own family's specific Union loyalties, he asked himself what good reason would be served to question that unshakable belief on his wife's part?

In the late-1880's, hero-worship of General Robert E. Lee was a living, breathing part of life for any "Southerner." It would take, in fact, almost another century before skeptical historians would try to determine (or postulate) Lee's flaws, mostly in an effort to bring the South's hero down off of his well-built and maintained pedestal.

Certainly, no one even in the later decades of the 19th Century honestly tried to assert that Robert E. Lee was perfect – militarily or humanly. After all, he had been defeated at Gettysburg in 1863, the high-tide of the Confederacy, where a victory might well have achieved independence for the Southern States. Lee admitted as much as he tragically met the remnant of Pickett's torn-to-pieces Division after their valiant but firmly-repulsed yet eternally famous charge, telling his troops, "This was all my fault..." The General had believed that his men could take the fortified center of the Union lines, despite hellacious artillery shell and canister fire and without any sort of shield other than the man in front or beside of another. He had severely misjudged the devastating effect of evolving modern military firepower. His failure in this regard had resulted in tragic consequences for the South, and any honest Southerner was fully aware of that fact.

No, Lee had not been perfect, and late-20th Century historians would almost cheerfully point that out. Another "hero" would be pulled down from his lofty perch atop Olympus!

However, lost amidst the glee of later skeptics was a fact well understood by good common people a century before and, in fact, by those who either had first-hand knowledge of or at least had listened to recent casual stories. No, it was not that General Robert

E. Lee had done no wrong; rather, he had not intended to do wrong.

This was a critical difference to plain, simple folks who understood the realities of brutally hard, non-stop work necessary not to provide creature comforts but simply to survive from day to day, month to month, and Lord willing, year after year. This was still a time when many diseases such as pneumonia, diphtheria, typhoid, and tetanus were routinely killers, when infant mortality was astoundingly high, where couples had many children because they would be lucky and profoundly blessed if more than half of their infants made it to age three.

In short, the common person in the late-19th Century didn't have time to waste on being skeptical or searching for "an angle." That was ultimately time that had to be spent in keeping themselves and their families alive. Taking "a sabbatical" for study and contemplation would mean starvation; a vacation meant an abundance of forward planning and amazingly good luck, as "Old Man Murphy" had plenty of opportunities to exercise his famous "Law", the consequences of which were often more severe than could be remedied simply by an irritated, "Oops."

No, General Lee, just like any other mortal, could be wrong. This was not only accepted but actually admired: therefore, he was "just like us." What WAS special and the reason for such devotion, almost veneration, was the essential purity of his actions: he meant no wrong, his actions had not been driven by political or personal ambition. In fact, he could have had command of the entire Union Army at the outbreak of the War. Instead, he had chosen to accept a far inferior position in the service of the State of Virginia as part of the Confederacy. It makes a person wonder what the prestigious MBA Schools of the 21st Century would think of let alone seriously consider such a career-destroying decision!

Yet this was precisely why Southerners loved and have forever afterwards loved Robert E. Lee. While not "the Perfect Warrior", he was and is viewed as probably "the Perfect Christian Warrior." That is, he meant no wrong, his actions were guided by his belief that he was doing his duty in the best and most proper manner possible.

His men truly loved him. I believe that it was not just because he was a brilliant military leader or divinely-lucky, if you will. They knew that he also loved his men, that he would not intentionally do the wrong thing at the expense of many of their lives, and most importantly that Robert E. Lee had essentially given up everything "for the Cause."

Soldiers are a bit unique in that regard. Lee's counterpart early in the War, Union General George B. McClellan, also had the love and admiration of his men. However, not only was McClellan unable (or unwilling; perhaps the fairest summation of McClellan's ability to effectively command a military force came from Ulysses S. Grant who, after trying to find a way to bring McClellan back into combat command confessed after the War, "McClellan is to me one of the mysteries of the War.") to lead them to victory, he ultimately showed his thinly-veiled personal flaws of ambition, running against Abraham Lincoln for the presidency in 1864. In fairness, though, McClellan was by no means the first military leader to aspire to political ambition!

His Democratic Party platform had called for the immediate cessation of hostilities with the South and a negotiated peace. Union victories in the fall of 1864, however, torpedoed that platform, forcing McClellan to repudiate its stated goals. Too, this platform, originally endorsed by McClellan, had to thoroughly shock and bewilder his many loyal troops. After all, it's generally considered "poor form" to negotiate settlement terms when you're royally kicking the enemy's tail. Perhaps, in McClellan's defense, his timing was simply, poor? However, his decidedly unflattering private and public comments concerning his Commander in Chief, Abraham Lincoln, throughout the General's time of command leave little to commend either his personal conduct or his calculating character.

Maybe though, McClelland as a soldier was best and accurately summarized by General Fitzhugh Lee, a Confederate cavalry commander and nephew of Robert E. Lee: "He had strategic but no tactical ability. Risks have to be taken when battle is joined, but he never took them. Broken, wavering lines were not restored beneath the wave of his sword, and his personal presence was rarely felt when it might have been beneficial. He had none of the inspiration of war."

But soldiers understand, sometimes immediately but always eventually, the ambitions of their leaders. They even perceive the fact that, no matter how well-intentioned their superior may be or sound his actions, the individual soldier is merely the means to achieve the end. And, under the trials of combat, death, and the lingering emotional scars for the survivors, soldiers are always capable of perceiving when their superiors have ulterior motives. In short, and with a soldier's beloved vulgarity, it's impossible to bullshit the common fighting man.

As a result, and considering the wide scope of near-recent American history, Wesley Kimmel simply and wisely let it be. His wife would forever love and cherish the supposed kinship to her "Uncle Robert", and he would never say anything contrary concerning the claimed genealogy or the character of "the Perfect Christian Warrior."

Besides, Wesley Kimmel knew that his own family had demonstrated their own devotion to duty and courage under fire. Kimmel men had fought on the side of the Union, even mildly-famous people like Colonel David H. Kimmel, the gallant commander of a cavalry regiment, the Ninth Pennsylvania Volunteer Cavalry, known as "The Gray Horse." Of course, the reason given for the nickname was simply that "the regiment rode gray horses." So much for romantic, well-reasoned, cerebral descriptions! One more additional example, I suppose, of soldiers' lack of time for and/or tolerance of bullshit.

Among the one hundred and four sharp engagements in which Col. Kimmel took part were many famous battles fought in the central part of the Confederacy, particularly those against the rugged Army of Tennessee: Shelbyville, June 27, 1863, Chickamauga,

Ga., September 19-20, 1863, and Cumberland Mountain, December 9, 1863. Other battles were fought at Lovejoy's Station, November 16th, 1863, Macon, November 20th, 1863, and as far north and east as Raleigh, NC, and Lexington, Ky.

Col. Kimmel and his regiment reportedly had made "one of the grandest charges on record" at Reedyville, Tenn. on September 6, 1864. There, with Col. Kimmel's 240 troopers opposed by a Confederate force of approximately 1800, the gallant Union officer had charged the Rebel cavalry, riding almost eight miles and, per eye witnesses, passing completely through the enemy's lines, capturing 400 horses and 200 men (incidentally, the author has been unable to ascertain an explanation regarding the horse vs. trooper numbers, other than it was apparently a rough day for cavalry mounts). Confederate losses were listed as 33 killed and wounded, while Kimmel's losses were seven killed and wounded.

According to the news articles, several days later the embarrassed Confederate commander, a Gen. Debarell, challenged Col. Kimmel to a "rematch" in which he would "severely whip" the Union commander along his valiant Gray-Horse troopers. Reportedly, the Colonel sent back word that he and his boys would gladly "meet him anywhere, and for him (General Debarell) to simply appoint a place, date, and time."

Colonel Kimmel had lived a charmed military life, unusual for junior officers in the Civil War. Again, it was reported that he had never been wounded in any of the many hot engagements in which he had fought, although his faithful mount had been killed instantly in a skirmish near Raleigh (further strengthening the author's contention that a cavalry horse's life was certainly harsh, dangerous, and often extremely short). However, in contrast to Kimmel's own apparently indifferent preservation of his own mortality, of the original 106 men in his original company, roughly 75% had been casualties. By the end of the Civil War, Colonel David Kimmel had reportedly in his possession, 34 captured "guide-ons and small flags."

As another note in Civil War history, the Ninth Pennsylvania Cavalry was listed as the only regiment of the State of Pennsylvania that took part in Sherman's famous "March to the Sea" from November 15 to December 10, 1864. By the way, Wesley Kimmel never chose to mention that highly inflammatory fact to Mary, even under the most intense of "marital debates", a feat that will certainly amaze and promote admiration from any other husband, past or present.

And, at the very end of hostilities, General William Tecumseh Sherman reportedly had remembered the brave cavalry commander, giving Colonel Kimmel and the Ninth Pennsylvania Cavalry the honor of participating in the final pursuit of General Joseph Johnston's sizable 87,290 Army of Tennessee force. As part of the separated left wing of Sherman's forces in North Carolina, Kimmel's regiment fought at the Battle of Bentonville, then hounded the beleaguered Johnston first to Raleigh, Greensboro, and finally to Bennett Place near present-day Durham. There, on April 26, 1865, upon hearing of Lee's surrender at Appomattox, Johnston effectively surrendered the remainder of the armed forces of the Confederacy.

Again, contrasting two military leaders who performed the same action under very similar, hopeless circumstances, Robert E. Lee's surrender at Appomattox was and still is viewed as a noble, humane, and fully honorable event viewed by friend and foe alike. For the remainder of American history, the word "Appomattox" will always conjure up feelings of pride, relief, and most of all, dignity, the devastated but to-the-end honorable Lee tenderly addressing the remnant of his gallant Army of Northern Virginia before riding off to an uncertain, potentially awful eventual fate. After all, he had been the unspoken leader of the Rebel Cause, the prosecutor of the hostilities against the United States of America, literally "the Commander of the Hosts of The Enemy."

Joseph Johnston tendered what was to be the largest surrender of Confederate troops in the Civil War at Bennett Place, a virtually forgotten location in American history. Confederate President Jefferson Davis considered this "undefeated surrender of so many troops" as nothing less than an act of treason. Fairly or not, Johnston disappeared into near-obscurity both after the war and into history. As an ironic footnote in his unfortunate personal history, he died in March of 1891, reportedly contracting pneumonia after serving as a pallbearer in chilly weather at the funeral procession of his once-bitter foe, and later good friend, William Tecumseh Sherman. This by itself likely did not endear Johnston to either his detractors or his surviving troops.

Both Lee and Johnston had ultimately done the same thing: surrender Confederate forces under hopeless circumstances and under honorable terms. American history has heaped laurels on the former and at best, indifference, on the latter. Lee was and is still respected and, yes, beloved. Johnston was and remains recorded but little-remembered, having had the misfortune to share the same space in American military history as Robert E. Lee.

Indeed, Benjamin Hill, a U. S. Senator from Georgia, reflecting in 1870 following Lee's death, offered the following: "He was a foe without hate, a friend without treachery, a solider without cruelty, and a victim without murmuring. He was a public officer without vices, a private citizen without wrong, a neighbor without reproach, a Christian without hypocrisy, and a man without guilt. He was Caesar without the ambition, Frederick without his tyranny, Napoleon without his selfishness, and Washington without his reward. He was obedient to authority as a servant and royal in authority as a king. He was as gentle as a woman in life, pure and modest as a virgin in thought, watchful as a Roman vestal, submissive to law as Socrates, and grand in battle as Achilles."

Similarly, although in much plainer language, perhaps the most respected and maybe the only worthwhile comment regarding a leader's conduct under enemy fire can come from someone who has been under the same maelstrom of fire. While in Kentucky in 1862, an officer of Co. F wrote, "One of the bravest and best captains in the Regiment was David H. Kimmel, of Mechanicsburg, Cumberland County. The troopers of his

Company are mostly Cumberland Valley men, orderly and brave.
I tell you, we Pennsylvania officers are proud of our men."

The same comment could likely have been made about any number
of Civil War veterans. In fact, many men in the border area of
central-Pennsylvania, Maryland, and Northern Virginia had found
themselves dressed in tattered gray or northern blue, not
infrequently former neighbors, friends, and sometimes family.
Mary's allegiance had been geographically-centered at Robert E.
Lee's home in Arlington, VA, not too many miles from south-
central Pennsylvania, and eventually a sacred and honored burial
site for national heroes. Similar to the Kimmels, many Lee family
members had populated the tri-state area, Mary among them.
Some of them had also fought on the Union side; all, however,
remained eternally and fiercely proud of their heroic ancestor who
had nearly brought the Confederacy victory. Often it was the
"fiercely" part of their demeanor that dominated.

However, before James Kimmel was born in 1893, Mary had
discovered the Lord and, almost as a private concession to her new
personal relationship with Christ, she had lost the angry edge of
her rebel fervor regarding, as she also once called it, "The War
Against Barbaric and Evil Northern Aggression". Still, young
James had been raised with stories of the courageous actions of his
ancestors in defense of the Country, however the Nation was
defined. Therefore, military service was not only accepted without
question but embraced almost as a matter of historical, deeply-
rooted family honor.

Family heritage seemed to follow young Kimmel into the Army.
The 318th Infantry Regiment had been organized on September 5,
1917 at Camp Lee, Virginia. Most of the original soldiers had
come from the eastern counties of Virginia but in April of 1918
men from the southern- and western-counties of Pennsylvania were
pulled into the Division to bring it to full strength, James among
them. Kimmel took to Army life relatively smoothly; after all,
ditch-digging (shovel-work) was second-nature for him, although
his buddies were not necessarily as uncomplaining about the
seemingly unending manual labor. To James, it was almost a

holiday, as there were three full meals daily, plenty of hot water and showers, and essentially a ten-hour day. Except for the lack of home and hearth, he found Army life, at least in training, almost a breeze.

Marksmanship was another skill that Kimmel already possessed, as he had literally been weaned with a rifle or shotgun in his grip and tasked to provide small game and deer for the daily dinner table. Compared to his weathered, semi-ancient Model 73 Winchester, the U. S. government-issued 1917 Model .30 rifle was a thing of beauty, a piece of gun-making that he could only admire and maintain with the care of a proud daddy. Best of all, the Model 30 made a very good marksman like Kimmel even better. That was one thing he knew the Germans were about to learn first-hand: American soldiers could shoot and shoot well.

However, the training and "banker's hours" were coming to an end. From Camp Lee the Division had gone by train to Hoboken, New Jersey and on May 22, 1918, Kimmel found himself on board the giant ocean liner <u>Leviathan</u> sailing for France. He had never seen anything bigger than a row-boat up until that time and he spent much of his time aboard simply gawking at the gigantic floating mass of steel plowing relentlessly east through the wild Atlantic. It was simply beyond his belief that something so monstrously big and heavy could possibly stay afloat let alone cruise at such speed through the water. James knew that an uncertain future was opening up before him in ever-closer wartime France but for now, he relaxed with the thought that a poor farm boy/coal miner from rural Pennsylvania could live his entire life within a 50 mile circle of his home. Yet, here he was, heading for another country aboard one of the largest ships built by man. It made him almost elated at his good fortune.

Many of his buddies aboard were too seasick to care about anything aside from their own misery. Unless one is somehow divinely blessed with immunity to motion-sickness, the seemingly unending wretchedness can make a strong-willed person accepting to the idea of, even praying fervently for, death.

Believe me, I know of what I write, being one of the many non-blessed human beings who suffer from seasickness. Although I had somehow become conditioned to semi-tolerating the rolling motion of movement in airplanes, boats still presented me with challenges. That was why, in November of 1984 and with great reluctance, I had accepted a plea from our Research Director to escort a group of good steel-buying customers on a Saturday morning fishing excursion out onto Lake Erie.

Now anyone familiar with the peculiarities of shallow lakes knows that a mid-autumn excursion with prevailing north-west winds can produce shall we say, interesting swells. In this case, our 20-person charter fishing boat had been out onto the lake for only an hour when most of the guests had forgotten about the sport of fishing, concentrating instead on keeping their heads hung over the ship's steel railing, retching uncontrollably.

Everyone, that is, except for the boat's captain, my Airborne buddy, Rich, and a PhD Mechanical Engineer, Dr. Kim, a native of Korea. I was about 70% seasick, but still managing to keep my gastric composure, due to a wise very light breakfast and an equally smart package of Nabisco peanut-butter crackers.

Dame Fortune would possibly have continued to smile on me and perhaps even the rest of the by now retched-out guests except for one single, seemingly innocent incident. Dr. Kim was really into the morning's fishing and, after snagging a nice lake Perch, reached into the bait-box to reload his line. Nothing unusual about that, I suppose, except that, with the brisk fall lake-air and the time reaching about 11:00AM, Kim was beginning to get hungry. Low and behold, there in front of him, chilled in a big red and white Igloo cooler, were "prime munchies", at least for him.

Without even a second thought, Kim grabbed a handful of bait and crammed the mess into his mouth, a contented look on his Oriental face. Unfortunately for me, hanging onto my breakfast toast and peanut-butter crackers by a thread to start with, the site of those oily, squirming morsels being force-fed into Kim's waiting mouth was more than I could possibly withstand. Immediately, I elbowed my way to the ship's railing, lowered my head, and proceeded to join the majority of the miserable passengers in a litany of physical despair. For any of you who are immune to seasickness, all I can say is that you are profoundly blessed by the gods.

James R. was one of those lucky souls as he had, for some reason, never been bothered by sickness resulting from rolling motion. Perhaps it was due to his spending so much time below ground in the quirky mixture of gas and unstable pressures that had somehow conditioned and toughened his inner ear structure. Regardless, he was able to marvel at the towering swells of the mighty Atlantic, tossing even the mammoth steel ocean liner about like a leaf on a storm-driven lake, and still enjoy hot chow though accompanied by the rancid smell of coal-oil and vomit which thoroughly permeated the ship's environment. Years later Kimmel would recall a short conversation at the time with an obviously distressed Army buddy.

"Where you headin' for, Kimmel?" the soldier asked, one arm clutching the ship's railing like a lifeline. He had that yellowish-green skin tone that only those that have suffered can sympathize with and remember, usually with a flutter of the stomach.

"Ah, Woody, I think I'm going back for more of that beef stew. The cook said there would be plenty left over." Now, James had meant no harm in his honest response. However, poor old Woody reportedly gave a gargled reply beginning with, "Kimmel, you son-of-a...", wrapped his body around one of the rail stanchions, and returned to his seemingly endless litany of gastric misery. From then on, James determined to keep his eating habits private out of respect, he claimed, for the almost-dead.

He had landed in France as part of General John "Blackjack" Pershing's 28'th All-American Division, 318'th Infantry Regiment, Company K, but upon their arrival on May 31, 1918 they had been quickly moved on to Calais and a British camp, West Camp No. 6. There, to their surprise, they had turned in their cherished Model .30 rifles and drawn British Enfields, gas masks, and bayonets, yielding up even their "Yank" steel helmets. Some of their heavier units had drawn British Lewis machine guns.

Kimmel remembered the men being uneasy at seemingly losing their American identity to become "just another band of Limeys." Still, in early June when they began training along with the British and Irish troops of the 34th British Expeditionary Forces (BEF), he and his fellow soldiers had begun to appreciate the experience and freely-offered wisdom shared by a number of their Allied combat veterans. In particular, he and his American comrades had been anxious to learn about their enemy, the common German infantryman: how did he fight, what weapons did he favor, where were his weaknesses, where were his strengths, had they actually cut the breasts off of Belgian nuns and proudly displayed French babies skewered on the tips of their bayonets?

The Brits had actually fielded the Yanks' questions with surprising ease and candor. "Yank," one English soldier had told him, "They're well disciplined, exceptionally well lead, heavily armed, and overall good fighting men. Still, they bleed red blood just like you and me. Don't worry so much about understanding Germans, Yank; worry about taking the fight to them. They've been at it since 1914, and they know what war is all about." That had made an impression on Kimmel. Here was an enemy that had been at this business for four years and was decidedly a professional fighting force, not a collection of ragtag militiamen; and after all, they had fought the British and French to essentially a stalemated standstill here on the Western Front.

Yet, he couldn't help but find himself itching for action. His impatience, however, was born of a desire to get things over with rather than a thirst for or illusion of "sport." Unlike many of his fellow soldiers, James Kimmel held no idealistic visions of glory and adventure. Subsistence farming, then coal mining up in the Laurel Mountains east of Pittsburgh had taught him that life, for the most part, was not built on dreams of fame and luxury earned via fantastic, heroic endeavors. Life for him was simple, uncomplicated; brutally hard work six days a week for as long as the body held up had been a way of life in the American mountains for generations of Kimmels back into the early-1700s. True, his parents had done their best to let James have at least a few years as a boy and he had made the most of the time hunting and fishing the cool Laurel Mountain slopes and icy mountain streams (even in mid-summer) while tending to the daily farm chores. He had cherished those carefree times, realizing even at a young age that they were fleeting.

Youth was a single-digit age concept in turn-of-the-20th Century south-central Pennsylvania. A ten-year old was expected to begin pulling adult duties, either in the fields or in the mines. Life in general was still fairly basic, far removed from the urban areas of Pittsburgh and Philadelphia where electricity and indoor plumbing had begun to make their own introductions. The Kimmel farmhouse had a hand water pump in the kitchen, a massive cast-iron wood stove, and a rather tiny gravity-feed coal furnace in the basement but little else to keep out the long mountain winters which essentially lasted from October until May. In fact, Wesley Kimmel sometimes remarked that he kept his long underwear out until Memorial Day, and then packed them away until mid-September. Hunting kept the family larder stocked with meat along with the ice-house back by a north-facing cave fed by a hard-water underground spring. James Kimmel never remembered going hungry although "store-bought vittles" were limited to canned-milk, flour, and beans.

Medical care too was also at extremely basic levels back in turn-of-the-century rural America. Doc James, a young general practitioner but always looking older than his years, did his best to provide medical attention to anyone within reach of his horse and buggy. Further, he was his own pharmacist, meticulously preparing his own pills and liniments for whatever ailed you. He would continue to dutifully practice medicine for the next 40 years ushering into the world children, then grandchildren of the kids he had ministered to at the turn of the Century.

And Doc James was awfully good at doctoring. Even into the 1950's, he would caution mothers to keep measles-infected children away from other kids, prescribing bed-rest and dark-glasses to protect sensitive eyes. The then-current (1950's "modern medicine") medical thinking had called for exposure to the disease and aspirin for any aches and pain. Doc James refused to recommend aspirin as a cure-all, especially to youngsters, choosing to provide his own inexpensive, yet carefully prepared pills when necessary. I can still remember the small 2" x 3" white vertical envelopes with the orange/red lettering on the front indicating the precise dosage and identification of their contents. Years later, Doc James would find many of his once-quaint practices vindicated, as newer modern medicine would determine that childhood diseases such as measles were not to be taken lightly nor exposed to needlessly, nor was aspirin a cure-all for every one of every age, particularly young children.

Of course, to be fair to medicine in the '50s, bacon, eggs, and sunshine were all considered to be good for you. So were cigarettes, for that matter; in fact, Life magazine regularly contained Camels ads with medical doctors extolling the virtues of Camels' "smooth, non-irritating" tobacco blend on smokers' throats. Somehow, seeing a little-black-bag doctor, seated at the bedside of a patient (in a private home, no less), stethoscope in his ears, a concerned look on his face, while drawing on a Camel cigarette seems highly comical.

Then, in the '70s and '80s, all of these were described as hazardous-to-your-health commodities. Instead, "twigs and berries" were the prescribed tonics for good health with coffee, and beer to be totally avoided.

Today, with the exception of cigarettes and other tobacco products, we're not quite so sure about any of these (except for bacon which, despite the scientific warnings, I still consider to be the original nourishment of the gods regardless of what anyone else claims). However, despite the debates and shifting sands of medical knowledge, I will vigorously dispute the notion that medicine has not improved over the last century.

Even with a remarkably practical Doc James around in those horse-and-buggy days, when diphtheria surfaced, you posted a "Quarantined" sign on the door and then walked on the other side of the street. Many diseases, now almost unknown to people of the 21st Century, represented a death-sentence, despite Doc James' effective country medicine. But, after all, living into your sixties was considered a good, full lifespan. Perhaps that was why church attendance was always so robust; mankind hadn't yet come to the point of discarding Faith in favor of what they believed (still?) was their own inherent personal command and control of physical circumstances along with their mortal souls, let alone their physical bodies. In other words, people of that day realized that existence was fragile, the going hard, and ultimately that life for the average person ended up relatively short in years.

As a result, for James Kimmel and most other country boys, life was simply too hard and short to allow children to waste time in non-productive enterprises. Every family needed each individual member to pull their economic weight and either do the farm work or make whatever monies they could to keep the Family above water. There were virtually no social or government safety-nets, no food stamps. If you ran out of money or fell on hard times, you either relied on local charity and/or your extended family. When the alternative to barely surviving day-to-day was starvation, the family needed all hands on deck.

But that didn't present young James with a tremendous adjustment. After all, he liked being on his own, finding his own way, relying on his own intuition and industriousness; and as a result, coal mining fitted him naturally.

So, after going through the 4th Grade in 1902, James Kimmel picked up a heavy square-bladed coal shovel, his short-handled pick, and proceeded to absorb the techniques necessary to mine coal. He was a quick learner, soaking up the lessons and experience of the older men who worked the area's small subsistence mines. For example, he learned how to detect and hopefully avoid the buildup of noxious gasses (if you didn't, you simply died), how to work a short-handled pick in a narrow, cramped tunnel shaft, how to efficiently transport the dislodged coal out the tunnel without wasting good mining time, and how to make sure that your tunnel was properly braced and supported. He learned rudimentary electrical skills (and how to consistently heed those lessons to avoid instant electrocution), the absolute necessity of paying attention every second underground, and most of all that nothing actually mined coal except hard human labor.

Mom Mary understood how hard life was for young James. As a firmly devout woman, she would stay awake on Saturday nights, kneeling in prayer, oil lamp lighting her room even at 1:00AM, waiting to be sure that her son would arrive home safely. After all, she knew that the one night of the week for young men to blow off steam, usually mixed figuratively and physically with alcohol, could lead to a wide variety of troubles to the physical body and immortal soul. Demon rum by itself could wreak havoc.

One late-Saturday evening James and Wesley had heard a crash followed by several thumps over towards old Route 53. Making their way by coal-oil lamp down to the local dirt road, they discovered an overturned Oakland automobile, sitting wheels to the sky. Inside was a thoroughly inebriated young man, suspended upside down and hanging by his pants belt, which had somehow looped around the gearshift levers, probably saving his life.

Completely unaware of his wildly good luck, and with gasoline dripping menacingly from the fuel tank, the driver was attempting to light a cigarette, dumbfounded by the fact that the lighter-flame insisted on going down – or up – depending on your point of reference. James snarled, "Get him out of there before he cooks all of us, the idiot!" Afterwards, he had thought to himself, "It doesn't get any closer than that!"

Now, hugging the trench walls, face buried as deeply as possible in French dirt, he had to smile once more. Closer, he mused, is relative. He remembered how frightened he had been initially of encountering poisonous methane-laced gas in the mines, a constant danger far more dangerous than the cigarette of an inebriated motorist. Nothing had invaded his dreams more completely than thoughts of suddenly smelling gas while cramped in a tiny tunnel, unable to move, holding his breath until his oxygen-craving lungs had to surrender to the deadly vapors. Well, he thought, at least I'm not crammed into a mine tunnel here. But then again, what he was now facing wasn't just methane gas.

Throughout the past several months he had done his best to avoid causing his mother added worry. He had just posted a letter home in which he had said: "Dear Mother and all, just a little letter to let you know that I am well and all right yet but I am getting tired of this life. I guess to tell the truth I am getting a little homesick but I think that it will not be too many more months until we will be back home. Tell Dad that I may get home this coming spring in time to help him get his spring work done. I guess Dad thinks I have forgot him but I think of you all (all) the time.

Mother, I saw Tad Barnhart the other day. He is with the 313th machine gun transport and he was awful glad to see me and it was the first time I saw him over here. Tell his Dad or wife that I saw him.

Well Mother, I don't know any thing much to write about. I could tell you a lot about going over the top and so on, but I will tell you all about it when I get home. I will close for this time as I am not thinking of anything more to write about. I am going to send a few post cards in the next letter as souvenirs of France. I am going to also send you a Jerry shoulder strap and buttons as a little souvenir. Will close with lots of love and kisses for you, Mother, from your son, Jim. PS – Please excuse, writing as best I can do, ha-ha." That was as chatty a letter as he could write, he figured. No need to try to tell her about the German machine guns, the close-no quarter fighting, or the terrible poison gas.

Indeed, James Kimmel had lived through three separate occasions in which the Germans had lobbed artillery canisters of chlorine and the even more-dreaded mustard gas in on the Americans. Each time, immediately upon hearing the frantic shout of "Gas!", he had instinctively reached into his canvas gas-mask pack and in one motion extracted the face shield, hose, and filter-canister, pulled the lip of the rubber mask first over his chin, and then over top his head. Tugging on the adjustment straps and then checking for a good seal, Kimmel had then turned to look for anyone who had either not heard the alert or had encountered difficulties of some kind. Either way, that individual was in a frightful position, as the cruel chlorine gas turned the lung tissue to a useless, gummy mess leaving the unfortunate victim to essentially drown in his own body's fluids.

On the other hand, while the blistering vesicant, mustard gas, simply attacked anything exposed (or not) on the human body, the burns it left were equally hideous. Almost as cruel were the lingering effects of mustard gas on virtually everything, the remnants of which could persist for weeks depending on the weather and terrain. He had seen the gruesome results of mustard-induced wounds and the excruciating agony of its victims in the rear hospitals. Worse than any of these, though, were the reports of the occasional use of "White Star", a dreaded mixture of chlorine and phosgene gasses. From that point on fears of mine-generated methane gas would never again dominate James Kimmel's dreams, not after the shell-pocked, poisonous gas-saturated, eternally soggy fields of war-time France.

From early-July into August of 1918, the 318th had found themselves supporting the British Army by individual battalions rather than as a unified regiment until late August. Then, after arriving in Domleger, they had happily turned in their British Enfields and other British gear and thankfully again drawn their own American weapons. Still, though, they had found themselves continually assigned to a reserve role even in the supposedly American sector. To make matters more irritating, instead of the rumored new Browning Automatic Rifles (BAR), they had received hand-me-down French Chauchat auto-rifles, of which the Doughboys were neither familiar nor did they trust.

Even in early-September, 1918, as the American Army had begun its offensive on St. Mihiel, the 318th had remained in reserve along with the bulk of the 80th Division. Kimmel and his comrades had begun to think that they might never actually see a live German again, although he had seen several dead ones lying along the road to Relamee Woods near Souilly. Up until this time, with the exception of a few limited but sharp engagements, the concept of all-out war had been just that – a still-to-be-experienced ordeal that had been feared, even dreaded, but not actually fully witnessed first-hand. But those few lifeless German corpses, faces frozen as if in an old, grainy photograph, had brought home the understanding to James R. Kimmel that this was a deadly serious business. He remembered thinking that perhaps being in a reserve role had some distinct advantages after all.

Almost as if responding to the 318th Division's pre-mature wishes, they had found themselves being brought up on-line to the Germonville-Vigneville Road on September 25th; the next day they found themselves fully part of the massive Meuse-Argonne Offensive. In the next 6 days, James R. Kimmel had found himself in an honest-to-God, non-stop shooting-war for the first time and, as the calendar changed, October 1918 had not shown any sign of presenting a reprieve. The sound of the Maxim machine-gun rounds cracking overhead, the shrill shriek of the whistle followed by the wild sprint out of the trenches and across "No Man's Land" confirmed Kimmel's thinking: this was wild, brutal, unworldly, insane. "How in the hell did I get myself into this?" he had found himself muttering countless times each day.

Now, on the evening of October 3, Kimmel had made the complete transition from trainee to combat veteran while living a lifetime in the space of a few weeks. As Company K had scrambled into their assigned trenches, he again found himself smiling grimly and reminding himself, "Remember to be careful for what you ask for." He had wanted action and to test himself under fire. Now, he was getting his opportunity and in more than ample buckets. War, it seemed, had a fiendish way of doing unpredictable things like that, he thought to himself. Then again, you had best think long and hard concerning what you asked for.

As if to add to the already present inferno of sound, the Allied heavy artillery was now responding to the German '88 fire. Kimmel hugged the front wall of the trench even closer, thinking, "Oh, great, more shell-craters to move through. Then again, more cover from the German machine guns." Yes, this was indeed what was being called "the machine gun war". Never before in the history of armed combat had such a wide variety of rapid, automatic-fire weaponry been so available down to the common foot-soldier on both sides. And although he had rarely seen them in great numbers, Kimmel knew of even bigger, more potentially devastating weapons of war just being introduced.

Originally introduced in 1916 by the British, the armored vehicles with steel tracks had appeared boasting the ability to effortlessly cross trenches and quickly breach the complicated tangles of enemy barbed wire. The oddly-rhomboid shaped monstrosities packed either "6-pounders" (57mm guns), or machine-guns housed in side-mounted "sponsons" and were protected with armor-plating up to ½" in thickness. Although hardly speed demons, when combined with good close infantry support and new artillery tactics, these "tanks" (originally referred to as 'Water Tanks' for security reasons; however the term 'tanks' had stuck) had proven to be full of future promise for the battlefield, although at the time they were still very prone to break-down and available only in relatively small numbers.

With the addition of the tank the battlefield had dramatically changed, albeit not in making it less deadly. While the proud columns of horse-mounted cavalry had quickly vanished from the World War I battlefields in the conflict's first six weeks, devastated victims of the ability of rapid-fire weaponry to cut down horse and human flesh in horrendous numbers, the new term "Armored Cavalry" was being introduced and coined.

No, Kimmel thought, along with the new airplanes (or "scouts", as they were known throughout the War) – planes such as the British Sopwith Camel and Nieuport, the French Spads and Morane-Saulniers, and the German Fokker's, both "Eindeckers" (single-winged) and the three-winged tri-plane DR-1's, plus their Albatross versions, coupled with their ever-increasing ability to effectively drop bombs on troops - war would never be fought the same way again. Armored and aerodynamically-shaped mobile gun platforms were rapidly replacing flesh and blood-mounted weaponry along with the usually unseen, until much too late attacks from the air. Then again, he mused, you could die just as quickly inside one of those sealed-up tanks or high in the sky, where the only escape from flame and wreckage was a prolonged and fatal fall. After all, mortality wasn't necessarily going to be cheated simply because of technological efficiency, human ingenuity, or sheer altitude.

Still, he knew, it would take the common soldier, the "grunt", the "ground-pounder infantryman" to finish the job, to take the fight close-in and occupy the enemy's territory. And it would depend on his ability to advance, close in upon, and seize the enemy by the throat, choking the human life out of him to complete the mission. Unfortunately for most of the survivors of such initiatives, the aftermath is never quite so easy to forget. The military planners seated well behind the front lines can simply take a map down, fold it up, and move on to the next specific operation – or war. The infantryman has no such luxury, either in 1918 or today.

Even after the physical map comes down, the hard, stark carnage and personal terror involved even in a successful mission refuses to be simply folded and put away undisturbed in a soldier's mental drawer. Kimmel had seen the guy next to him crumple up in agony, stunned and frantic to stop the life from draining out of his machine-gun riddled body. He had seen the horror, shock, and even pleading of the enemy soldier as the thrust of the bayonet or muzzle-flash exploded directly in front of him in a final glimpse of life. Yes, he thought, it was the eyes, always the eyes that he would remember. And Kimmel would remember them until he drew his last breath on earth some 60-plus years later.

The shrill shriek of the whistle signaling "over the top" always made him momentarily chuckle. Whistles were for children at play and to start picnic games, he had always thought, not to signal grown men to race to their deaths. By now, more by drill than instinct, he was over the top of the trench before the whistle's echo had ceased rather than being frozen for a few seconds as had happened the very first time. "In a hurry to get yourself killed, Jimmy Kimmel," he found himself muttering once more as he weaved his way through the shattered landscape, his calf and thigh muscles straining pushed by the superhuman urge for self-preservation. But he was also a good soldier and the key to any frontal assault, at least a marginally successful one he knew, was getting enough troops on-line to attempt to achieve and maintain fire superiority. Otherwise, being by yourself was not a good thing, as the Krauts would have much fewer targets to train their guns on. And being a single target, Kimmel knew, was never desirable.

Only 50 yards from the relative safety of his own trench and the German machine guns were already cutting up the ground around him. He dodged the spits of dirt launched by the German slugs, stumbled momentarily, and then hugged a shattered tree stump, trying to blend his slender body around the stubby root crown. Amazing, he thought, how low to the ground or close to even the skinniest tree a man can force himself when lead-death is flashing inches above or around. He was constantly reminded of the old soldier's adage: "If you hear it, it's missed you. It's the one you don't hear that's the killer!"

Still, he found himself bringing to bear his 1917 Model .30 and, with target-acquisition aim in shooting practiced since his boyhood while hunting in the deep Pennsylvania woods, he managed to lay down seven or eight rapid fire shots that sent the nearest entrenched Jerry machine gun crew scrambling for cover, one German soldier frantically clutching his right leg. With equally Army-practiced smoothness, Corporal Kimmel seamlessly re-loaded and chambered a round. Others in his platoon had now managed to bring to bear semi-effective cover fire, at least enough to make the Germans pause momentarily before re-manning their gun emplacement positions.

Now, however, almost on cue the friendly '75 artillery fire began to tear chunks out of the entrenched German guns' positions slightly to their rear and Kimmel used those few seconds to lunge forward, taking added advantage of the stunning effect of the high-explosive rounds in and around the enemy soldiers. Time slowed to a crawl with the enemy moving, it seemed, in exaggerated slow-motion; but Kimmel's legs appeared to churn in a blur. Almost calmly he thought, "It would really annoy my parents if I got killed by our own friendly fire."

Corporal Kimmel dashed the remaining 25 yards, bayonet at gut-level. With one last, extended lunge, he leaped into the enemy trench, landing directly in the middle of five startled, shell-shocked German troops, wide-eyed, almost is if they were seeing an avenging, apocalyptic demon. Kimmel, however, was a flurry of motion. There was no time for rifle fire; everything at that point was hand-to-hand – rifle butts, fists, boot-kicks, and the rest of the savage eyeball-to-eyeball, kill-or-be-killed maelstrom of violence that made up trench warfare.

****

Epilogue

James Rubert Kimmel (no one is sure where the spelling of the middle name originated, including himself; one story was that his father, Wesley, simply disliked the name "Robert" but tolerated "Rubert"), my maternal grandfather, survived the end of World War I and was mustered out of the U. S. Army in June of 1919. He returned to Somerset County in south-central Pennsylvania – Stoystown, to be exact - to his wife, Ethel Carrie (Miller) and within the next three years fathered two children, James W. and then Jacquelyne Anne (my Mother). After exiting the military service, James R. initially helped on the family farm, then returned to coal mining for several years.

Despite the downscaling of post-wartime industry, earned money was good in the early part of the "Roaring Twenties", as the steel mills in Pittsburgh churned out the critical materials for consumer manufacturing and building: steel sheet for automobiles, thick steel structural plate and beams for commercial buildings, bridges and cargo ships, and steel tubing for oil pipelines to feed the Country's thirst for energy. And, of course, one of the key raw materials for steelmaking was coal, converted to "coke" in the "beehive ovens" scattered throughout western Pennsylvania or the newly-introduced coke-ovens, then fed to the ravenous iron-producing blast furnaces to provide the molten feedstock for steel. Using a phrase that soon became attributed to the upstart automaker General Motors

Corporation, Kimmel often heard: "What's good for U. S. Steel is ultimately good for a coal miner."

The early-to-mid 1920's economy remained reasonably healthy and the Family lived modestly but comfortably; however, the severe economic distress later in the decade impacted the Kimmel Family as well as most every other mining family in Pennsylvania. The fires in the blast-furnaces and Bessemer converter steelmaking furnaces were almost completely extinguished, as the mills struggled to put three-day work weeks together. Following the stock market crash that fall, Christmas of 1929 was especially bleak, with the mines being idle adding to the early-winter mountain cold. James R. fretted concerning the upcoming holidays and the prospect of very few gifts from Santa under the Christmas tree for nine year-old James W. and little seven year-old Jackie.

He wasn't worried about Ethel; she understood that even her occasional seamstress work had been scaled back to almost nothing due to the economic gloom. New clothes were now an extreme luxury and "making do" with patched and hand-me-down clothing was a way of life for almost every family.

The Kimmel children, however, still expected to wake up on Christmas morning to find brightly-wrapped presents under the tree and the Standard-gauge Lionel electric train circling the mountain-moss-decorated scenery, including the cardboard-house town with one new building being added each year. This, along with the "reindeer hoof-prints" and obviously huge heavy-weather boot tracks visible in the snow atop the house roof, courtesy of James R.'s pole with a mountain-deer hoof nailed to the end and bulky Woolrich galoshes, was Christmas for his little son and daughter.

As a result, early December of 1929 created a semi crisis-of-conscience for Kimmel. Desperate to earn a few dollars for Christmas, he overheard scuttlebutt regarding driving old horse-drawn wagons down over Bald Knob Mountain to Bedford. The complication: the trips were at night and the cargo was bootleg whiskey, "white lightning." James R. had never felt tremendous support for Prohibition to start with; simply, he always had enjoyed having a drink and believed that attempting to outlaw the practice was impractical, as most working-men liked to have a drink – some much more than others. However, since it was "the Law of the Land" since the passage of the Volstead Act back in 1919, he had grudgingly abided by it.

But now, he was considering not only violating the law but also aiding those who were profiting in that violation. It wasn't the act itself that bothered him the most; rather, the fact that he would be openly breaking a law of his Country. Of course, there was also the small but very real consideration that he could be caught participating in the clandestine transportation activities, and spend the holidays in jail. These concerns were all balanced against thoughts of the faces of his children as they would bound out of their beds and race into the living room on Christmas morning.

As a result, on Christmas morning of 1929, the Kimmel children basked in the joy of a cornucopia of presents under the Lionel-surrounded Christmas tree, and Ethel purred contentedly as she sat in the over-stuffed blue chair surrounded in her new, warm, high-collar wool winter coat. All of this bounty was funded by three icy-wind, blowing-snow trips over Bald Knob mountain in a four-horsepower wooden farm wagon loaded with bootleg hootch, minus a few bottles for "family medicinal purposes." In this instance, Family had decidedly won out over conscience.

Despite the seemingly unending depths of the Depression, in early 1930, James R. scraped together enough cash to buy a small pool hall and single-bay service station, to which, after Prohibition ended in 1933, he added a modest restaurant along with a bar and dance floor. Located barely a quarter of a mile from the Family farm, just outside of Stoystown on old Route 53, the entire Kimmel Family including Wesley and Mary helped maintain the business. Even during the height of the Depression, the south-west road heading towards equally small-town Somerset provided a meager but relatively steady clientele. Interestingly, the non-descript town of Somerset became a stop along the first "Superhighway" in the

Country, the Pennsylvania Turnpike, following its opening in 1939.

Through the Depression years, he and the family managed to eat and survive thanks to the proceeds of the food, drink, and gasoline business plus some outdoor entertainment courtesy of the local creek. Perhaps harkening back to his days aboard the Leviathan, James R. dammed the northeast corner of the creek bed, purchased two small wooden shallow-draft power-boats along with several 10 HP Mercury outboard motors, and proceeded to offer cruises around the created lagoon and up under the concrete bridge of Route 53. His warning cry of, "Low bridge!" added to the excitement of the ride along with the barely six inches of clearance between boat deck and bridge bottom. He charged ten-cents per occupant; today, this wouldn't even begin to cover the insurance premium – if anyone would begin to consider offering liability coverage!

A few picnic tables, meticulously manicured grounds, and a covered outdoor dance pavilion also created a popular family recreation area, particularly on summer holidays, and the entire complex became eventually known throughout the area as "Kimmel's Park."

James R. Kimmel always was known as a man's man. He had no need for a bouncer at the bar; even into his sixties, James R. could still keep order. One time in the early-'50s, a young miner had come into the Park already drunk and when James R. refused to serve him, the young ruffian reportedly had shouted, "Now, Jim Kimmel, I'm gonna' give you the worst licking you ever had and right here in your own place!"

The words were all that the lout got out of his mouth, as a crashing right cross from James R. sent the drunken bully ass-over-tin cups; end of the fight. I remember my Grandfather commenting in characteristic understatement, "I had whiskers embedded in my knuckles, so I guess I caught him pretty square."

Through the years of World War II James R. continued to work, both supporting the War rationing efforts and having his son, James W., serve as an Army Ranger in both that war and in Korea. We will hear more concerning James W. a bit later.

In 1955, James R. and Ethel sold the "Park" and retired, living on a very meager World War I soldier's pension and Social Security. He was eligible for a miner's "Black Lung" benefit/pension as well which would have been more than his soldier's pension and Social Security combined. James R. refused to apply for it. When routinely asked concerning this decision he would simply reply, "I don't have 'black lung'; why would I apply for benefits on account of it?"

While he had avoided coal-induced lung disease, 50-plus years of two packs of Camels per day did manage to give him several serious bouts of pleurisy, the last one in 1962 almost taking his life. He managed to recover, but also came out of that illness a changed man. First, he completely gave up smoking. He claimed that, after he had recovered from the pleurisy, he and Ethel had made a trip to the local grocery store where he had purchased a carton of Camel cigarettes. After pulling the black 1951 Chevrolet Deluxe Coupe into the garage and carrying groceries into the house, he stood at the garage entrance and lit up a Camel. He said that he was immediately light-headed and sick to his stomach, so much so that he crushed the cigarette out and never lit another from that day on. Of course, there were always a multitude of peppermint LifeSavers lying wherever an ashtray had once been. Still, and successfully, he did it "cold turkey."

Maybe it was the brush with pleurisy-death; maybe it was creeping age? Somehow, though, I doubt either of those reasons. Rather, I think James R. realized that regardless of his own physical and mental toughness, life would and could always out-maneuver him. Even in France, he claimed that the knowledge of his mother, Mary Lee McDevitt Kimmel kneeling by her bedside in fervent prayer for him, provided him with a gentle nudge to question his "master of my fate, captain of my soul" beliefs. Whether it was the wisdom of age finally bringing him face-to-face with his own mortality or perhaps him finding a measure of peace and wholeness by acceptance of God in his life, James R. walked forward in the Reading Brethren Church in 1963, confessed his faith in his Lord and Savior Jesus Christ, and became a devout Christian for the rest of his life. I was always touched and awed to see him bow his head in reverent prayer before a breakfast or lunch meal, whether alone or in company.

I became very close to James R. in the last ten years of his life, particularly after my own service in the U. S. Army. Upon returning from my Basic and Advanced Individual Combat Training and realizing that I would likely spend my time as a reservist (first in the Ohio and then Pennsylvania Army National Guard), I had approached our first meeting back home with genuine anxiety. I felt that I had somehow broken the chain of Family combat veterans dating back to the Civil War (or again, as Mary Lee would have called it, "The War Against Northern Aggression" – she was always a little bit put-out when Mom had announced that she was marrying "a Yankee", which still constituted anyone coming from a "blue" state such as Pennsylvania.). Now, in 1972, freshly-trained troops were being sent to Korea or held State-side for other non-combat assignments as the southeast-Asia conflict in Viet Nam was in its final ending stages for the vast majority of American combat troops.

I remember walking hesitantly into my grandparents' kitchen, wearing my Class A "greens" along with a light-blue Infantry Cord and brand-new Private First Class (PFC) stripes on each shoulder. I wondered what he would say, or if he would say anything at all, this battle-tested combat veteran of a war long before.

Grandma Ethel called out, "Jim, your soldier's here!" A moment later, James R. walked into the kitchen. Not knowing exactly what else to do, I reached my hand out saying simply, "Hi, Grandpa." We shook hands in a "decidedly manly manner"; our family had never been the huggy/smoochie kind. However, in an instant and to my amazement, I saw tears in his eyes and he reached out and pulled me close. As he hugged me he whispered, "You done good, Slim. You done it right." I remember closing my eyes, hugging him tightly, and feeling waves of relief roll over me, smoothing the hardened ridges of worry and anxiety that I had built up for many months. In those few moments, I found all the validation I would ever need for my military service along with other parts of my life. Those eight words are probably the sweetest I have ever heard.

James R. lived until July of 1979. He was in robust health up until about 4 months prior to his death. We hunted together each autumn up until his last, savoring the times when we could wander the harvest-picked bare corn-fields looking for pheasant, grouse, and rabbit, then joining James W. for the opening of "buck season" the Monday after Thanksgiving. On Memorial Day of 1978 following the annual Stoystown parade, James R. and I stood together in front of his flag pole for a picture, he in his Doughboy uniform (yes, it still fit after 60 years) and me in my khakis, jump-boots, and black beret. After the picture was taken, I turned to him and said, "Well, we'll take one next year – same day, same place." He answered, "If I'm living, Slim; if I'm living."

New Years Eve of 1978 Janet and I had driven up to Stoystown from Pittsburgh just to sit and celebrate the coming of 1979 with my Grandparents. James R. sat with me in the quiet of his tiny basement recreation-room as the sun had long since set, disappearing early even for December behind a bank of low-lying stratus clouds beginning to form from the west over the Alleghenies. I had just finished a cold Iron City beer and a shot of Imperial (in "Pittsburgh-ese", that's called an "Imp and Arn") and he was sipping a glass of red Chablis. I remember him saying that he was finding it harder to stay warm so far that winter and I had reminded him that the Arctic cold had swept south faster than normal this past December.

"I hear you, Slim," he had said. "But I've seen cold winters before. I think that maybe this one will be my last one." I had laughed, perhaps a bit too gaily, telling him that he was just getting the "New Year's Blues" and that before he knew it we'd be getting our uniforms out again along with the barbecue grill for our summer picnics. I remember him rubbing his back, grimacing slightly; he had commented that, for the past month or so he had resorted to taking a nap lying on the dining-room floor radiator grill, letting the heat soothe his mysteriously chronic sore back. Involuntarily I had shivered, realizing that he was in pain and suddenly looking very, very old. I remember pouring another shot of Imperial and thinking about those words from the past Memorial Day, "If I'm living, Slim; if I'm living…"

By Memorial Day of 1979 James R. Kimmel was living but only barely, lying in a rented hospital bed that we had placed in the living room of the house. Through the late winter and early spring of that year the pain in his back had spread into his stomach region. As the weeks went by he grew weaker and correspondingly more despondent. On a Sunday afternoon in late-May, I had taken the picture of him and me from Memorial Day of 1978, reminding him that we had a date for a re-take coming up. I remember he took the picture, stared at it for almost a minute, handed it back to me and said, "Yes, them's were happy days." Then he looked out the front window of the house, up towards the IOOF Cemetery which a month later would receive his earthly remains, and quietly whispered, "I was a soldier once…" and I saw the tears slowly trickling down his weathered cheeks.

Perhaps he was thinking the farewell thoughts of General MacArthur: "…I could see those staggering columns of the First World War, bending under soggy packs, on many a weary march from dripping dusk to drizzling dawn, slogging ankle-deep through the mire of shell-shocked roads, to form grimly for the attack, blue-lipped, covered with sludge and mud, chilled by the wind and rain, driving home to their objective, and for many, to the judgment seat of God."

"Grandpa Jim" passed away at home on July 7, 1979. The official cause of death was listed as "old age". Somehow, though, I think it was also partly due to "aged memories".

The year before, in a completely out-of-the-blue moment, James R. had turned to me and remarked, "It's the most terrible thing a man can do – take another man's life." And I knew that, for a few brief moments, he had been back in France, charging forward into that line of German trenches and seeing the stunned, terrified eyes of the Kaiser's troops as an American Doughboy scrambled towards them like the Pale Horseman of The Apocalypse. The two of us – soldiers – sat there for over a minute in silence. I simply nodded, knowing that true peace free of those kinds of demons would not come to him this side of the grave. Indeed, I've come to understand that this is the eternal curse carried by any combat soldier who, by the Grace of God, survives the battlefield only to face the remainder of life burdened with a private-hell of memories.

SSG Barry A. Lauer and CPL James R. Kimmel –
Memorial Day 1978

Col. David Kimmel – 9th PA Volunteer Cavalry

A Soldier's Question – Battle of the Ardennes Forest (AKA – The Battle of the Bulge) – December, 1944

It wasn't as if Sergeant Merle B. Lauer, 101st Airborne, 506th Parachute Regiment had never experienced cold weather before. After all, the Allegheny Mountain region in south-central Pennsylvania could get Arctic-frigid in late-December. Temperatures lower than -30°F were uncommon but not unknown at the higher elevations and the future misery index known as "wind chill" was as yet un-named, but still a reality. Yet, even at those freak Pennsylvania winter temperatures there was always the solid, unmoving protection of the 3-story beet-red brick house on Clark Street in the once-booming coal-mining town of Hooversville, population roughly 300. Even in the most bitter winter conditions, the old coal-fired furnace would still manage to keep the most distant upstairs rooms and attic reasonably warm (and the central rooms closer to the furnace maybe just a bit too sultry), and the coal supply was not a problem as the nearby mines still generated a near-endless supply of acceptable house coal.

No, it wasn't just the cold, the unrelenting wind, or the fact that it was December in Western Europe; human beings had been dealing with such climatic facts for 20,000 years or so, if Lauer's high school history memory was still lucid. Mankind had (usually) found ways to shelter in, curl up, and wait out frigid weather. But this December, 1944, things were not quite as simple; and the enemy prevented holing-up. Jamming his toes into the soles of his leather combat boots for about the three-millionth time and still barely registering a hint of feeling, Sergeant Lauer felt totally exposed, utterly vulnerable, and except for the few men of the 506th left around him, for whom he would willingly give his life just as he knew they would for him, completely alone.

In December of 1944, this was not just "Europe in winter." Rather, this was eastern-France (or was it southern-Belgium?), Bastogne, to be more precise. And, with a surrounding, superior-numbered enemy army intent on exterminating the stubborn, thoroughly frozen "Screaming Eagles" of the 101st, holing-up would probably get you a bayonet in the back or a viciously sharp trench knife across your vulnerable, bare throat. Lauer fingered his field jacket pockets once more, again coming up with not even the shredded butt of a cigarette. "What I wouldn't give for a half a pack of Lucky Strikes – no, I'd settle for a pair of smokes! Anything to feel some warmth somewhere on my body!" And he also knew that even if he had a smoke he wouldn't light up, not out here, where even the faint glow of a cigarette would be like shining a beacon into his face. Amazing what a combat infantryman learned in months of battle; assuming, that is, you survived to contemplate and continue to apply the lessons. What was it that his seventh-grade English teacher, Miss Clark had said? "Experience is an excellent teacher, but she can sometimes submit horrific bills."

Unfortunately, mortal combat has its own way of dispensing experience: a soldier learns that carelessness – the snap of dry winter underbrush beneath tired boots, voices instead of hand and arm signals – can get your mortal check stamped "paid in full" for eternity. Further, it's not just Privates (or even Sergeants) who are susceptible to carelessness, although maybe they are not as prone to underestimating a determined, still-dangerous enemy. Going eyeball-to-eyeball day after day will do that to a line combat soldier.

In mid-December of 1944, it hadn't been "Privates" who had gotten careless and far too casual regarding an enemy that they had presumed powerless, devoid of battle morale, already defeated. Now, the 101st and other Allied units were reaping the savage dividends of that failed upper-level notion. Nazi Germany's Wehrmacht may have been severely wounded but, as nature taught daily, that's precisely when the danger may be the most acute. Instead of the "Home for Christmas" mantra that had pervaded the Allied Armies in the autumn of 1944, the Germans had now replaced it with a repeat of that supposedly neutered Teutonic method of war called "Blitzkrieg." In a classic case of counting chickens before the chicks are hatched, the Allies had ignored the obvious signs of a Wehrmacht armored buildup until their Panzer columns, under the cover of atrocious winter weather which de-clawed the superior Allied air power, crashed with devastating swiftness through the dense forests of the Ardennes.

Once again in World War II, an enemy had struck with force through an area deemed "impenetrable", just as the Japanese had done at Singapore 4 years earlier, slogging through "impenetrable" jungle to quickly capture the stunned British defenders. Abject surprise, paralysis in command, confusion in tactical operations and communication, then the instinctive scramble for survival had once again been the result throughout the Allied lines along with, in many cases, capture and death. Again, Miss Clark's "Dame Experience" had submitted her ghastly bill regarding "experience - learned."

The 101st had been hastily thrown into the onslaught in a desperate attempt to block the avenues of Panzer movement, whose obvious intent was to split the Allied lines and charge northward through Belgium and ultimately the port of Antwerp. With its extensive dock facilities and strategic position on the North Sea, not only would Germany potentially gain a strategic port location but also conveniently split the Allied front in two. Achieving this would not necessarily "save" the war for Hitler; however, it could alter the Allied "Home for Christmas" mantra to "Home for Christmas in 1945…maybe."

The Allies had subsequently been presented with perhaps the most serious military challenge of World War II, and squarely in the middle of the potential catastrophe the 101st had found themselves formed around the vital crossroads and communication link situated at the village of Bastogne. There, they dutifully had dug in, fashioning hastily-constructed field trenches guarding the confluence of rough roads with what they hoped would be effective overlapping fields of fire.

The situation would have been grim even in favorable weather. But when the gale-force driven winds of a North Sea-bred snowstorm, fog, and viciously frigid temperatures had fully settled in, exposed and static defensive positions had also become amazingly and deadly cold. Huddled next to Private Henry Stevens at roughly midnight on December 20, Sergeant Lauer couldn't help but remember something he had learned in high school science regarding the thermal properties of earth and how below-grade basements stayed at constant moderate temperatures thanks to materials, depth of soil, and thermodynamics. "Maybe conventional thermodynamics don't work too well in wartime," he murmured to no one in particular.

"You say something, Sarge?" Stevens asked with a start. Sleep was virtually impossible in the intense cold, although the soldiers found themselves slipping in and out of light dozing sessions, shocked back to full consciousness by their own violent shivering.

"No, just moving a bit, trying to stay warm," Lauer replied. For about the 10-millionth time he found himself asking, "Whose bright idea was this to join a parachute outfit, let alone the 506'th?" The answer was always the same: from the beginning of World War II Merle Lauer had wanted to get into the fight and do it with "the best of the best" and when he had arrived at Toccoa, Georgia in early 1944 he had been assured that he would indeed be among "the best". That is, if he conquered the training, the physical and mental abuse, and demonstrated the personal toughness required to wear the coveted paratrooper "jump wings".

Lauer had seen smart, educated men, already in excellent physical condition, wash out of the Airborne. He had wondered about that at the time. After six months in combat in France, he fully understood. It was ultimately the mental toughness that mattered most, the ability to still function effectively when bone-tired physically, when carnage descended all around, and when giving up, while maybe an attractive option, was simply unthinkable.

It was something that Sergeant Lauer would try to pass on to future generations: you could silently carp about general conditions of life as long as you kept putting one foot in front of the other. If "I've had enough!" was part of your personal vocabulary, you had no business being in the Airborne.

As another frigid gust swirled the snow in front of his position, he dipped his head to let his steel pot block the blast and smiled grimly at the fact that all he had been concerned about in the Toccoa days was qualifying as an expert parachutist. He had given little or no thought to the possibility of getting killed – the gracious gift of God to all young human beings, who always tend to over-weight the rewards and ignore the risks. Nothing will ever "happen" to me, if it does it will happen to someone else and, besides, I'm going to live forever!

Even after the night jump before D-Day he hadn't paid much attention to the possibility of being blown out of the sky along with the rest of his buddies or catching an enemy round upon landing, probably because everything had happened so fast and was also so new. After all, night jumps required full attention and, along with the prospect of first contact with an enemy looking to snuff your life out, he had not really had time to mull things over philosophically. Generally this was because you found yourself obcessed with repeatedly muttering such mindless profound expressions as, "Holy ____!"

At any rate, Lauer mentally noted that after Normandy, men usually began to find religion – truly or at least rationally. Essentially, most everyone grew up after D-Day. They realized that not only was death a distinct possibility in combat but that there was no effective way to shield oneself. Being a poor soldier definitely hiked the odds of meeting the Grim Reaper but Lauer had seen "good soldiers" perish simply because Death could be a capricious shrew. Sometimes, it all came down to numbers.

On a night-jump in early-August of 1944, Sergeant Lauer had found himself gathering his gear before takeoff when an obviously distraught buddy approached him.

"Hey, Merle B.," the man said, surprising himself with his own half-shout, "What'd you draw?"

Lauer flashed two fingers twice, indicating a "nice" distance back from the door.

"Switch with me, Merle? I'm number two and I just can't shake this feeling…" Lauer shrugged and nodded as nonchalantly as possible. After all, he figured, out quick or out later, it didn't really matter. Besides, there was nothing worth looking at going down other than night and he didn't know if he really wanted to see anything else.

As the C-47 droned on, the distant, still-muffled sound of flak began to intrude on the solitude of the twenty-four men. Flashes of dark-fire began to appear in the sky ahead of the troop plane. Two minutes before jump time, the C-47 was rocking unsteadily as the anti-aircraft fire seemed to escalate by the second. This is about as bad as I've ever seen it, Lauer muttered to himself.

At the command of "Stand in the door", the sudden noise of rushing air and straining engines mixed with the savage blasts of enemy fire. It appeared that he was jumping into a dark, jumbled cauldron of hell. Still, training and practice were kicking in as he shuffled towards the door.

Suddenly a metallic-sounding explosion rocked the airplane. Six inches from his left boot, Lauer saw a jagged hole showing in the C-47's floorboards. A moment before, he had been adjusting his right pack strap a bit tighter, his left arm occupying the same space a mere second before the jagged chunk of flak had torn through the floor.

He was still calmly pondering that thought when he heard "One!" and saw the soldier in front of him disappear into the blackness. Caught in mid-thought but thoroughly trained, Lauer shouted, "Two…" and stepped through the door. As he fell forward, he heard another deafening explosion and felt the concussion flip him sideways. Somehow, he managed to untangle his chute lines and felt the jolt as the main canopy opened.

Looking up, all he could see were pieces of C-47 encased in flame, the victim of a lucky but deadly shot. Hurtling down were also the mangled remains of his buddies; only the first two men had made it out of the doomed troop carrier. Numbers three through twenty-four had perished, including his doomed number twenty-two. Sometimes, nothing made any sense at all, including a soldier's premonition.

Sergeant Lauer had never pictured himself in quite such a predicament – then, or now, in the frozen fields outside Bastogne. Then again, he mused, if you wanted predictability (and far less risk and/or adventure), you would never, ever have joined the Airborne, let alone the 506th Parachute Infantry Regiment. As if anyone had needed a hint of things to come, shortly after the Regiment had been activated in July of 1942 their commander, Lt. Col. Robert F. "Bounding Bob" Sink, had established the standard for the unit: everything took place "on the double."

But besides the grueling training at Camp Toccoa, Georgia (and the simmering, steamy heat which was foreign to a Pennsylvania mountain-raised boy) the 506th PIR began to adopt the spirit of the Currahee Mountains nearby. To the local Indians, "Curahee" meant "stand alone". To the men of the 506th, it became not only their Regimental motto but also their implied mission, namely, to fight and stand alone behind enemy lines. Sergeant Lauer always chuckled at that thought. It indeed seemed that he had spent most of his time in Europe looking at enemy uniforms rather than Allied. The unspoken creed – "Never give up" – also became part of their being.

In late November, 1942, the 506th PIR had departed Toccoa for Fort Benning, GA where their parachute training began. Lauer had never really liked heights but quickly found that you could not like to be high off the ground but still function; in other words, you could be scared spit-less but still do your job! Learning to pack your own chute was a unique and special experience since knowing how it went together could clearly help if things happened to go "badly" on the way down. And there were a great deal of things that could go wrong on a parachute jump, particularly in the all-surrounding blackness of night.

After graduating from jump school, Sergeant Lauer and the rest of the 506th PIR had been moved to Camp Mackall, NC for additional tactical training plus several additional night parachute drops. In June of 1943 the 506th had been attached to the 101st Airborne Division and, after several additional months of training, headed for Camp Shanks, NY, the last stop on American soil, as they knew. By September of 1943, they were aboard the S. S. Samaria bound for Liverpool, England.

Stationed in Wiltshire County, Sergeant Lauer had found the surrounding English villages strikingly similar to those in the small Pennsylvania coal towns except for the infernal clouds and ceaseless winter fog. It was there that, in May of 1944, he had been assigned as a Rifleman to Regimental HQ functioning also as a combat medic. But, as with most elite fighting units, the 506th was growing restless for action; or at least, a respite from the often gloomy English spring. Their period of restlessness had ended on the night of June 5th, 1944, when they were given their first combat mission opportunity – D-Day, The Normandy Invasion.

Lauer quickly found out how difficult coordination of a large-scale night-operation could be, despite rigorous training and meticulous mission preparation. Training exercises had included perhaps a single rifle company and four airplanes; this operation, however, would be much bigger. Although the 81 troop carrier aircraft had lifted off shortly after midnight on June 6th, 1944 in relatively decent order, low-clouds and anti-aircraft fire had effectively scattered the formation. As a result, only 9 planes had managed to drop their troops on the Drop Zone (DZ). Actually, that had been a providential event, as the Germans had previously recognized the area as a likely location for a parachute assault and quickly annihilated the few on-target American troops. The remaining units including Lauer's had hurriedly consolidated upon landing, organized what was left of their combined-arms groups, and begun moving independently towards the beaches of Normandy. As morning dawned on the 6th, the 506th had seized the high ground overlooking the beaches just as the first wave of landing craft was approaching.

At the end of June the 101st had been relieved and sent to Cherbourg as First Army reserve before returning to England for re-fitting and additional training. That stay had been short-lived, though, as British Field Marshal Montgomery, fascinated by the German airborne assault on Crete earlier in the war, had devised a bold "breakout plan" to include a daylight airborne assault. On paper, the plan had been fairly straight-forward: airborne troops would capture the roads and bridges in the Holland cities of Eindhoven, Nijmegen, and Arnhem. Essentially slicing Holland in two, British armor would plow their way through the gap created and rush for the German border.

The flaw in the plan – or at least the grossly overlooked and underestimated part - had simply been: the Germans, and the "plow their way through" part. Ultimately, it took until November of 1944 for the 506th PIR along with elements of the 82nd Airborne to reach all of the objectives in Montgomery's plan, first securing one small Dutch town, then another, each time facing ferocious German counter-attacks. It is always amazing how a general and a front-line combat soldier can look at a map and see completely different views.

Actually, it had been during the Market Garden operation that Sergeant Merle B. Lauer had encountered his first real taste of terror and gut-paralyzing fear for his life. Things had started off badly the moment the 101st stepped out of their aircraft. Sergeant Lauer had never felt so thoroughly helpless than he did that 17th day of September, 1944, dangling from his chute in complete daylight and feeling as if he were wearing a neon sign saying "Shoot the duck – win a prize!" From the moment he hit the ground it seemed that he was part of a wild, running firefight. Clearly, the element of surprise – if there had been any to start with – had long since vanished. The Germans knew that the 101st was on the ground and had rushed infantry and armored reinforcements to the region. As dusk settled in, Lauer and his comrades found themselves cut off from the main force, running low on ammunition, and quickly lost in the unfamiliar Dutch countryside.

Realizing that the Germans had succeeded in securing the major roads in the area, Lauer's squad had taken to the cover of brush and found itself slowly working along a low-cut hedgerow, practicing "best" infantry tactics of slow, measured movement mixed with plenty of stop-look-listen interludes. He sometimes marveled at the way experienced infantrymen could communicate without a word being spoken as compared to the early days of training when everything still seemed like play and men jawed and played grab-ass on patrols. Of course, he knew, everything seems far less important when you know that no one is out there looking to snuff your life out. In life-or-death combat, you either practiced your craft extremely well or you ended up extremely dead. There was nothing casual about being a good infantryman, let alone an Airborne combat soldier.

The other complication in this deadly serious and potentially lethal game of hide-and-seek was that sometimes the enemy possessed very, very good soldiers as well. Pausing along a thick section of hedgerow, Lauer had paused to glance at his watch; it was still well before midnight. The platoon leader Lieutenant – fresh from OCS (Officer Candidate School) in the States - had been just two steps ahead of him, moving slowly and almost noiselessly in a semi-crouched position. Unfortunately, there was a mortal difference between "almost" and "noiselessly". Vaguely silhouetted against a near-new moon, Lauer saw a black-clad arm reach through the bushes and expertly slice a wicked-looking combat knife across the Lieutenant's throat region. With only two or three animal-like gurgles, the officer's body had slumped back into the Sergeant's lap. Frozen into stillness, Lauer had endured the longest 10 seconds of his entire young life as he waited for the black arm to plunge through the hedgerow once more, aiming at his own throat. After an eternity, he could hear footsteps retreating up the hedgerow path, but it was a full ten minutes or so before he could will his legs to work again. Since that night, he had dreamed of black arms intruding into all aspects of his dream-world, waking him in pools of cold sweat terror. The reality of warfare for Sergeant Merle B. Lauer had found its roots at Market Garden.

The failed Dutch operation had also nearly ended Lauer's military career as well. After the Germans had begun pouring reinforcements into the Eindhoven area, his entire company had been split up with individual squads ceasing to function as coordinated units due to the frequent fire-fights and communications breakdowns. Plus, as the fleeing night sky began to show streaks of ragged dawn through the columns of smoke, their cloaking protector, night, was quickly stealing away. Now, the scattered units of the 101st began to frantically look for someplace –anyplace – to dig in and hide. Each man knew that, behind the strengthening numbers of Wehrmacht soldiers would quickly follow the dreaded SS units and Gestapo, and not a man in any Allied unit wanted to take a chance on winding up in the custody of an individual SS squad with an especially bad attitude regarding Americans.

Sergeant Lauer and his buddy, Stevens, tried to hug the low bush rows as they scanned several streets of neatly-trimmed Dutch houses, trying to find one with a naturally nondescript out-building that they could commandeer for at least a few hours. Fatigue was beginning to sap their well-conditioned strength along with pervasive animal fear, and at least an hour of sleep would seem like a weekend getaway, assuming of course that they didn't awaken to a harsh voice screaming, "Achtung, Amerikaner! Hande hoch!" Either that, or not awaken at all – ever.

Suddenly a face appeared at the top panel of a neatly-painted white and blue Dutch-door. "Hier! Hier!" a low voice whispered. They could see a white-haired man in a dark-red shirt and brown, calf-length trousers opening the bottom door panel and motioning them forward. Without any thought of consequences, the two fugitives darted for the open door. The old man quickly closed the two-paneled door, threw the deadbolt, and motioned the tired soldiers over to the fireplace, where he piled on two extra spruce logs. From the room off to the right, a slightly-built woman's worry-lined face appeared; then she smiled, and moments later returned with two steaming cups of bitter black tea. Tastes better than the best whiskey, Lauer thought, as he savored the feeling of warmth beginning to radiate from his throat and stomach on out into his chilled extremities. As he sipped his hot drink, the elderly man and woman sat quietly and calmly, not saying a word.

As the two GI's greedily finished the very last of their tea, the old man stood and said, "We find you place to sleep, hide from Germans for while." Sergeant Lauer nodded, slowly beginning to realize the grave position that this brave old couple had placed themselves in. If the soldiers were caught on the premises, he had no doubt that there would be harsh reprisals on not only this gallant couple but likely the entire neighborhood. The Germans always tended to do things that way, to reinforce and punctuate corrective behavior lessons.

Speaking as slowly as he could, Lauer said, "No, but may we hide in your shed (he motioned towards the back of the house and formed a roof-shape with his hands) for just a few hours? Then we will leave and you will be safe." The elderly gentleman shook his head slowly.

"No, Americans, you stay here. We will hide you in root cellar if Gestapo come. But now, eat a little, sleep a little. My name Matthias Gröot. Marta and I watch for Germans." For the first time in two days, Sergeant Lauer managed a smile.

"Okay, sir. We thank you very much," he said, already feeling his eyelids beginning to flutter. But as he fought to avoid nodding off, he couldn't help but notice as the old woman noiselessly moved to the kitchen, removing a small covered bowl from the back of a worn but well-kept corner cabinet. She then reached into a square wood pantry drawer to the left of the stove, withdrew a full cup of flour, a tiny covered bowl of sugar, added a splash of water, and began to knead small but neatly-formed Dutch cakes.

The questioning look from Sgt. Lauer's eyes spurred a quiet but firm response from Frau Gröot: "We have two sons in the Dutch Army. They are somewhere – England, we hope – and we pray for them every night. I was keeping sugar and flower for when they someday return, but now is a good time to use them." Lauer started to protest but stopped, overwhelmed by both the generosity and firmness of the response. All he could do was nod and mouth a quiet, "Thank you." Years afterwards he would claim that he had never tasted a more wonderful feast.

Then, almost as quickly as they had devoured the cakes, the elderly Marta spread two thick down comforters on the kitchen floor well away from the single room window. The weary Americans literally fell onto them and into immediate sleep.

The late afternoon sun was trying to find its way into one corner of the kitchen when a hushed voice woke him along with a gentle shake. "The Germans, they are searching neighborhood." Instantly alert, Sergeant Lauer reached for his M-1. "No, no, you hide in root cellar," Matthias whispered. Lauer and Stevens scrambled to the side of the kitchen and down three wooden stairs where Matthias was lifting a fourth stair-board. There was just enough room to slide underneath the upper stair-step and into a shallow dirt-walled cellar. In the dim light from Matthias' oil lamp he could see cords of radishes and turnips hanging along the cobweb-laced rafters along with dried greens of some kind. The earthy smell mixed with a faint starchy tinge reminded him of his parents' own earthen cellar back in Hooversville, except for the fact that this one was barely the size of a linen closet. He also realized that it could also end up being his tomb.

Clutching his M-1, Lauer tried to remain calm, forcing himself to breath slowly and noiselessly. Stevens was hunkered against the rear wall, back to the slit-like entrance. Lauer chose to be facing anything or anyone that happened to appear in front of him.

A loud banging at the front door brought the two GI's to full alert. "Achtung! Kommen sie hieraus, schnell!" a decidedly unfriendly voice shouted. They heard the deadbolt at the front door slowly being withdrawn and Matthias saying, "Ja, was wunschen sie, mein Herren?" Immediately they could hear heavy boots thudding on the living room floor with muffled commands and a harsh, "Hier! Setzen sie sich! Hast due ein Amerikaner versehen?"

Again, Matthias' calm voice answered, "Nein, mein Herren. Wir haben nichts gesehen." The thud of Mauser rifle butts was evident as the Germans rapped on walls and floors. Lauer could hear boots scrape on the rear steps, then a series of sharp thuds on the steps. He slowly raised his M-1, finger noiselessly flicking the safety off. A voice suddenly sounded, "Gehen sie hieraus!" They could hear the rear kitchen door open and the sound of boots trudging across ground heading towards the small out-building in the rear of the house. We'd be sitting ducks if we'd have gone in there to hide, he thought to himself. Almost immediately a voice called out, "Nexte haus! Schnell!" At that moment, Sergeant Merle B. Lauer allowed himself to take a full breath.

That night, after a hurried but heartfelt goodbye and under cover of a light drizzle and fog, the pair of Americans carefully picked their way through quiet back yards and brushy woods. Shortly after midnight, they literally walked into an advance American patrol that cheerfully provided them with Lucky's and two Hershey bars. As he inhaled deeply, feeling the warm haze filling his lungs and granting him the first truly relaxed breath of the past 48 hours, Sergeant Lauer silently vowed that he would somehow repay the courage of the elderly Dutch couple. Of course, he half-chuckled, that assumed that any of them were still alive at the end of the war. At this point, though, he was beyond excessive worry on the subject. Instead he concentrated on the sensation of sweet chocolate in his mouth and the security of a half-smoked cigarette in his fingers. Sometimes, on some days, you just didn't look beyond the tip of your nose – or fingers.

Following their relief and the German pull-back into Germany, Sergeant Lauer and his squad rejoined the remains of his unit, marveling at the toll enemy action had taken on the 506th. In a letter home he would subsequently write, "George McKinley is one of the original Toccoa men here. There are only six of us left in this Company of 110 originally. Naturally, being an old Toccoa man means quite a bit now because there are just about 84 of us remaining in the whole regiment. We started out 3 years ago with 2500 men. Sometimes I look around and wonder where they all went and the thoughts of the many battles we were in makes me begin to feel terribly old. I've been lucky, though. One night 57 of us went into an attack in the Bastogne region and the following morning there were 3 of us left to tell the tale. We reached our objective but had to withdraw that same evening. The only thing that saved me was a 536 radio. I had it on my back when the bullets hit."

It seemed very unlikely that Sergeant Lauer and the 101st could ever find themselves in more desperate or hopeless consequences, but 1944 was not about to let the Screaming Eagles (famous for their jet-black shrieking eagle head and yellow AIRBORNE script; other Airborne units referred to them as "Screaming Chickens" or "Puking Buzzards", although not entirely with disrespect) off easily for the holidays. By October, the "Home for Christmas" scuttlebutt had seemed almost believable as Patton's Third Army dashed across France like an unstoppable juggernaut and seemed poised to charge straight into the heart of Germany. It was rumored that Hitler was considering an armistice to avoid having Third Army Sherman tanks storming down the DammerPlatz hell-bent for the Reichstag. Perhaps the 101st had indeed seen their last battle, Lauer had mused.

But all of those dreams disintegrated on December 16, 1944. In a stunning surprise offensive, two German Panzer armies had struck through the seemingly impenetrable Ardennea Forest charging headlong into the U.S. First Army front. Specifically, the 28th and 4th Infantry Divisions along with the 14th Cavalry Group and 9th Armored Division had been hurled back while the surrounded, greener-than-new-grass 106th Infantry Division was virtually cut to pieces. The 101st had been rushed to the area around a small Belgian town called Bastogne on the night of December 18th in an effort to stall the Panzer advance and hopefully relieve the 28th and 106th.

Quickly, however, the 101st found that they were not relieving anyone but simply fighting to save themselves from being completely over-run, having been surrounded by General Hasso von Manteuffle's Fifth Panzer Army under the overall command of the vaunted Field Marshall Gerd Von Rundstedt. The operational orders to General McAuliffe, General commanding the 101st, were simple and direct: "Hold! Hold! Hold!"

All around, however, the situation was growing more disastrous by the hour. On December 19th, two of the three regiments of the 106th Infantry, surrounded and overrun, were forced to surrender. Meanwhile, white snow suit-clad Wehrmacht elite troops were continuously assaulting the 101st advance outposts near Bastogne. Fighting was desperate, savage, and brutally hand-to-hand. Sometimes, as Sgt. Lauer crept forward to scout the forward positions, he could immediately tell where the Germans had been – the bodies of dead Americans were lying still, usually with several Wehrmacht troops lying all around. A few times, though, the only sign of the enemy's past presence was the bodies of soldiers – his buddies – sprawled on their backs, fatigue-shirt collars a pale red from the congealed, frozen blood that had spurted from their slit throats. It was kill-or-be-killed, and fortune obviously did not favor the friendly or the enemy.

Each of the next two days became a continuous nightmare of chronic fear mixed with unrelenting physical pain. Sleep was impossible; only fatigue-induced snatches of semi-consciousness broke the monotony of dull, aching pain in frozen feet and fingers. But the memory of frozen, grotesque GI corpses stained with faded-red tended to keep Lauer alert, despite the personal agony. Strange, he thought, how long a single hour can seem. Occasionally additional, obscure thoughts would cross his mind – I wonder if a frozen bullet will still fire? Or even – I wonder if you still feel cold when you're dead?

Then, Lauer would find himself falling back on his training, the clearing of the mind that comes from focusing on the situation immediately at hand. Of course, if anyone needed any additional incentive for focus and alertness, the Germans were constantly present to provide it. The artillery shelling continued seemingly without pause, but that was only because the intervening periods of dead silence were so rare. In between the '88's barrages, it seemed that life kicked into a higher gear to permit a shoring up of a foxhole and a water run, and even a quick yielding to nature's call – as if anyone really had anything left to be "evacuated."

Of course, whenever they allowed themselves the luxury of brief conversation, the talk always centered on food. Lauer could recite his Mom's holiday dinner table menu, starting with shrimp cocktail, fresh oysters, hot from the oven corn-bread, toasty buttermilk biscuits, roasted turkey, absolutely lump-less mashed potatoes, pond-smooth turkey gravy, sweet-potato stuffing, and a three-part cut-glass dish heaped with homemade sweet-pickles, pimiento-stuffed olives, and oversize, pitted black olives. Desert for the already stuffed-full would be pumpkin, blueberry, and apple pies, fresh and fully-fatted whipped cream, and IXL Creamery vanilla ice cream. Of course, if anyone cared, the crystal toothpick holder was always within arm's reach.

He found that strange as well, that desperately hungry men could somehow find that talking about food was in some way semi-satisfying. Maybe, he figured, it gave them hope that they might possibly survive? Or maybe it was just that talking about food brought a measure of momentary comfort in a wilderness of distress. And, as the Winter Solstice arrived on the 21st, the men of the 101st were indeed living on memories; the last of even the most meager rations were now gone.

Funny how a soldier thinks that things are as bad as they can get, then find it just ain't so. In fact, they could be worse. Early on the morning of December 22nd, Lauer and his buddy, Paul Miller, found themselves part of a particularly grisly detail. It was, however, something that had to be done. In just one hour, a delegation from the surrounding Germans was to arrive, their obvious purpose: to demand total surrender from or vow certain annihilation to the 101st, or as they were now being called in the State-side newspapers, "The Battling Bastards of Bastogne." The Germans knew that the Americans' situation was desperate. What they didn't precisely know was exactly how desperate things were.

And the surviving soldiers of the 101st were determined not to tip their already terrible hand any further.

Casualties from the previous three days had been so heavy that bodies, now frozen in the cold, had been stacked gently but tightly like large wooden logs. It was the best that could be done for the dead while under constant enemy fire. Now, however, the soldiers found themselves carefully but quickly dismantling the "human firewood stack" and hiding the bodies away from direct view – anywhere, in ruined shell-blasted barns, mangled tool sheds, anywhere quickly out of sight. The living soldiers meant no disrespect to the dead; however, even the deceased could serve one last time by not being present to expose how dire the Screaming Eagles' predicament had become.

Shortly after the "tidying up" exercise, as expected the Germans sent a truce party into the American lines demanding that the 101st surrender or face "absolute, complete annihilation." Reportedly, when commanding Brigadier General McAuliffe read the note, he had simply replied, "Aw, nuts." The puzzled German delegation had feverishly discussed between them, "Was ist das 'nutzen'?" As they were taken back to the front lines, an American officer clarified the response with a, "That means NO, g___-it!" Sergeant Lauer had chuckled upon hearing the exchanges. Apparently Von Rundstedt and McAuliffe had both remembered an ancient saying, albeit from different viewpoints: "Victory is found in the mind of the enemy commander; defeat lies within yourself." Said another way, you can sometimes win a battle merely by convincing the defending commander that he is doomed to defeat.

But Lauer knew that there was no way that the 101st would hoist the white flag; they never had before and, he knew, as long as there was one troop left alive, there would be no discussion of surrender. The orders had plainly said, "Hold!" not "but, however…at your own personal discretion feel free to pack it in if the situation looks too rough." Heck, if you were so inclined, he thought, you shouldn't have joined the Airborne anyway. "'Nuts', huh?" he said out loud. "Well, I guess when you're destined to die it doesn't cost a plug nickel more to go first class!"

Normandy, Market Garden, and all of the other battles had been savage, primal, and seemingly unrelenting. But even in those operations, the enemy had been singular – the German Army. Here, around this poor shot-to pieces little Belgian town, there was the armed enemy to the front (and all around) and an "unarmed enemy" that invaded every part of your being, namely, the weather. When the Germans would open up with their devastating '88s the ground would shake while everyone prayed that their luck would hold and that their rat-holes would shield them from all but a direct hit. But even then, there would be a quick resolution to the situation – immediate death or staying alive. The pervasive cold, however, was another manner. Scuttlebutt had said that this weather front would stick around for two weeks. That meant continued grounding of the vital supply and ground-attack/defense fighters that for the past several months had been tilting the odds heavily in the Allies' favor; without those vital equalizers, the feared Tiger Tanks of the German Panzers were especially fierce foes, more than a match for the American Shermans and bazookas.

The real devastation of this weather was the all-pervasiveness of it. There was no respite, no going inside to warm up, not even a chance for hot chow (that is, if there were any); simply, hour after hour, then day after day of bone-chilling cold that seemed to extract strength along with heat out of a soldier's body. Sergeant Lauer fingered his thin-fabric field jacket. Well, he thought, it's certain that this coat wasn't made to see below-zero weather! In fact, none of their gear had been winterized. He had seen the photographs of the winter fighting on the eastern Russian front in '42 and '43 but nothing, he decided, could convey yet alone prepare a soldier for the utter, energy-consuming frigidness of unrelenting cold.

Huddled in the two-man foxhole, struggling to hold the tattered blanket over top in a fruitless attempt to keep the infernal wind out, Merle Lauer found another determined annoyance seeking to intrude – the nagging question of, "Why me?" Going Airborne and in particular qualifying for the 506th had been, admittedly, an ego trip. But even the hardiest of troops would never have dreamed of the horrors of the past six months. It was one thing to learn to treat a battlefield casualty, to be the one individual to stand in the breach between life and death, as he had been cross-trained to do. It was something completely different when the casualty was your close friend and you tried your best to keep his internal organs and fluids from spilling out following a chance hit from an '88 round and all you could do was press hard on the bandages and pray.

On one occasion, he remembered a private, new to the unit, cut down by the blast of a German "potato masher" (grenade). Lauer was the first to reach him and found that he could actually see daylight through the wounded man's midsection. The helpless soldier was in agony, alternately crying and begging for water. Lauer reached for his canteen, only to hear an equally-new lieutenant shout, "Don't give water to a man with a chest wound!" With thoughts of murder in his own mind, Lauer gently slipped the canteen into the wounded GI's mouth, watching him sigh as the water reached his parched throat. A few seconds later, the man was still. For about an hour afterwards, Lauer debated in his own mind whether he hated the Germans more than fresh, stupid lieutenants.

By early-November of 1944 it had begun to appear that maybe, just maybe the ordeal would shortly end. The Germans were falling back in undisciplined and full retreat towards the heartland of Germany. For the first time, Lauer had begun to allow himself the possibility that the war could be over by the New Year. But then, in mid-December, the frantic calls had come through saying something about "a breakthrough. The next thing he knew, he was kneeling in a foxhole, wondering whether he would be killed by the attacking Panzers or the frigid winter blasts.

But the real question – the deep, personal, unspoken one - was, "Why? Why me, why here?" He had always been a student of history, focusing special interest on the Greeks and Romans. For some reason, the Spartans at Thermopylae came to mind; what were they thinking about as they strapped on their skimpy plates of crude body armor and battle shields, preparing to hopelessly

defend the pass with 300 versus thousands of crack Persian troops?
Or more recently, even those intrepid Texans in a crumbling adobe
church mission down just north of the Rio Bravo penned up by
5,000 Mexican regulars. Did they also wonder, "What the heck am
I doing here? With my own mortality staring directly into my face,
with cessation of existence hours or minutes away, does any of this
matter, let alone make sense?"

Strangely, though, these thoughts also provided some sort of
comfort to Sergeant Merle B. Lauer, even if only as a brief
distraction from the arctic winds. It mattered to him that other
men, soldiers of the ages, had grappled with this same question in
equally perilous and even hopeless situations throughout history.
He remembered a mortally-wounded West Pointer at Eindhoven
reciting "Duty, Honor, Country" with his dying breaths. Was that
perhaps the key? When it was all said and done, when all of the
ego, bravado, and politicizing had been dispensed with, were these
three simple words the essence of all the soul-searching "Why's?"
Or did those words somehow magically make any other attempt at
reason irrelevant?

As the sun quickly set in the almost-winter evening, Sergeant
Lauer found himself somehow and in some way at peace with
himself. He checked his M-1 for the umpteenth time, patted the
full inserted clip, then his lone spare semi-full magazine. There
were two lonely rounds left in it. "Well," he said to himself, at
least it's not empty! Now," he thought, "If I could only reason my
way out of this damned cold!" Two days earlier he had
remembered an old hobo trick and stuffed some newspaper strips
into his combat boots. Strangely, the paper had indeed helped
keep some circulation flowing in his feet and legs. Today, he
would have given ten bucks for just one section of the Johnstown
Tribune Democrat newspaper! "Wonder what Mom would think
about all of this?" he thought. She had always been the proper,
calming influence in his life.

Actually, the usually unflappable Nell Lauer was near-frantic. She
had read the local Johnstown Tribune Democrat daily newspaper
voraciously, memorizing the facts and details regarding the mid-

December German Offensive. Somehow, she knew that her son, Merle, would be in the middle of everything, just like the 101st always seemed to be. Why, she kept wondering, would her seemingly intelligent son want to join an outfit nicknamed "The Screaming Eagles" anyway? And then there was this business about jumping out of airplanes! Where, she wondered, had this desire for danger and adventure originated in her rather ordinary younger son, brought up in an average American family in small-town America?

Her husband, 61-year old Ed Lauer, ran a general store over across the stone and concrete bridge that connected both sections of Hooversville, Pennsylvania on opposing sides of Stony Creek. He had operated the store since the late-1920's, supporting his family through the Depression years (and also his neighbors with food on credit; when he died in 1968, over $2000 in IOU's were found in his old oak roll-top desk, uncollected) while also serving as Volunteer Fire Chief, Town Burgess, and Notary Public. Between raising her two sons, Merle and Frank, activities in the Ladies Auxiliary at the Hooversville Christian Church, and running a household, Nell Lauer had always been relatively busy. But until this Ardennes thing, she had never found herself totally pre-occupied physically and mentally. Mercifully, on D-Day and at Market Garden, it was weeks before she had even known that Merle had been involved.

December of 1944 had been different. The newspapers and radio had fed almost hourly updates as stunned Americans found themselves looking at the new possibility of continued war in Europe into 1945 and perhaps beyond, rather than a wished-for speedy end. Of course there was still the Japanese war to deal with but they didn't have the "V-weapons" and Messerschmidt jet aircraft which had suddenly appeared so menacing and invincible in the European skies. No, it was Nazi Germany that everyone really feared and now it appeared that Hitler had somehow pulled yet another lucky rabbit out of his old campaign hat and soldier's coat. It was indeed looking like a glum Christmas in 1944, particularly for the Lauer family. Nell Lauer could only imagine the struggle for life in that little village in Belgium that until a week ago she had never even heard of.

A movement, barely perceptible, brought Sergeant Lauer back to full alertness. In the deepening dusk, his eyes quickly adjusted and focused on what was now obviously a human being slowly, slightly stooped, moving haltingly along the tree-line about 200 yards away. Then, he caught more movement, this time picking out the unmistakable shape of German kettle-helmets against the snow-covered trees in the background. Lauer eased his M-1 upward simultaneously flicking the safety off. With the precision of a soldier who has done this same thing countless times before he instantly drew up a site-picture and squeezed the trigger. The sudden report of his rifle sounded like that of the Angel's Last Trumpet. Almost instantaneously he could hear the deep thud-thudding of the Browning Automatic Rifle (BAR). And almost as quickly he could see the muzzle flashes of the flushed Wehrmacht troops attempting to lay down defensive cover fire.

Sergeant Lauer was now focused on one thing only – the enemy to his front and his own survival. Thoughts of home were distant memories, now drowned-out by the acrid smell of expended ammunition, the sound of small-arms and light-automatic weapons, the muffled screams of pain, and the flashes of tracer-fire in the now-dark winter air. His world now was composed of the length of his M-1 and his ability to eject and insert a last clip of ammo. The question of "Why me?" was, at least for the time being, irrelevant and completely forgotten.

■■■

Epilogue

The telegram that had arrived at the home of Nell and Ed Lauer on December 29, 1944 was devastating. Both of them understood that the words, "Missing In Action", were usually meant to be encouraging to the receiving family, holding out a glimmer of hope for the survival of their loved one. And, as the message had stated, with the associated chaos of the battle area, Sergeant Merle B.

Lauer could eventually turn up alive. Left unsaid was the mutually acknowledged implication of, "But that chance is admittedly slim."

New Year's Day 1945 came and passed with Nell lapsing deeper and deeper into a mother's anguished depression for her presumably-lost child. There had been no word from the War Department or anyone else since that stark, abrupt telegram a week earlier. Ed had tried his best to gather family and close friends during the holiday evenings in an attempt to distract Nell from her smothering dread. The evening of New Year's Day brought bitter cold weather sweeping in from the northwest across the Alleghenies. Nell spent the next few days huddled in the Clark Street brick house's back parlor, seated in the cushioned oak rocker next to the gun-metal gray radiant-heat floor radiator, growing increasingly despondent and silent.

As the first week of 1945 drew to a close, Ed Lauer determined to protect his wife in whatever manner possible should the dreaded news arrive. He made sure to come home from the store each day for lunch simply to provide his wife with company. As a realist, though, he also made a trip down the main street to the Western Union office where he instructed that any further telegrams be delivered directly to his store and not to Nell over at the house. Funny, he thought, people always say that it's the waiting that's the hardest compared to the actual news. But that's crap, he thought. Even no news at least provided some possible hope against hope that Merle was still alive. But as each day slowly dragged by the Lauer family members increasingly resigned themselves to being in effect on a death watch.

On January 17, Ed Lauer opened the store promptly at eight o'clock and made a pot of coffee on the small gas stove in the storeroom off the back counter. Then, steaming cup of joe in hand, he absently flipped through the pages of the day's Tribune Democrat. As he gingerly sipped his scalding-hot coffee he noticed an article on page 5 of the first section entitled, "Belgian Nurse Treats Wounded GI's." The lady in white was spoon-feeding a reclining soldier in the foreground while two of his comrades sat in the background. It was then that Ed Lauer noticed.

"That's my son!" he half-shouted to no one in particular. Immediately he reached for the crank-phone perched on the wall directly behind the cash register on the oak-topped counter and, holding the receiver under his arm, dialed the Johnstown newspaper circulation phone number printed in tiny numbers at the bottom of the second page. It seemed as if the phone rang twenty times before a gruff voice answered, "Hello?"

Now almost breathless, Ed Lauer half-shouted his story; the startled voice on the other end of the phone line quickly took on a softer tone as the words poured out. Quickly he was transferred to a very helpful receptionist at the Tribune Democrat who immediately took down Ed Lauer's store telephone number and then at once contacted the national AP office who subsequently located the photographer who had taken the picture. Reportedly he had checked his notes from his photo shoots and, yes, the soldier on the right of the picture was indeed a Sergeant Merle Lauer, wounded in the hip and leg from both shrapnel and rifle fire.

About a half-hour later, Nell Lauer sat quietly in the rocking chair in the rear parlor, holding the Johnstown newspaper close beside her, smiling contentedly and feeling all of the fear, dread, and tension built during the former 30 days unwind like the rubber band of a child's balsa-wood model airplane. Now, there would be time, she thought, a chance to say things that had been left unspoken, simply assumed. She realized that it was a compassionate gift from God. She would indeed get to see her son again.

Merle Lauer recovered from his wounds received at Bastogne, then participated in the final wartime operation of the 506th PIR, that of capturing Hitler's "Eagles Nest" at Berchtesgaden. I have pictures of himself and several buddies holding up strings of trout caught in Hitler's private lake (the article was titled, "Hitler's Golden Trout") using surgical needles as fish-hooks. Merle claimed that only a few months earlier such actions would have generated summary execution by Hitler's elite SS guard. Simply, you didn't mess with "Der Fuhrer's" fishies!

Actually, there was a story even behind this particular escapade. As well as the soldiers, the nearby townspeople were all seriously short on food. Sergeant Lauer spoke to several of the town elders and persuaded them to have a number of the German women hold an impromptu "fish fry." The Screaming Eagles trotted out a few sacks of flour, sugar, and good old Maxwell House coffee, continued to snag trout, and soon the entire town was gratefully feasting on Hitler's Golden Trout. Apparently, the fish had been strictly off-limits even to loyal Germans! Plus, coffee had been completely unavailable for over a year in The Fatherland. The soldiers watched in fascination as the townspeople savored their first taste of real coffee in recent memory, taking delicate sips in an effort to make one cup last forever.

Afterwards, the German women headed for their homes and began returning with small cups of flour. The stunned soldiers realized that the grateful people were dutifully "returning" scarce war-time food materials. The GI's quickly shook their heads, "Nein, nein."

Sergeant Lauer remembered the comment of one elderly white-bearded German who, shaking his head slowly said, "America must truly be a rich land to provide such things to its fighting soldiers." Perhaps, Lauer mused, the general German population had been doing their own "hiding of the bodies" for these last few years of the war. Or at least, they had hidden the dire situation of lack of coffee!

For its heroic actions at Bastogne, the 101st Airborne Division was awarded the "Distinguished Unit Citation", marking the first time that an entire Division had received this prestigious award. As General Dwight D. Eisenhower remarked, "This marks the beginning of a new tradition in the American Army!"

Sergeant Merle B. Lauer returned to Hooversville in June of 1945. Family pictures at his homecoming reflect his parents' mixture of joy and pride along with the thrill of seeing someone who had literally come back from the dead.

Sergeant Lauer did not forget Matthias and Marta Gröote, the Dutch couple who had shielded him from capture by the Germans. In the summer of 1954 he sponsored their son, Hans, his wife, young son and two daughters into the United States. I remember him bringing the family of five up to Hooversville on the train from Johnstown, where he had arranged for them to acquire a small farm over towards Windber, PA. Upon their arrival, Nell and Ed Lauer held a dinner in their honor, after which we kids introduced the Dutch children to American treats – Orange Cream Sickles. The youngsters marveled at the ice cream and orange shell wrapped around a flat stick and, although the cream dripped down onto their suspender-held shorts and bare legs, they refused to give up until they had licked every last drip of treat from the sticks. Nell simply chuckled and wiped off the sticky drippings with a damp towel. We American kids were amazed; we couldn't conceive of anyone not knowing what to do with ice cream on a stick!

Prior to World War II, Merle B. Lauer had joined the Citizens Military Training Corps (1937) with training at Ft. George Meade, MD. In between, he had attended college and studied Accounting while maintaining a Reserve status in the Army.

He qualified as a Sr. Parachutist in November of 1942, along with ratings of Expert Machine Gunner, Rifleman/Carbine, and .45 Caliber Pistol. He also graduated from the Army Medical School, first assigned to the 506th's Medical Detachment, then as a Combat Medic.

At the end of World War II, Lauer was commissioned as an officer in the Army Reserve, retiring in January of 1963 as a 1st Lieutenant, 2380'th Logistical Command.

In the post-war years, Merle B. Lauer married Pearl Clifford in 1946, spent several years in public school teaching, and then turned to the booming steel business in Johnstown's Bethlehem Steel Car Shop, where he worked 30 years in railroad-car steel shop operations. Along the way, he developed an interest in scuba diving and also geology, particularly gemstones and faceting, eventually becoming a "licensed facetier." I know this because he made Janet's and my wedding rings.

In the early-'70s, he expanded his geology interests to include rock-hunting trips to the American Southwest. On one such trip in Utah, he had hiked roughly 30 miles into a remote section of mountainous terrain north of Bryce Canyon National Park and, while rock hunting, discovered an ancient cave-dweller settlement. He remarked regarding his feeling of awe knowing that civilized Europeans had likely never set foot on that ground. Subsequent calls to the National Park Service and his accurate report of the map coordinates have helped preserve the site for history.

In the mid-'70s, Merle Lauer embarked on a Caribbean scuba-diving trip in the company of a local Johnstown diving club. The sea had been unusually calm that day and eventually he found himself with two other divers exploring the ocean floor at a depth of about 150 feet. Suddenly, one of the other divers began to frantically signal that he had experienced a regulator failure. Exactly as trained, Merle swam over, motioned towards his own mouthpiece, and signaled for his comrade to share air while breathing normally as they rose slowly to the surface.

As is often the case with human beings in emergency situations, not everyone has the clear head to remember the routine; rather, animal instinct takes over and self-preservation trumps everything else. Merle's partner took the mouthpiece eagerly, then immediately began to claw towards the ocean surface, leaving Merle dragging helplessly behind. As the two divers broke the surface, Merle savagely gasped for air, feeling his lungs almost turning inside out as they sucked in oxygen.

Unfortunately, that was virtually what had happened to his lungs, a condition known as "lung burst". Since he had been breathing compressed air, as the two divers rapidly ascended the gas had expanded along with the decreasing external pressure causing his lungs to over-expand in what is called "pulmonary barotrauma."

It was almost a full two minutes before he knew that something was seriously wrong; initially he had felt no pain from his over-expanded lungs. The embolism that had formed traveled quickly although not instantly; still, it had moved inexorably. The paralysis spread like a wave on flat beach and within five minutes, he was having trouble breathing. Racing against time, his friends on the surface frantically radioed the Coast Guard for assistance. One location had a hyperbaric chamber and facilities that could handle such disasters and the powerful Chris Craft thundered its way toward that 30 mile distant port.

Merle Lauer survived, although he spent months in the hospital. Gradually, he regained a good portion of the use of his arms and upper body; below his waist, though, the traumatized nerves and muscles refused to move out of their embolism-induced damaged state.

For the next 30 years, Merle Lauer taught geology courses at the University of Pittsburgh – Johnstown and continued to take rock-hound trips West in a Chevy pickup truck with a small camper in the bed. Inevitably, the poor truck would return resting on the suspension support stops, crammed full of rocks. He reported that on one trip he and Pearl had noticed a distinctive rock formation just off the Interstate and, upon stopping for investigation, found a small lode of precious gemstones. Taking a quantity of the minerals and then restoring a shallow layer of covering ground, they continued on their journey. The following year, mostly out of curiosity, they stopped at the same location. There, still undisturbed, was the lode of gemstones. Upon being asked by his students as to why someone else had not discovered the gemstone site literally 20 feet from an Interstate highway, Merle reportedly answered, "They obviously didn't know what to look for."

Although I never knew about it until near the end of his life, Merle Lauer never forgot his experiences in France, Holland, and Belgium. Nor did he forget his comrades in arms. My aunt recounted to me that every Christmas Eve he would attend midnight mass with members of his rifle squad from Bastogne. Then, afterwards, they would gather at one member's house for a late dinner, coffee, and drinks. Aunt Pearl remarked that these were very private get-togethers with wives purposely excluded. One year, though, when the post-church meeting had been held at their house, she had crept out into the hallway to try and catch just a glimmer of the conversation.

What she heard, in her own words, were hushed stories of terrible ordeals, gruesome recollections, and occasional choked sobs. Alternating between shared laughs over "spending the night in a hog pen" and other light moments were brief flashes of anguish and terror such as "and then that d___ '88 round tore them to shreds and all I found was a piece of an arm." She recalled sitting there dumbfounded, having never heard even a hint of those experiences from Merle's lips.

Sometime in the 1990's the group had become so diminished by disablement and death that the Christmas Eve tradition had fallen to simply an evening phone call. But even then, according to my aunt, the conversations remained hushed, almost reverent. Time is reputed to heal all wounds, it's said; but I know that my aunt would beg to differ. Some, it seems, fester un-mended forever.

Sergeant Merle B. Lauer was awarded numerous citations. He won the Silver Star for "...heroic action against the enemy...", two Bronze Stars with Oak-Leaf Cluster, the Combat Infantryman's Badge, the Combat Medical Badge, the Belgium Fourragere, the Belgium Croix de Guerre, the French Fourragere, the Netherlands Orange Lanyard, and 4 Battle Participation Stars including the Arrowhead for the Invasion of Normandy.

A May, 1945 Johnstown Tribune Democrat newspaper article stated, "His experiences are many and the narrow escapes he had from D-Day to V-E Day are enough, he said, to turn his hair snow white. Before too long, Lauer anticipates being discharged for his point rating is now far in advance of the number required for discharge. (However) at the end of the War, Lauer was declared "essential" and remain(s) overseas." He was officially discharged on November 30, 1945.

One year before his death, Merle Lauer received an email from an unknown e-bay seller. Apparently, the individual had come into possession of a World War II-era field jacket with a label inside saying "Sergeant Merle B. Lauer." Reportedly he had purchased it from a Belgian farmer who claimed that his father had found it in his barn stuffed behind some farm implements sometime after the War. The e-bay seller brazenly asked Merle to confirm his previous ownership of the field jacket and also write a letter explaining the history of the garment.

The jacket reportedly sold for $4,500. I don't know that Merle B. Lauer ever composed the letter, although knowing my uncle, I suspect he did. I do know that the e-bay seller never offered to let him have the first opportunity to re-obtain the field jacket. Then again, I suppose that it wouldn't have been the first time that "coin-of-the-realm" trumped patriotism, duty, honor, or humanity. By the same token, perhaps the fact that I'm taken aback by it speaks volumes by itself. In short, I guess Michael Corleone, alias *The Godfather*, was right when he insisted, "It's strictly business; it's not personal." Of course that was right before cold-blooded murder was committed.

A month before his death, I ran across a historical site listing World War II parachute jump wings, several of which had names attached to them. One set was listed as "Belonging to Merle B. Lauer." I contacted the owner, identified myself as the nephew of Merle, offered to purchase the wings at whatever the owner considered a fair price, and asked that, if my request was accepted, the wings be sent to a rest-home in Geistown, PA, to the attention of Sergeant Merle B. Lauer, complements of Staff Sergeant Barry A. Lauer. Not that I was terribly surprised, I never received a response.

Merle B. Lauer with his father, Edward Lauer

A Soldier's Question – Korea, 1950, Chosin Reservoir

"Sometimes life really fights dirty," James W. Kimmel remembered thinking as the trucks pulled out through the gate at Fort Indiantown Gap in central-Pennsylvania. He had watched as other Reserve and National Guard soldiers waved farewell – the lucky ones, he had thought – feeling as if he had been back in the ring on the receiving end of a kidney-jarring rabbit punch. And as he had watched the rest of those fortunate soldiers roll off into the distance towards home, Kimmel couldn't help but ask himself, "Why me? Why again?"

His own Ranger battalion of the 28th Infantry, however, had not been so fortunate. They had been quickly mobilized and activated for immediate service in Korea, eventually to be part of the unlucky "cannon fodder" being thrown in to try and stall the rampaging North Koreans now sweeping aggressively south and threatening to quickly swallow up the entire Korean peninsula including the democratic South.

He remembered having to consult his dog-eared pre-World War II National Geographic map to even locate the place – a fairly small projection of land extending out of northern Asia, across the Yellow Sea from Japan and adjacent to Red China. Talk about an unlucky (and potentially unhealthy) place to be located in history, he had thought at the time, being a ping-pong ball between Japan and China.

Most of the rest of the United States had never heard of Korea either. Worried preoccupation with Russia and then more recently-Communist China had been the focus of everyone's concern following the end of World War II and on through the late 1940's. For that reason, the events of late-June 1950 in Korea had been a thorough surprise to the USA – citizens and politicians alike -

along with a roller-coaster ride of emotions and events as the North Koreans had swarmed into the South.

For the first forty days or so of the conflict called by different names by the individual combatant countries – "The Fatherland Liberation War" by the North Koreans, "the 6-2-5 War" to the South Koreans (reflecting the date of the start of the conflict, June 2), and "The War to Resist U. S. Aggression and Unite Korea" by Communist China. – the Communist North's troops ("Korean Peoples Army", or KPA) had surged forward, quickly pushing the hastily-organized United Nations troops (by far made up of U. S. combat troops) back to the Pusan peninsula.

In a chilling preview of the Communist philosophy that would be played out once again a little more than a decade later in Southeast Asia, as it pushed southward the KPA made it a point to search out and assassinate those in government and instructional capacities. Of course, this was not a KPA invention; Stalin's Soviet Union had patented that brand of "social re-engineering" a little more than a decade before, only to find that those very people might have come in handy when Hitler's Wehrmacht plowed into Russia in 1941, very nearly conquering the Soviet Union. But skilled, intelligent human beings tend to not want to take things at face value, though, which clearly make them potential risks to totalitarian regimes, especially when they are part of the conquered enemy. So, essentially, "when in doubt, rub 'em out!"

The Americans thrown into this meat-grinder grimly realized that they were conducting a holding action and, although greatly outnumbered and out-gunned, they did their best to delay the advancing hordes. Just like Pearl Harbor nine years before, it would take time to revive and build an effective fighting force, certainly more than a few months. Still, it was a shock to those GI's – many, like Kimmel, veterans of World War II – to be retreating in the face of an enemy onslaught.

Kimmel had wondered about all of this at that time, specifically why Americans always seemed to be taken by surprise when it came to deceit and treachery in military actions. Perhaps, he figured, we tend to want to rely too much on the other nation's "good will" and their seemingly reasonable natural abhorrence of violence and death. We want to believe that negotiation and a handshake will settle conflicts and guarantee that both sides will keep their word. Americans always seem to find it hard to comprehend how another culture or people would end up being downright duplicitous, saying "Yes" when all the time they meant and were doing "No!" Apparently, the lesson of December 7, 1941, where Japanese peace negotiators were still in Washington as the bombs and torpedoes dropped on the U. S. Pacific Fleet in Hawaii, had been another in a series of history-forgetting consequences.

But, Kimmel figured, there was something else at work as well, something more fundamentally human in disconnect. The average American mind had never seemed to comprehend the concept that another modern, 20th Century culture or people would treat life as a dirt-cheap commodity. Modern weaponry and tactics had, on several occasions, slaughtered thousands of attacking Communists, reminding the Marines of the bloody island battles against the Japanese. But it didn't seem to matter much in the overall scheme of the North Korean military moves. Simply, the enemy had overcome superior firepower with shear volumes of soldiers; eventually, they must have figured, the enemy runs out of bullets and if you don't run out of human bodies first, you win!

This makes a certain amount of accounting sense unless, of course, you happened to be one of the sacrificial bodies fed into the high-velocity lead meat-grinder of automatic weapon fire; then, he supposed, it would make a great deal of difference both physically and philosophically speaking. But, despite Communist promises of a "workers' paradise" and the condemnation of "bourgeois" Western ways, the average Communist soldier found, just like common foot-soldiers down through ancient military history, that an individual life was an expendable, disposable, and quickly forgotten commodity to the Communist political and/or military hierarchy.

The saying had sprouted among the GI's, "Life is cheap to a Red!" Kimmel had treated that concept with some serious disbelief. Perhaps, he rationalized, the Communist military commanders were simply inept? Surely, no one, not even staunch Communists, would simply sacrifice the lives of common soldiers so casually! And at that time, he had honestly believed it.

Events in the fall of 1950 had tended to make Kimmel's musings seem academic and also outright naïve. Thousands of dead bodies have a way of separating fact from hope and dreams. However, when General MacArthur had engineered the daring but highly successful Inchon amphibious landing behind the Communist lines and the North Koreans had begun a ragged retreat back along the way they had come, Kimmel was convinced that his own involvement in Korea would be both brief and simply as part of a mopping-up exercise. In fact, by mid-autumn the Allies had appeared ready to push the Communists completely out of Korea and over the Yalu River into Manchuria.

Naturally the Red Chinese had protested over this move but, after all, the United Nations had sponsored the counter-attacking military action and surely, everyone figured, neither the Chinese nor the Russians would dare to brazenly interfere with a joint United Nations initiative. Even General MacArther had assured President Truman that Chinese military intervention was "Improbable." And, as the troops enjoyed their hot Thanksgiving turkey meals along with scenic if bone-chilling cold positions overlooking the Yalu, it had appeared that everything would indeed be wrapped up well before 1951 made its first appearance.

In fact, what was to be the final offensive of the then-short Korean War, called the "Home-By-Christmas Offensive", had just begun on November 24, 1950. Certainly, everyone on the Allied side figured that the end was clearly in site. However, they had seriously miscalculated the determination of the Peoples Republic of China and the PVA (Peoples Volunteer Army).

On November 25, 1951, in a strategic move of both unmitigated treachery and brass-beans boldness, Communist Red China –

2,000,000 troops strong – had suddenly invaded across the Yalu from Manchuria, threatening to roll-up and possibly annihilate the stunned Allied armies. In simultaneous blows, the PVA rolled-up the ROK II Corps along with the U. S. Second Infantry Division, inflicting appalling casualties. In the east two days later, the PVA Ninth Army Group launched a three-pronged attack against the 1st Marine Division and the 3000 member 7th Infantry Division Regimental Combat Team. The massive shock and swiftness of the sneak attack had been like a sledge-hammer blow to the head for the United Nation troops.

As in any military action throughout history, there were immediate lessons to be learned. First, the old saying, "Familiarity breeds contempt", had been once more confirmed. The PVA had been underestimated, both in number and combat readiness. And, once again Americans discovered that even concentrated, well-placed automatic weaponry was conquerable by the overwhelming weight of sheer human numbers, and fanatical determination to use those numbers regardless of the costs. In what became known as "human wave assaults", the Chinese Communists resorted to massive charges by wave after wave of infantry soldiers to wear down and eventually over-run under-manned Allied positions.

The ensuing Communist casualties as a result of the concentrated Allied fire-power had been horrifyingly appalling to be sure; however, no supply of ammunition is endless, no individual defending soldier can carry an infinite load of ordinance. Therefore, in many cases, the weight of sheer numbers had overwhelmed even the most determined defenses – assuming, as a Communist commander, you had no particular squeamishness about sacrificing hordes of humanity. And clearly, squeamishness regarding human sacrifice was not a failing quality or personal weakness demonstrated by the enemy commanders. Kimmel had quickly realized that his preconception of all mankind's sacred concern and reverence for life had been either delusional, misplaced, or at least in grievous error.

The Americans had evacuated their wounded, particularly the Airborne and Ranger outfits, refusing to leave them behind to the "clemency of the enemy." Apparently, the Communist commanders had no such hesitation. Signaled by a lone, tuneless bugle call, the "human wave" would move forward, often climbing over the carnage of decimated comrades, but ever on until they could physically fight hand-to-hand with the now-ammunition depleted, hence weaponless GIs. And although the U. S. Army and Marine soldiers were well-trained both in weaponry and physical combat, troops driven by determined, ruthless commanders could eventually accomplish their purpose, albeit, with a count of killed and wounded that would have stunned and sickened most sane military leaders – at least by any reasonable, civilized definition of sanity.

Sergeant Kimmel had heard all of these stories even before he had entered Korea, although he had continually found it hard to believe. After all, he had served in World War II including the final stages of the assault on Germany, first across the Remagen Bridge, then into the German heartland. He had met desperate resistance in several instances but even the most fanatical SS troops had usually blanched at wholesale slaughter of other Germans including the children-soldiers that had been conscripted out of desperation at the very end of the war.

He remembered a push through a small German town where they had encountered sporadic sniper fire. As they had closed in on the suspect house, a frightened child's tear-streaked face had appeared at a window crying out, "Nicht schiessen! Nicht schiessen!" Apparently, he had been ordered to stay behind and fight "to the last bullet and drop of blood" by his SS commander. Of course, Kimmel thought ruefully, that SS guy was more than willing to sacrifice someone else's last drop of blood! Kimmel and his buddies had taken the young boy's beat-up Mauser from him, given him part of a Hershey bar, and quickly passed him back to the rear to join other demoralized, defeated Wehrmacht soldiers.

Even the fanatical Japanese soldiers, who often had fought savagely on Tarawa, Iwo Jima, and Okinawa to extinction, were not totally without a sense of self preservation. Kimmel remembered hearing one Marine tell the story of a brutal battle on

Okinawa in 1945, at the end of which a single wounded, tattered Japanese soldier had emerged from his cave-bunker staggering forward, hands in the air. He had gasped, "We were ordered to fight to the last man!" The startled Marine had asked, "Well?" The Japanese soldier had calmly added, "I am the last man."

No, World War II – at least in Europe – had seemed almost "civilized" at times, if any war could be insanely labeled as such. Of course, he knew, maybe that's how it was once the Germans realized that they actually had no hope of victory. After all, he had heard the tales of the Nazi concentration camps after their liberation. He knew that he had been in on the very end of things in Europe. The more seasoned troops in the 28th had reassured him that, when it came to war and kill-or-be-killed, the Germans, Japanese, or anyone else could be inhuman, heartless, and horrific. Indeed, Kimmel was coming to the conclusion that no one culture had a monopoly on humanity; as for chivalry, the days of The Knights of the Round Table were long gone, if they had ever existed in the first place.

But now, in the bitter December Korean weather, "civilized warfare" seemed a distant and far-fetched fantasy. The Communist onslaught had been brutal enough; but on top of that, the badly outnumbered GI's were facing savage, Arctic cold straight off the frigid wastes of Central Siberia. November weather in Korea had been bad enough, about 16°F. But when December blasted its way onto the peninsula, the temperatures had quickly plunged below zero. Cold-weather parkas, quilted mittens, and heavy winter boots had all been rushed to the front lines, often by determined C-47 and C-119 "Flying Boxcars" navigating through fearful storm fronts. Lurking above them, perpetually weaving their combat patrols, flew the Air Force's P-51 Mustangs, "the Queen of World War II Fighters", constantly vigilant for any armed intrusion originating from a Communist YAK fighter, courtesy of Joe Stalin's Russian arms arsenal.

Sergeant Kimmel had talked to one of the P-51 jockeys only a few weeks before. Jake had fought over the skies of Germany in 1944 and 1945 against the cream of Germany's Luftwaffe. In early

1944, he had flown the heavy, punishment-hardy P-47 Thunderbolt, seven tons of 2000HP Pratt & Whitney radial engine and a rugged airframe that was loved for its ability to absorb punishment in the form of Messerschmidt 109 and Focke-Wulf 190 20mm cannon fire. However, although a good match for the German fighter planes, the P-47 had lacked the range to escort the B-17 Flying Fortresses to their targets deep into Nazi Germany. Therefore, when the big "Jugs" as they were lovingly called or "little friends" to the bomber crews reached their limits in range and peeled off to return to England, the German fighter planes seized the opportunity to wreak havoc among the unprotected, slower Flying Forts.

It always upset Jake personally to see the damaged B-17s returning, literally shot to pieces, grievously-wounded crewmen often pulled from the wreckage of those Forts just barely able to reach England but not one mile further. Of course, he knew, the ones that returned were actually the lucky ones. Too often the end result of a damaged B-17, one or two engines gone along with hydraulic damage to the controls, was a quick and fiery death at the hands of the Messerschmidts and FW-190s and their lethal cannon fire. If an unfortunate crewman managed to safely parachute before being riddled or fried, he would be leaping into enemy-occupied territory and usually end up a prisoner-of-war for the duration.

But then, in early-1944 the Army Air Forces had received the sleek P-51, faster and far more maneuverable than the massive Thunderbolts, but most importantly, able to escort the vulnerable B-17s all the way to targets deep into Nazi Germany. It had been the dawning of a new day for the Allies and in particular the Fortress crews, who had watched their losses plunge as more and more of the agile Mustangs became operational and their pilots gained air-combat experience. Hermann Göring, "Generalfeldmarschall" of the Luftwaffe, commented after his capture in May of 1945 that he knew the war was lost the first time the P-51's had escorted the B-17s as far as Hanover.

Slowly too, the superior P-51s had not only afforded protection to the bombers but had begun to whittle down the number of able, experienced German fighter pilots. Month by month into late-1944, Jake had seen the capabilities of the enemy fighter pilots markedly deteriorate, as more and more inexperienced German men were rushed into the rapidly thinning Nazi pilot ranks. Inexperience coupled with the superior American P-51s often proved to be lethal combinations for first-time Luftwaffe pilots, and when applying those once-in-a-lifetime (the enemy's, that is) lessons, Jake had proven to be a harsh schoolmaster. He had scored eight confirmed kills in Europe and had been confident of more, despite the increasing lack of Luftwaffe aircraft daring to come up for battle.

However, eventually Jake had encountered lousy "technical" luck in the form of one of the few Me-262 jet fighters that the Luftwaffe had managed to get into operation. Military historians agree that with enough of these vastly-superior twin-engine jet aircraft, Germany could have very likely turned World War II around by making Allied bombing missions once again both bloody and virtually defenseless. The result could have been a resurgent industrial capacity in the Rhineland, hence more jet-fighter plane production, and an eventual re-born and re-armed Third Reich. Coupled with a Teutonic interest in nuclear fission and a revenge-driven Hitler being really, really, well, highly angry, (the p___ed-off expression would fit better here), and this manuscript, if ever written at all, would likely be in German.

Fortunately for the Allies (and the World), delays in production, in part due to decisions straight from Hitler himself, who wanted the Messerschmidt jet plane to be a "vengeance bomber" instead of an air-defense fighter aircraft, ultimately crippled the overall fighter aircraft availability of the Luftwaffe. Coupled with the dearth of able pilots, the Me-262s were simply too few, too late.

Nevertheless, the deadly potential of the jet Messerschmidt had been demonstrated first-hand to Jake and his unlucky Mustang. Although the P-51 was arguably the best fighter plane of the Second World War (the British might argue in favor of the famous

Supermarine Spitfire), it was simply no match for the 100-mph quicker, more powerful German jet.

Fortunately for the American Army Air Corps, there were far too few Me-262's in the air in early-1945, their capable pilots dwindling, and the Mustang and Spitfire pilots usually took great pains to avoid head-to-head encounters with the Nazi jet fighters. Instead, the prowling Mustangs would employ both altitude and cloud cover, stalking the limited fuel-range Messerschmidt jets until forced to land, then pouncing on them as they slowed, wheels down. Given the altitude advantage, patience, a fuel-thirsty Messerschmidt, and a considerable portion of luck, this technique worked reasonably well for the P-51 pilots.

A shortage of any of those previously mentioned advantages, though, could decidedly wreck a Mustang pilot's day, or even life, as Jake was to discover. While flying high air-cover for the B-17s on a deep-penetration raid into Germany in March of 1945, before he even sensed potential danger, a bogey was on top of him, out of the sun, and in the form of a camouflage-patterned Me-262, later said to have been flown by one of Germany's few remaining brilliant fighter pilots (possibly Luftwaffe ace Adolph Galland). As Jake was reminded some time later by a downed Spitfire pilot, "That was bloody poor luck, old boy!"

Before he could even say, "What the...?", the Mustang's Rolls-Royce/Merlin engine had been ripped to shreds by the jet Me-262's twenty-millimeter cannon rounds, pieces of jagged metal slamming furiously against the armored forward canopy glass. Jake barely had time to roll the stricken P-51 on its back, slam the canopy back, release his seat-straps, and fall clear before sheets of flames surged over the just-emptied cockpit. As a result, he had sat out the last several months of the war in a Luftwaffe Stalag prisoner of war camp.

Like all of the World War II veterans, regardless of their branch of service, Jake had looked forward to returning to "normal life" post-war, having a family, and some day bouncing a grandchild on his knee while answering the question, "What did you do in the War, Grandpa?"

But in a continued run of military bad luck, the P-51 pilot had been pulled back on to Active Duty in Korea, again flying the venerable Mustangs. James Kimmel, as a fellow-World War II veteran could sympathize with the fighter jockey; after all, the experiences in one war were far more than enough for a man's lifetime. Several weeks before, they had met in Pusan, and Kimmel remembered what the fighter pilot had told him.

"I'm not worried at all about tangling with a bunch of those d___ YAKs, even when I know that the pilot is 100% Russkie, which about half the time they are. They're here to gain combat experience and usually I'm only too happy to oblige them. The only thing that gives me the shivers is me running smack dab into one of those new Commie MIG jets. Getting my butt flamed twice by a d___ jet would just about match my bum luck!" Plus, of course, he had no desire to be taken prisoner by the Chinese Communists.

They had both laughed about their perceived equally poor luck, smoked a couple of Lucky Strikes (Kimmel could never understand where from and how the fly-boys always seemed to have cigarettes coming out their ears, although they were equally generous in sharing them), wished each other good luck, and moved on. Now, Kimmel thought about the combat air patrol flying far above them in the even more frigid winter air, constantly vigilant for armed Communist intruder YAKs or, worse, MIGs. He wondered if his buddy's luck would hold out until the Air Force could rush their new F-86 Sabre jets, made incidentally by North American Aviation, the same maker of the P-51 Mustang, into combat operations and the aerial fray against the Russian-made jets.

"Why are we always showing up late for the party and in old clothes?" he said to no one in particular.

Kimmel couldn't help but shake his head slowly, remembering how the United States had shipped millions of tons of military supplies through the frigid and highly dangerous, U-boat-patrolled waters of the North Atlantic via the dismal port of Archangel to keep the Soviets from being conquered by the Nazis. That had been only six or seven years before.

Even as the war in Europe was ending, though, Joseph Stalin had begun laying the iron foundations of a Communist Eastern Europe. Tensions had escalated month after month, then year after year, with Russia threatening a new war in Europe, even blockading the Western Sector of Berlin in 1948. American airpower had thwarted that move with a massive, determined airlift of supplies to keep their sections of Berlin supplied. Unfortunately, that temporary setback had not deterred "Uncle Joe" for long.

Now, two years later, all past friendships and services thoroughly forgotten, the Russians were openly supporting both the Chinese and North Korean Communists. Blatantly and without any thread of guilt, they were directly helping kill American soldiers, their late-allies in conflict. Heck, Kimmel wouldn't have been surprised to find "Made in USA" labels on some of the Communist Chinese ordinance and supplies!

Then again, he thought, Joe Stalin was the same treacherous, murdering dictator that had ruthlessly purged (a euphemism for murdered) his army of their commanders in the 1930's, virtually wiping out whatever potentially capable military leadership had existed in pre-war Russia. When war did come to the Soviet Union, this lack of leadership cost countless lives and had almost led to utter annihilation of Mother Russia.

The murdering dictator had ignored the writings of his fellow-murdering dictator, Adolph Hitler in which Germany's ultimate plans for those countries to the east had been fully and clearly proclaimed in a hideous, hate-filled document called, "Mein Kampf." In explaining what he hoped to accomplish in "My Struggle", the Fuhrer had explained "Lebensraum", or living space, and the need for it "in the East." Apparently, Stalin and his fellow Communists had not connected the dots leading east and the geographical location of the Soviet Union.

He may have been a slow-learner but once "Uncle Joe" had realized the full intent of the Germans and seeing the abject lack of preparedness in his execution-devastated officer corps, he had signed a peace accord with Adolph Hitler in 1939 on the eve of World War II. Shortly after that on September 1, 1939, Germany had invaded their neighbor, Poland.

Within the month, the Poles had found themselves in the proverbial middle. The two "wolves" – Hitler's Germany and Stalin's Soviet Union, with the Polish "lamb" in the middle – were making dinner plans, and only two of the three potential diners would be satisfied. Stalin jumped in and hurriedly grabbed the eastern part of Poland within a few weeks of the Nazi invasion. He had gained his buffer with his supposed-ally and, even more valuable, time.

Then, a little more than a year later, in perhaps one of the least surprising events in military history, Hitler had sent his battle-hardened Wehrmacht against Russia in "Operation Barbarossa." The Allies had, not entirely altruistically, saved Stalin's neck by sending massive amounts of supplies and arms to the Soviets. But throughout all of this, Stalin had not given up on his desire for Communist conquest. Apparently Uncle Joe had written his own "book". He had finally declared war on Japan merely days before the war's end in order to grab eastern territories as spoils of war; within months, Eastern Europe had quickly fallen behind what Winston Churchill had called, "an Iron Curtain."

There was a clear pattern of repeated behavior with Stalin and the Soviet Union – deceit and treachery. A war-weary world had hoped, just as they had hoped to satisfy Hitler by obliging his blatant territorial grabs in the late-1930's, that Stalin would somehow be finally satisfied. Once again, the world – including most Americans - proved to be poor students of history. The Soviets' support for the Communist North Koreans was, therefore, no surprise. The only startling fact was that so many supposedly smart people in the West were indeed surprised.

Kimmel shivered again involuntarily as the wind gusted to gale force once more. Allied air power was doing its best in the stormy weather conditions, valiantly providing close air-ground support, dropping the jellied-gasoline Napalm to slow the Red troop advances and armor, and adding rocket-fire to tear-up supply vehicles and roads. And the Air Force's cargo planes continued to fly whenever possible. But despite the determined air-drops, the GIs and Marines had found themselves having to curl up in the open, often finding themselves and their sleeping bags buried by several inches of snowfall each morning. Then again, they had told themselves, at least we have sleeping bags. The silent, running joke was, "No Red is gonna get warm curled up in my bag!"

As an aside, a little less than 20 years later, embattled Army Rangers would again be battling Russian-supported Communists, this time in southeast-Asia, the once-French Indochina and eventually Viet Nam, defending a particular firebase while chowing down on gallons of ice-cream. Manning their weapons in one hand, a spoon in the other, they would be equally determined that "No Red is gonna get warm curled up in my bag", in this case, "they ain't getting our ice-cream!" When that battle had ended, the Rangers still had their weapons, spoons, and many empty ice-cream drums. Sometimes victory comes in many flavors, the pun intended.

The Chinese Communist offensive in Korea had penetrated the Allies' front, boxing Kimmel's 3rd Division along with the Marine 1st against a frozen wasteland known to the locals as Chosin Reservoir. Knowing that it would be tactically impossible to hold the area against the hordes of invading Reds given limited defensive manpower and armament, along with the atrocious weather, the order had been given to retreat southeast down the Changuin Road with the Rangers providing rear-guard cover for the Marines. The trick, of course, was to keep the enemy from over-running the retreating troops' rear while still retaining the ability to extricate themselves as well. After all, they were, in fact, the rear of the rear.

On the particularly frigid morning of December 3, 1950, Sergeant Kimmel couldn't help but again wonder at the apparent naivety of diplomats, particularly American. At that very moment, he knew, frenzied and pointed debates were going on in the halls of the United Nations in New York City. Three Chinese diplomats were simply sitting there quietly, he had heard, not choosing to respond to any of the barbed accusations. Why should they, Kimmel thought? They had pulled off, essentially, a fait accompli. What were they expected to do – say, "Oh, sorry, please don't be angry with us; we'll now withdraw all of our troops and give up the huge gains we have made. The last thing in the world we desire is for the West to continue to be angry with us."

Actually, the only thing that made sense to Kimmel was the reported request from General MacArthur for permission to commence the bombing of airfields and staging areas across the Yalu in Chinese Manchuria. Anything would help, he felt, to take the pressure off of the surrounded Americans. Of course, he knew, the argument was that in doing so, the United Nations risked an all-out war with Communist Red China backed by the Soviet Union.

Just then a burst of automatic weapon fire burst over top of his concealed position behind a shallow levee. "Glad to know that this ain't a war," he muttered, "Just a 'police-action'." I wonder, he thought, if getting killed in a 'police action' was any better than in an actual, all-out, by-gosh-war? Maybe you end up less-dead if it's a 'police-action' rather than an "all-out war? Sort of 'kinda killed in somewhat of an action?'" Funny how the definition of "war" has different meanings depending on whether you're in a comfortable heated room in New York City or freezing your tail off huddled behind a shallow dike in frozen Korea, he thought!

The crackling voice from the radio brought Sergeant Kimmel back to attention. "Charlie 2, this is Gray Ghost. Pull back 2 clicks south to the wrecked half-track, dig in, and establish a defensive perimeter." Damn "Majors", he thought. Too far removed from the situation to be good company commanders but close enough to issue orders that defied the facts of the present situation. After all, the reason that there was a wrecked half-track in that place along with a number of other Allied vehicles was that the Reds had zeroed in on that position the day before. Somewhere, some Commie commander had that spot circled in red – ha, funny – just waiting for the chance to call in a fire mission on those coordinates (and anyone foolish enough to encamp there) one more time. Think that some Red major doesn't have that location locked-in?

Plus, "digging in" with that frozen ground was simply a concept; instead, looking for a slight rise to act as both a wind-break and protection from direct fire on the ridge about 4 clicks away would have been the smart move. Plus, although he liked the M-1 Garand rifle, he'd have given about 2 months' pay for three or four Bazooka's. At least if the Reds came with any armor, those babies could possibly stop even the Russian-built T-34's dead in their tracks and anything else with armor plating less than 9" in thickness. But Majors, buzzing around in light choppers, were oblivious to simple but obvious infantry things like that. After all, bayonets and Red hordes don't usually reach up several hundred feet.

Plus, the sub-zero cold itself was as much of an enemy as the Reds. Sergeant Kimmel forced himself to wriggle his toes inside his snow-encrusted combat boots. He hoped he was being successful; he had lost much of the feeling in his feet the night before, realizing that frost-bite had likely begun to set in. He knew the symptoms, having suffered the same conditions during the relief of Bastogne in World War II, and had subsequently lived with the aches and occasional numbness in his feet and hands for years afterwards. Alternately, he kept one hand inside his heavy field jacket in a feeble attempt to keep the blood flowing. Feet he could function without for brief periods but with the Communists sure to attack shortly, having feeling in his fingers, he knew, was a life-or-death matter.

Kimmel was not new to frigid weather; the cold in the Laurel Mountains in Pennsylvania could be downright brutal as well. But even in the deepest weeks of January, there were usually days where the daytime temperatures crept up to near freezing. Here, though, he could sense the gale winds had started in early November, gathering strength deep in the wastelands of frigid Siberia and naturally channeling their bitter-cold nonstop blasts across the defenseless Korean peninsula. The problem was, once they began it seemed that there was no end; just day after day of mind-numbing, body-freezing cold. There was no way to hide from the blustery gusts, no shelter that was even remotely effective. It was almost as if the winds had their own spirit, finding ways to burrow deep into a man's body and mind. Even the simplest and most automatic tasks, like taking a leak or opening a can of K-rations, or even removing one's gloves, seemed to require monumental effort and intense concentration. Kimmel had never thought at all about the word "bone-chilling" until Korea but that was exactly what he was experiencing now. The cold was permeating every fiber of his being, working its way beyond his extremities deep into his body to create what he could only later describe as a dull heaviness. It was almost as if his physical system was pulling inward, hunkering-down, ready to yield extremities in trade for stark survival. James Kimmel knew that the Chinese Communists were not the only life-threatening force facing the retreating Americans.

The shallow slopes beside the road were glazed with a semi-shiny layer of ice, the blowing showers of icy snow accumulating, then occasionally being blown loose by the Siberian gale blasts. Facing into the wind was excruciatingly painful to exposed flesh. And, a soldier had to be careful in handling ice-cold metal gun barrels without gloves as well unless one felt the need to be permanently attached beyond the normal fondness of a soldier for his weapon. What a God-forsaken cold and desolate place to fight a war, Kimmel thought to no one in particular! Using K-Ration cases, back-packs, ammo bandoliers, and anything else stackable, his platoon began to prepare a hasty, rough V-shaped defensive position, the left-flank anchored on the roadway. Kimmel figured that this would give them the best chance of protecting their flanks, always in jeopardy as the Commies liked to attempt strategic envelopment and penetration of the Allied lines in an attempt to isolate and overrun undermanned units. It could work if the enemy was, again, determined and willing to make appalling sacrifices in soldiers. The Reds had shown that they were indeed that determined.

Sergeant Kimmel positioned the lone Browning .30 CAL machine gun at the "tip of the spear" to be able to cover the widest field of fire unobstructed. The handful of 4.2 mortars was arranged in the rear to assist in flank security plus provide cover in the likely event that the platoon needed to fall back; or, in other words, if/when they were overrun. He grimaced at the thought of having to call in mortar rounds on top of his own position, knowing that the ensuing hell of exploding steel was not particularly selective in differentiating friend and enemy. What was needed, he knew, were about a half-dozen more .30's and a whole lot more ammo, as enemy soldiers were outnumbering the number of bullets available. Of course, he would have settled for another full battalion of Rangers and maybe a platoon of well-armed Shermans.

Glancing at his watch which showed 10:55 hours, Kimmel marveled at the lack of Red attacks even as the cold winter sun tried to poke itself through the low clouds. Maybe, he thought to himself, the Chinese were as cold, miserable, and desperate as the Americans were. After all, everybody, regardless of political persuasion, bled the same red blood and felt the same frigid temperatures. The Reds did not possess anywhere near the personal equipment the GIs were still holding on to. Could the icy gusts of the Korean early-winter possibly take the passion and bravado out of even the staunchest Commie's determination?

Almost in answer to his unspoken question, the sounds of a score of bugles began to fill the air, taking on an almost-metallic sound in the cold as if the notes were loath to leave the enclosed warmth of human-generated breath to blast into the frigid morning air. Kimmel had heard these sounds about a half-dozen times in the past 4 days; a tuneless series of bugle tones meant to signal one and only one thing only – Attack! The Chinese didn't have standard, prepared bugle commands save this single one and its meaning was absolutely clear to every Chinese soldier – forward, ever forward, into the face of the enemy's fire, over the bodies of fallen comrades, stumbling, staggering, probably falling many times, but rising, and always closer until face-to-face with the enemy! Either that, or mowed down like so much winter-wheat.

Although he would try on several occasions in the future to articulate what it was like to withstand a Communist human wave assault, there was no way Sergeant Kimmel could adequately express the scene, other than as "an attack originating from the gates of hell." The advancing gray-clad hordes looked like an approaching hurricane-driven, froth-topped ocean wave which emitted a low, unintelligible roar as it rolled forward.

The fighting overhead was just as hot and savage. High overhead, Jake and his Mustang pilots were busy keeping the Communist YAK fighters occupied; below, a flight of deep-sea blue Navy F4U Corsairs attempted to brave the blowing snow and savage cross-winds and drop their Napalm bombs in an effort to break up the Communist infantry formations while still at a distance from the defenders. The gull-winged dark Navy-blue fighter-bombers made repeated low-level passes through brutal small-arms and light-caliber but fiercely concentrated anti-aircraft fire, dispersing Napalm, rockets, and .50-caliber machine-gun fire with remarkable accuracy. Scores of Red infantrymen would disappear in sheets of flame or blasts of bullet-shredded snow. Still, although terrible breaches were being carved out of the Red lines, the seemingly-unstoppable wave of Communist soldiers continued to surge forward, closer, with each step, closer.

The thud of the 4.2 mortars began to make themselves known along with the corresponding chaos caused in the Red lines, while the Browning began barking into action. The Communist lines were just at 300 yards out when the platoon began to open up with individual light-weapons fire. Like a wave attempting to spread itself around a beleaguered seaside sand-castle, the Red hordes were probing the platoon's flanks while searching for any obvious weaknesses in the GIs' front line. Kimmel's men were taking a fearful toll on the enemy, firing virtually non-stop with often practiced, now near-instantaneous Garand ammo clip re-loads. Huge clumps of gray-clad troops seemed to melt down into the snowy fields as they withered under the intense GI weapon barrage.

But the Communist formations, though decimated, had not been completely dissipated. At about 100 yards out the survivors broke into a dead run looking to quickly close the gap between themselves and the murderous American weapon fire. Kimmel glanced over at the constantly hammering Browning, stunned to see the Swiss-cheese barrel noticeably glowing orange from the self-generated heat. The assistant gunner was desperately trying to dog-paddle snow onto the steaming barrel and Kimmel could actually hear the hiss of water turning to steam above the low groan and roar of battle. He quickly thought, we can't lose the .30 caliber - it's our only longer-range automatic weapon! But he also knew that by now the glowing gun barrel was essentially useless, destined to generate a full stoppage at any second. They had all been taught to fire in short bursts to control heat buildup but no one in their wildest imagination had considered fighting off wave after wave of armed soldiers who were bent on charging directly into the teeth of automatic weapon fire. Then again, no one had considered that there could be so many Communist Chinese!

The gunner's curses instantly told Sergeant Kimmel regarding the .30's status. And then, the Communist line was directly on top of them. Kimmel caught the lead Red soldier in the left jaw with a rifle-butt uppercut, then rammed backwards directly into the face of another charging soldier. From then on it became a mindless litany of swing, slash, kick, and club, followed by taking a few steps backwards, then repeating the process again – and again. In the melee the Red troops were stumbling over fallen comrades yet still trying to move ahead. The Americans were doing their best to intercept the off-balance enemy soldiers and drive them backwards, tumbling clumsily into the next wave of advancing troops. Still, it was savage, merciless, unrelenting, and completely desperate hand-to-hand combat.

Near miraculously, the Communist troop advance began to falter, haltingly broken by the renewed Corsair bomb drops and now 105mm Howitzer fire from the Marine rear-guard. In the few moments of confusion and indecision among the Reds, Sergeant Kimmel signaled a hasty fall back about 50 yards, all the while dragging wounded comrades along with whatever ordinance and supply they could salvage on the move. He knew that this would in all probability be a short lull and that soon the hated bugles would sound yet again and replenished Communist soldiers would once again attempt to sweep forward and permanently overrun the Americans. Buy time, buy time, he found himself muttering to himself. Give those Navy planes a chance to try to break up the assault waves before they could get too close.

But he also knew that it was equally imperative to provide at least some momentary respite for his own platoon, as even men who know that they are fighting for their very lives can reach the limits of human physical endurance. And Kimmel knew that those limits were rapidly approaching. Desperately, he inter-wound his frozen hands around the web-gear of two wounded GI's, dragging the dead-weight across the frozen road and back to a make-shift first-aid area where the equally all-in combat medic was doing his level best to sustain life in five beat-up, stabbed, and/or bullet-riddled soldiers. Kimmel rubbed his left shin where a Red boot heel had caught him during the melee. Looking at the bright side, he reasoned, apparently his left leg was not frozen solid. Regardless, he knew that he'd been lucky.

The bugles began to sound once more, the brash wailing sound that by now had lost its threatening tone to the frozen GI's, who realized that they were simply fighting for their personal existence. The rain-cloud-gray-clad masses of Chinese Communists again appeared to move like a dull, uneven wave against the snow-speckled ridgeline that had up until a half hour earlier been the platoon's defensive perimeter. It now seemed strange to Sergeant Kimmel that he felt a sense of calm as he tucked two full ammo clips in his belt and cleared his Garand of the rapidly accumulating snow and ice. He momentarily admired the glistening shine of the wet gun barrel, even in the deepening overcast of the Korean sky.

Everything now seemed to be happening in slow-motion with the individual faces of the advancing Reds becoming visible, square-shaped Oriental heads beneath obviously Russian tri-flap winter hats, their breathing generating frosted puffs of clouds as they pushed ahead. Kimmel let loose a burst of automatic fire at about 50 yards and the lead Communist element stumbled and fell, their trailing comrades lurching and sliding sideways in an attempt to move around them as well as hopelessly escape the spray of lead death. Kimmel ejected the spent clip and seamlessly slapped a full one in just as the first three Chinese troops stumbled over his scattered gear two steps in front of him. He lunged forward with the butt of his M-1, wooden stock meeting yielding flesh with a muted thud, then turned to face the next threats. His mind clear, completely and utterly focused, he allowed his hand-to-hand training to take control as the swing-club-slash-fire movements repeated themselves over and over again. Strange, Kimmel thought, how quiet it is without sustained weapon fire. The only sounds were those of human exertion, impact, and a low groaning.

The gale-force Siberian winds and the sub-zero cold continued, unassuming spectators of various individual human duels-to-the-death on the frozen slopes of the truly God-forsaken northeastern corner of Asia known as Korea.

■■

Epilogue

Sergeant James W. Kimmel survived the savage fighting in December of 1950 and into the early months of 1951 when the United Nations forces, made up of U. S. troops by far, regrouped, fought the Chinese Peoples Volunteer Army and North Korean masses to a standstill, and then slowly began to push them back to the North just beyond the 38th Parallel by June of 1951. Two years later on July 27, 1953, an Armistice Agreement was concluded in Panmunjom.

The full story of the Korean War including the complicated, interwoven politics on all sides, the various military movements and strategies, and the general attitude of all of the combatant countries is admittedly well beyond the scope of the story told here. The Chinese called it a "War Against U. S. Aggression", just as the Confederacy (and Great-Grandma Mary) had referred to their conflict as a "War Against Northern Aggression." Thus, there are obviously many viewpoints and opinions regarding the Korean War, depending on whose side of the 38th Parallel you happen to be on.

I've tried to tell my Uncle's story from his perspective, including his determined hatred of Communism and any political doctrine that would threaten his beloved United States of America. Sixty years later, it's much easier or, maybe, just more convenient to gloss over the conduct and policies of such Communist nations as simply the product of the Mao-led Peoples Republic of China, the (former) Stalinist Soviet Union, and the seemingly frozen-in-historical-time up to today, North Korea.

However, those that have fought against those regimes, sometimes at the cost of their own blood and lives, held no doubt as to the savagery behind all of "The Peoples..." slogans. That includes those who stood against later Communist movements years later fighting future-clients of China and Russia.

As a result, I am admittedly unashamed to tell this story as James W. Kimmel would have told it, in the context of a just battle against godless armies ruled by merciless dictators like Joseph Stalin and Mao Tse Tung. History has eventually shown these murderers to be exactly what their crimes displayed. There's no way to sugar-coat or apologize for their actions. Hitler got all of the richly-deserved "bad press", but Stalin and Mao ultimately deserve every bit as much horror and revulsion. They were monsters and their political philosophies – no matter how passionately and vigorously defended - demanded the lives of millions of human beings.

The social activists in the '60s and early '70s, who fashionably sported "Chairman Mao" side-bags (or purses, if you will) and "Mao's Little Red Book" (aka the "Sayings of Chairman Mao") unfortunately, or conveniently - tended to ignore those minor details. Maybe it's because of the daunting number of zeroes in "a million"? Then again, the Communists always did make it a point to eliminate the "intelligentsia"…

So, in regard to how my Uncle and, I believe, those other GIs, Marines, Air Force crewmen, and Navy seamen including those who made the ultimate sacrifice in those early-50's years in that little-known area of the world known as Korea felt, and if they could send a message to us today, it might simply be, "Can you hear me NOW?!"

Uncle Jim, I can feel you smiling and nodding.

Oh, and I didn't want to forget about Jake, whose last name I confess is lost in the mists of time and war. Uncle Jim did hear that Jake survived his missions in P-51s and gladly was among the first to trade in his venerable Mustang for one of the new North American F-86 Sabre Jets. Leaving his fears behind him concerning the repeat possibility of being the victim of a propeller vs. jet combat engagement, Jake reportedly flamed three MIGs in his new jet-mount, before being sent state-side to spend the remainder of the war in the relative safety of instructor-hood.

Although he had avoided Communist-inflicted wounds, James W. Kimmel carried the legacy of frozen fingers and toes with him for the rest of his life. As a little boy, I remember him grimacing as he massaged his hands after coming inside my Grandparents' house on cold January days. It seemed that normal circulation had exited his extremities permanently.

He made the Army his career, taking the assignment of First Sergeant of C Company, 1st Battalion, 103rd Armor in Somerset, PA with the Pennsylvania National Guard. Upon his retirement in December of 1980 after 37 years in the Army, and as he had watched recruitment in the military dwindle for most of the previous decade, he wistfully remarked, "People aren't as patriotic nowadays as they used to be. For anyone to come into the Guard, you've got to want to join." He added, "I can find lots of faults with our country but I can't find a better one."

Born on January 17, 1921, James W. Kimmel began to follow in his father, James R.'s footsteps even as a young boy, a physically fit specimen who, despite his relatively small size, refused to be cowed or bullied and, therefore, was always ready for a fight. He was a rugged outdoorsman enjoying hunting across the mountains of south-central Pennsylvania, a pursuit he continued for the rest of his life, later with his son, Douglas. For a brief time after graduating from Stoystown High School he had pursued a boxing career under the tutelage of his uncle, Alvin Miller from Lorain, Ohio, known throughout the boxing world at the time as "Lorain's No. 1 Boxer."

"Uncle Alv" had fought professionally for 11 years from 1912 through 1923, with three title-fights for the Featherweight Championship of the World against the then-world-champion, Johnny Kilbane. At one stretch in 1914 through 1916, Alv had run up a streak of 28 consecutive fights without a defeat before dropping the first title-fight to Kilbane. The second fight in 1917 went 12 rounds and it was only upon a doctor's examination after the fight (which had been ruled a decision for Kilbane) that it was found that Alv had fought the last seven rounds with a broken jaw. Alv told young James W.'s mother and father that he saw "professional potential" in the young boy in the late-1930's and subsequently took him under his tutelage to train as a prize-fighter. Young Kimmel reportedly showed promise and prepared vigorously for a boxing career. Pearl Harbor, however, quickly put a temporary end to his embryonic prize-fighting aspirations.

He did his Basic Training at Ft. Bragg, NC, in 1944; then after a period as an instructor, he found himself disembarking at LeHavre, France just in time to be swept into the Battle of the Bulge as part of George Patton's 3rd Army. Despite frost-bitten fingers, he participated in battles across northern France and into Germany. At one point he reportedly had turned down a battlefield commission, explaining simply, "I felt I could do more as an enlisted man than as an officer."

In Europe, Sergeant James W. Kimmel received, among other citations, the Bronze Star for his actions in "...delivering ammunition to American soldiers behind enemy lines" along with what newspapers described as "numerous other commendations and medals." He also was awarded the Soldier's Medal for rescuing a German boy from drowning in a Bavarian reservoir. Ironically, this brought to his Family's mind a somewhat similar situation early in young Kimmel's life.

As an active 11-year old in the early 1930's, he had enjoyed the extremes in south-central Pennsylvania's fickle weather, skiing one day, then watching a brief warm-spell alter the previous-day's frigid conditions. However, on one occasion and with the inexperience and typical lack of caution of a youngster, these changes in the mountain weather almost proved fatal.

Young James had decided to go down to the dammed creek just below Kimmel's Park and spend an hour or so after school alone ice-skating. The mid-February air had turned frigid almost immediately following sunset but he felt comfortable dressed in his heavy woolen coat, rabbit-fur-lined cap, and green wool mittens. On the creek bank, the family collie, Laddie, paced nervously, occasionally barking as if to say, "It's time to go inside now."

James had been out on the ice for about 45 minutes and decided to take one last swing around the south-facing edge of the dammed creek. About 30 feet from the creek bank, the ice suddenly splintered and gave way. Instantly, young James felt his body immersed in the incredibly cold water up to his chest; he could not feel the creek bed underfoot. Instinctively he spread his arms, attempting to distribute his weight out onto the semi-solid ice and keep his head above water. But the ice simply continued to fracture, even under his barely 100 lbs. of weight.

With his back to the creek bank, young Kimmel could feel the soaked woolen coat add what felt like lead weights to his flailing arms. He shouted out, but knew that he was well outside of hearing range even of the service-station at the front of the Park building. Within two minutes, he could feel the hopeless desperation building in his chilled, weighed-down young body. For the first time in his adolescent mind, he found himself musing, "So this is what it's like to die?"

The by-now frantic collie, however, had moved into action. Approaching the stricken youngster, gingerly, feeling the ice cracking even under his own much lighter weight, Laddie inched closer to the by now violently-shivering boy. Then, in a short lunge, the brown-and-white collie snagged young James' coat fur collar in its strong teeth and began haltingly to pull backwards.

At first, young Kimmel could feel no movement, as the valiant collie's paws clawed frantically for traction on the glazed ice surface, animal frenzy and determination pitted against seemingly equal and unmoving natural resistance. Then, in a few agonizing seconds, Kimmel could feel something solid beneath his nearly frozen legs – the creek bottom! Summoning up one last surge of self-survival energy, he willed his almost immobile legs to push. Combined with the backward momentum of the determined collie, young James was suddenly pulled up onto the icy surface and, moments later, could feel the dried grass of the creek bank. With Laddie still pulling with every last ounce of his collie-strength, the half-drowned and frozen boy finally managed to slide his whole body out onto dry land.

It only had taken one look at this thoroughly soaked son and the frantic collie dog for James R. Kimmel to realize what had happened. Shortly afterwards, with young James wrapped in a wool blanket and seated next to the coal stove, the heroic collie was feasting on a choice cut of steak, probably wondering what all of the commotion as well as the delicious treat were about? For James W., the near-death incident as a young boy in a half-frozen pond had fashioned a lasting memory.

Following Germany's surrender in May of 1945, Sergeant Kimmel subsequently anticipated action in the Pacific as the plans for

Operation Olympic (the assault on the southern Japanese island of Kyushu) and Operation Coronet (the main assault on Japan along the Kanto Plain just south of Tokyo) were being developed for the invasion of the Japanese home islands. These operations were scheduled for late-1945 and then into 1946 and he knew that they would likely be horrendously costly. He was on-board a troop ship heading for the Pacific when they received the news of the dropping of the atomic bombs on Japan, followed by the Japanese surrender in September of 1945.

Years later Kimmel remarked, "There wasn't a single man on those ships that regretted the decision to drop 'the bomb.' We were told that, after the bitter fighting and jaw-dropping losses at Iwo Jima and then Okinawa, the invasion of the home Japanese islands would likely cost over a million American lives and maybe three-times that many Japanese, most of them civilians. Our own estimated casualty rate was 50% or more in the first-assault waves. No, not a one of us was sorry to hear the news regarding the atomic bombs."

Historians, pacifists, and other social moralists have debated and often decried the use of the atomic bombs to bring the Pacific war to a quick conclusion. As with most any "Monday-morning quarterbacking" conducted with time to spare and in a non-threatening environment, it's unjust to make pronouncements unless you were squarely in President Truman's shoes, or those of the troops heading out to the Pacific after just defeating the Third Reich. Just one more instance, I assume, where the difference between being "in the game" versus simply "keeping score" can profoundly change your perspective. It's a bit like the old ham-and-egg breakfast gag – the chicken was involved, the pig committed.

Upon returning to the United States, Sergeant Kimmel was discharged in early 1946 and once more considered a professional boxing career. In mid-year, boxing as a middleweight, he knocked out the Tri-State Golden Gloves champion in a fight held in Washington, DC. But, perhaps not coincidentally, he married

Edyth Steckman that same year and subsequently hung up his gloves for good.

The military, however, was still in his blood and he quickly re-enlisted in the 322nd Topographical Engineering Company based in Somerset, PA. Surveying and mapping became desired skills when the Korean War began in 1950 and Sergeant Kimmel spent 10 months there as part of the 48th Topo Battalion, nine of those months involved in combat. Much of his time was spent in mapping and plotting friendly and enemy lines as they shifted unceasingly from one day to the next.

Korea had apparently made more of a lasting effect on James W. Kimmel than just physical. Upon returning state-side, he began to come to grips with his own mortality, if you will, and subsequently met the Lord in the early 1960's, becoming a devout Christian and very active in the Reading Brethren Church (Reading Mines was a very small coal-mining hamlet eight miles down the road from Somerset). He once claimed that if Korea was in any way a preview of hell, he wanted no part of it in any way, shape, or form.

James W. Kimmel, my uncle (brother of my Mother), rarely spoke about his Korean experiences except for the few times when, unexpectedly, the words seemed to spill out like a steam pressure-relief valve finally opening. When he spoke about those experiences, the words had such stark clarity to them that you could literally feel the bone-chilling cold and hear the tuneless Chinese bugles sounding clearly in the frigid air. He claimed that, occasionally at night, he would awaken in a cold sweat "hearing those bugles, those gosh-forsaken bugles!"

I never really got to know my uncle well either as a man or a soldier; he was mostly a very private individual, choosing to keep to himself and his wife and son. Two incidents, however, have stuck with me, one before and then after I went into the Army. Following the assassination of Dr. Martin Luther King Jr. in April of 1968, several American cities were stung by "race riots" and Pittsburgh, PA was among them. Sergeant Kimmel's National Guard unit was activated during that time and late one night he was on patrol in the "Hill District", a notoriously "tough" slum neighborhood and, reportedly, the model for the '80s TV series, "*Hill Street Blues*". That evening, while guarding a major intersection, a young black man walked up to Kimmel, stood directly in front of him, and spit on him. On hearing of this (and, at the time, being an amateur Golden Gloves boxer myself and, therefore, not big into pacifist concepts of non-retaliation) I asked him what he did next.

"Nothing," he answered, and before I could ask he continued, "I figured it was a lot easier to clean my uniform than to start a fight over a little spit." That told me, a proud young man, much about the military and about the character of my uncle, James W. Kimmel. Here was a prize-fighter, a combat veteran of two wars, and yet he could turn the other cheek, demonstrating Dr. King's universal call for non-violence even in the face of direct provocation. More than that, my Uncle would not let his own personal pride spark "justified" retaliation, particularly over a bit of saliva. It's said by Christians that they sometimes "see Jesus" in the actions of others. I know I did by my Uncle's conduct that summer night in the simmering streets of Pittsburgh.

In 1977 I served with him during the weeks of the aftermath of the Johnstown Flood as the Pennsylvania National Guard attempted to cope with a horrific natural disaster which had once more demonstrated the helplessness of humans and their creations in the face of nature's superior elements, specifically flowing water. I began to get a first-hand glimpse of him as a soldier as I watched him calmly but firmly direct his men in an efficient, no-nonsense manner while surrounded by confusion, danger, and an overhanging pall of death. Again, there were few words, just directed action and I began to appreciate how he likely performed during the height of fierce combat in frozen Korea.

As a First Sergeant, I'm sure that he was not always without trouble. As the primary non-commissioned officer in charge as a buffer between enlisted men and their superiors, I suppose tension and turmoil go with the territory. In the mid-1970's, one of his men filed a complaint against him. Apparently, the man was

choosing to resign following his six-year enlistment in the
Pennsylvania National Guard. First Sergeant Kimmel reportedly
made the statement that walking away from service to one's
Country was "unpatriotic." I never heard under what
circumstances the comment was made but I know that my Uncle
was verbally reprimanded for the remark. But that also told me a
great deal about the man and the soldier. For First Sergeant
Kimmel, you didn't casually walk away from the Army like you
did from a club or some other civilian organization. The bonds
were simply too tight, too sacred to merely unfasten, the
responsibilities too important. Obviously, though, he could never
understand those that would do so, even with seemingly good
reasons.

Later in life, he developed Parkinson's disease and it eventually
proved completely debilitating, finally sentencing him to a life
with strap-restraints to help keep his head upright and body stilled
as a respite from the tremors. It was pitiful to see such a robust
soldier reduced to the fate of a complete invalid. It was infinitely
harder on my Aunt who had to endure the day-by-day decline of
the love of her life.

James W. Kimmel died July 17, 1999 in Somerset, PA and was
buried with full military honors. It was the single most impressive
ceremony that I have ever witnessed. The haunting trumpet call of
"Taps" echoed across the sloping cemetery lawn in mid-summer
Somerset as I stood at attention, right hand over my heart. The
honor guard removed the Stars and Stripes from the casket, then
meticulously folded the flag 13 times to represent the original
thirteen Colonies, finally forming the ensign into its tri-cornered
shape.

At the end of the gravesite service, the Battalion Commander of
First Sergeant James W. Kimmel's unit presented the precisely-
folded blue-field-with-white stars American flag that had draped
over his casket to my aunt, saying, "This flag is presented on
behalf of a grateful nation and the United States Army,...I am
honored to present the flag of his Country in memory and honor of
the faithful service of Sergeant James W. Kimmel..." Then, the

A Soldier's Question – Ft. Polk, LA, 1971

Times of crisis probably precipitate the most intense periods of questioning for a soldier, those desperate moments when Religion suddenly becomes all-important and the "bargaining of life" takes place. These are the secret times when the soldier offers God a shopping list of vices to be potentially sacrificed in return for a chance at continued existence. I admit that those moments probably happen in every human being's life, not just for soldiers, although mortal combat situations certainly increase the opportunities for sharpening the human-versus-Divine bargaining skills.

Simply, when faced with trying times, up to and including our own mortality, all of the intellectual barriers to approaching God quickly fall away, and we stand emotionally naked, without even a logic-contrived fig-leaf for cover. The singular plea is: "Get me out of this in one piece, Lord!" Of course, once the crisis has passed and, assuming we survive whatever was threatening our immediate and ongoing existence, we often get forgetful and find ourselves lusting after the knockout-blond in the string-bikini, swearing like a drunken sea captain (no, not the blond), or doing whatever we had fervently agreed to never, ever do again. The crisis has passed, all is well with the world, and we forget about our bargaining session until the next crisis event – and one always comes along, eventually.

For me, a hint of the initial questions a soldier might ask began in earnest in the fall of 1971. It didn't hit me like the savage, sudden strike of a lightning-bolt but more like the fall of a maple leaf in a windless, quiet October afternoon. But like one leaf on top of another, before long you can suddenly find yourself knee-deep in a large pile of autumn foliage.

The following story describes a brief period early in my 7 year military career when reality had finally begun to settle in. It's set in west-central Louisiana, the Fort Polk Military Reservation, if you will, about half-way between Shreveport and Lake Charles. I suppose that the muddy bayous and assorted dank swamps of the region seemed to make sense for providing a prelude to and training for jungle warfare in Southeast Asia.

After all, there were wide assortments of particularly nasty snakes and poisonous insects plus the indigenous alligators and wild pigs which, by the way, can make a hellacious racket coming through the tall swamp-grasses. Not being able to see the porkers until they either crash by like a runaway B&O freight, or, if you're incredibly unlucky, they steer a collision course with your body, just makes the experience that much more exciting and/or downright scary. From one day to the next I alternated between fear of snakes, spiders, scorpions, and wild pigs. Actually, I feared the alligators the least. Too, I began to appreciate the one significant advantage of living further north: a lack of the aforementioned varmints due to the several-month deep freeze cycle of real winter.

But in reality, Ft. Polk was, I think, meant as a gut-level reality check for an Infantry soldier, with each week of Advanced Individual Training meant to remind the trainee that very soon it likely wouldn't be just a training exercise. Conceivably, in a few months those weaponless pop-up olive-drab silhouettes out in the firing-line fields could be shooting back. The booby-traps skillfully set for the soldier-in-training to confront and (hopefully) disable would have no scoring NCO nearby in Southeast Asia to both grade and coach the soldier. Carelessness and/or failure would be potentially life-threatening or – ending. All of these realities began to set in as the weeks passed in the fall of 1971 and the days became literally and figuratively "shorter." And, of course, I found myself more frequently asking, "Why me?"

Ultimately, the U. S. Army shaped my own life in profound and fundamental ways. I went in as a young 22-year old college-graduated engineer, "technically proficient", or at least documented to be so in Metallurgical Engineering, but in many ways lacking in personal self-confidence. Yes, I knew what my diploma said regarding having "satisfied the requirements" and the scripted "Bachelor of Science in Metallurgical Engineering" was duly impressive. But even diploma-in-hand, I wondered what exactly I was qualified to do? Suddenly, the world looked much larger and significantly more menacing that it had when viewed behind sheltered, ivy-covered walls.

Seven years later I exited the Army decidedly older, but also far more mature, and highly-confident – both in myself and what I could accomplish if I truly set my mind and efforts to work. I completed an Associate Degree in Electronics Engineering Technology and several graduate Electrical Engineering courses, never with anything but an "A" grade. The study materials and concepts were no less difficult technically than anything I had encountered in under-graduate college; however, I was approaching my post-Army education with persistence, focus, and self-confidence. The experiences as an Infantry Squad Leader and then Combat Engineer had toughened and sharpened my ability to both think on my feet and with specific attention to the task at hand. In short, the Army had taught me much more than just shooting and marching.

I also ended up eternally proud. There was never a day that I put on the uniform of my Country that I was not proud to wear it. I guess wearing a subdued-green patch that simply says U. S. Army does something almost magical to you. Ultimately, you stand just a little bit taller, chest puffed-out just a little bit more. You are a soldier of the United States of America.

In the late-'60s and early-'70s, wearing any sort of military attire in public was not necessarily a socially-admirable thing to do. Upon returning home through the airport in Houston, TX, following my Advanced Individual Training, I remember being jeered by some young ladies because of my decidedly military appearance – clean Class A's, spit-polished combat boots, and one-fourth inch-maximum short hair. Yet, even in those anti-military times, I remember feeling, well, proud. I suppose it seems beyond reason to a civilian; it makes absolutely perfect sense to a soldier.

Today, I still put my "khaki's" and "Corkies" (my Corcharan jump boots) on for Church on Memorial Day. Although I always claim that Janet has washed my uniform in extra-hot water, I understand that while I went into the Army with a 29-inch waist and received trousers with a 29 inch waist, one of us gradually grew to a 36-inch waist and, no, it definitely wasn't my khaki trousers. After Church we take a picture of me with my wife and daughter underneath the Flag staffed at the corner of our front porch. Then, on Memorial Day itself, I go outside at 8:00 AM, raise Old Glory, and stand at attention in silence for a minute. It's my annual special "private time for remembrance".

And daily, I pray for our Men and Women in the Armed Forces, wherever they are serving. Once you've worn "The Uniform", you're always "kin", not just with those currently serving, but with every other soldier/sailor/airman who has ever "stood in the breach" for the United States of America. Again, it probably sounds corny to civilians; it's anything but for a Veteran.

The transition, though, from civilian to soldier is never instantaneous; pulling on your first set of Army fatigues does not miraculously create a military person. Neither is it without questions along the way; at least that's the way it worked for me. Fortunately, although there was much in our training to be firmly serious about, there was also humor; the kind of things that you look back on and laugh about fifty years later. Maybe this is because a soldier is always looking for an island of perceived respite in a sea of real insanity.

The following story was actually written several years ago, shortly after I had watched a Hollywood movie interpretation of an Army AIT unit going through training at Ft. Polk, LA, coincidentally in 1971. It's not a very good movie; the script writers apparently tried to cram as many trite "Army clichés", more myth than actual stories, and extreme but highly improbable situations as humanly possible into a film. Portraying realistic, believably human situations is always commendable; in this movie, the intent seemed to be to make almost everyone appear to be lacking even a single redeeming character trait, let alone anyone possessing any semblance of genuine military behavior. You ended up feeling sympathetic to no one along with a decidedly negative impression of the U. S. Army. Which, I guess, is what the writers had set out to do in the first place?

I kept turning to Janet, saying, "That's crap; you'd never get away with that!", or, "That wouldn't happen, not in a million years!" We weren't "choir boys" and, yes, there were a certain number of jerks, but you knew who and what they were. However, most everyone else was just a soldier – trainee, Non-Com, Officer – trying to do his duty in the best way possible.

A few days afterwards, still fuming about the decidedly unreal and unfair representation of Army life, I found myself with a pad and pen in hand, beginning my own true-to-life description of experiences at "Tigerland USA". My personal story sure isn't even remotely Hollywood; it is, however, scripted after my own saga in AIT at Ft. Polk, LA, in the autumn of 1971, and inevitably includes those eternal questions which always present themselves to soldiers at various cross-roads in their Military lives.

So, with this preface, walk back about 40 years with me to the Sovereign State of Louisiana and Ft. Polk, Louisiana - aka "Tigerland USA"…

"A Unique Curriculum from Peson Ridge, Ft. Polk, LA – November 1971" (aka "Post-College Education")

Mention "The Ridge" to any late-'60s/early-'70s U. S. Army graduate of Ft. Polk, LA's Infantry Advanced Individual Training (AIT) in "Tiger-Land USA" and you'll probably get a response that includes things such as, "Sure, good old Peson (pronounced "pea-sawn") Ridge," plus a few descriptive adjectives, most of which would be of the unprintable variety. Then again, you might even detect a slight smile as well.

You see, "The Ridge" was situated at somewhat of a crossroads for Infantry training, or maybe just a good old fork in the Army road. Take the left-fork and within a few days everyone is playing for keeps in the jungles of Southeast Asia. An "oops" can be fatal and "Charlie" is definitely not predisposed to providing second-chances. Take the fork to the right, and you get a reprieve of sorts, maybe, depending on the mood of the Military gods and fates. The problem with that particular path was simply, you never knew when the general mood or confluence of international intrigue and threats might change for the worse. Then, you might easily return to the Army road-fork and head off to the left.

But for the typical eighteen- or nineteen-old male with a typically-short perspective on life and its potential complexities, "The Ridge" was simply a "final exam", something to struggle with and overcome so that you could get on with the rest of your life. The fork-in-the-road symbolism was beyond our thinking at the time; after all, we figured, pondering the meaning of life was best left for old people, that is, anyone over 25.

As I sit here in my warm home, reclining back in the Lazy-Boy close to 40 years later, I guess I was no different, although without question the years have seen my Country and myself change (such as, both have grown "bigger"). And, now I certainly confess often taking to contemplating the various nuances and meaning of life.

However, looking back over the decades past, and remembering that particular 22-year old recruit, actually an "old man" from an Army-enlistee standpoint, fresh from Engineering School, and suddenly a "buck private", I can't help but smile too. To think that I had assumed that all of my education was behind me and what could anyone else possibly teach me, especially the U. S. Army, as I walked off the University of Pittsburgh campus for the final time...

Now you've got to understand something here. I really had not seriously included the Military as part of my Life Plans. Up through 1968, college graduates, particularly in technical fields, had been receiving "deferments", essentially a "Get Out of the Military Free" pass card. I remember graduates in 1967 and 1968 walking off the campus, diploma in hand, and straight into good, high-paying (over $700 per month!) Engineering jobs, with never a worry. That was certainly the expectation as well when I began college in 1966.

However, the mood of the Country, both in regard to the Viet Nam war and also the tenets of social-equality were quickly changing. Specifically, people were questioning as to why "the sons of the Proletariat" were the only ones to face military conscription? Personally, I wasn't sure exactly who or what comprised "the Proletariat", but I did actually agree that deferments for college graduates were inherently unfair – even if it included me.

As a result, the conscription rules were eventually changed in the late-60's: you would keep your draft-free status as long as you were a full-time student. However, the moment you stepped off the graduation stage with cap, gown, and diploma, (or happened to flunk-out of college; actually, I credit the draft for a renewed interest in academics by college males at the time) you were immediately draft-eligible, as long as you had been classified as "1-A" by your local Draft Board. And I was 1-A. Just as a note, I never made my graduation ceremony in 1971. Instead of a black cap and gown, I was wearing U. S. Army "tiger-stripe" jungle-green fatigues and combat boots; but that was far down my life-path, unbeknownst to still-in-college me.

I can honestly say that I had not ignored the possibility that I'd be called to serve in the Military. Several of my high-school classmates had already gone to Southeast Asia and one, a basketball-buddy of mine, Joel, had already been killed. It was one thing to read a casualty list in the newspaper; it was something completely different and much more personal to lose a friend who you had grown up with. But Joel had gone into the Army directly from high school. At the time of his death, I was still almost two years away from graduating. I suppose I was hoping that by then the war would have wound down and that occupational deferments would once again be available. Too, like most other typical college students, I wasn't paying particular attention to the ongoing national debate regarding military conscription. Or maybe it was just that my head was too full of concerns for passing Differential Equations and Dr. McGruer's infamous Physics 16, 17, and 18. (One particular test had a class average of 25; there were four problems, no partial credit, and Dr. Mc graded "straight-percentage.")

That's why the Draft Lottery was a slightly unexpected event for me. Apparently, the Powers that were in charge decided to take the selection process out of the hands of the local Draft Boards and, in order to further enhance the fairness of the draft selection, it was decided to do the selection process by conducting a Draft Lottery. And, as an apparently "adopted son of the Proletariat", this time it quickly came as absolutely no surprise to me that I was to be included in the very first Draft Lottery in November of 1969.

For this "if you win, you lose" endeavor, all 365 days of the year would be assigned an individual "ball", the group of which would be tossed into a huge barrel, turned several times for hopefully thorough mixing, and some responsible person from the Draft would then pull out "birthday balls" starting with Number 1.

If your birthday corresponded to Number 1, you were virtually assured to be personally hauled from the college graduation platform the moment your diploma met your fingers and quickly drafted into the Army (and likely "sent directly to Viet Nam", as Drill Sergeant Malkowski threatened us many times in Basic Training – but again, that was in my future...). The higher "birthday number" drawn, e.g., the 300'th ball, the less chance of being fitted in Army green. No one could really argue regarding the fairness of the process; it put everyone at equal risk with no special favor for college guys or any other perceived advantage of intelligence, breeding, or influence, e.g., knowing someone on your local Draft Board.

That first Draft Lottery had several similarities to today's State Lotteries, although again, winning in this case was essentially NOT seeing your "ball" pop up. Here's what the "pre-game" line had read: those drawn first (say, 1-100) would essentially be immediate draft bait. From 100 to maybe 150 we figured your chances of being drafted would be "iffy"; in other words, you'd best be studying the waxing and waning of diplomatic overtures in Southeast Asia because if things went poorly, more troops would likely be needed. Over 150, everyone felt one would be safe. If I remember, they eventually drafted numbers 1-125 within six months (or immediately upon college graduation) of that first draft lottery. No matter....ultimately, I wasn't even close to being borderline, which is probably fortunate for me, as I was never well-versed in waxings and wanings..

It was interesting for me to observe that there was a noticeable upswing in the number of young men interested in the intricate mathematics of Probability and Statistics at that time. After all, your life-plans (and possibly your life, period) were tied to your birthday and the luck of the draw from that barrel. A single day's difference in date of birth could literally alter your life. I guess that, in the end, Biology was the key factor in life, just like Mr. Fusko had categorically insisted back in 9th Grade at Wilkins Junior High School. His other famous quote: "You only get what you receive."

I remember that it was a weekday evening for the drawing and that Ken, I, and two other Engineering guys had gathered in Ken's tiny, off-campus apartment (yes, I know, they're ALL that way) to watch the televised live drawing that would have a direct bearing on the future of millions of young men. In keeping with the historical significance of the evening as well as to provide the necessary fortification in regard to the upcoming event, Ken had graciously stocked a generous supply of Old Bohemian (if I remember, it ran about $3.00 per case in 24 snap-top cans) and the other staple of college students' refreshment, Wise Potato Chips (you remember them, don't you – the bags with the Owl on them; get it?). Oh, and yes, I was 21, although just barely.

As the undertaker-somber Draft official, dark suit, white shirt, and black tie about 1-1/2" wide, described the rationale and rules of the drawing, all of us opened fresh cold Old Bohemians (I wonder if there could have been some perverse sort of irony to have been watching the Draft with a draft?), then sat down on the floor to watch our individual fates being decided by a bunch of little balls clattering around inside a big rotating Plexiglas barrel.

About 4 sips into my Bohemian draft I heard Ken groan. His birthday had been drawn as Number 4 (out of 365 possible dates; talk about crummy luck!). We all slapped him on the back, then immediately toasted him generously and loudly with a chorus of, *"You're in the Army now..."* Come on now, we were Engineering students as well as young males, and sensitivity was not strongly in our makeup at the time.

As a matter of fact, Ken graduated in August of 1970, was immediately drafted, and by January 1971 was sending me short letters from Viet Nam while serving as an Infantryman. I remember him writing: "We were out on patrol yesterday and I was carrying the M-60 machine gun. Suddenly, gunfire burst from the tree-line to our left and immediately we were in the biggest fire-fight you could imagine. When they send YOU over here, remember to keep your weapon loaded and your head down!" Another letter simply had said, "Crappy place to be. Glad you're not here – yet!"

I guess at the time I should have been comforted by the fact that the system had worked as advertised. But all I could think of then was, "Get past the first ten, then twenty, then...and make it to over 100." Besides, the odds just had to be getting better for me, right?

Please understand that this televised drawing had no resemblance to the NFL Draft or any such star-studded ESPN extravaganza. Instead, I remember watching the decidedly stern-faced "older guy" stoically pulling "birthdays" out of the barrel one at a time, looking very much like I would have imagined the Angel of Death reviewing, then confirming his list of future "clients." In retrospect, I guess we should have sprinkled lamb's blood over the apartment door lintel, as apparently we were all quite "uncircumcised" or something like that (you DO know your Old Testament story of The Exodus, right?).

Before I could take two more sips, it seemed, one of the other guys went, "What the...? NO!!!" He had just been drawn Number 13. We repeated the hearty toast and rousing song as he muttered, "My Mom was in labor 28 hours with me. Why couldn't she have had me right away the day before?" It was a shame, I felt, that now even our poor mothers were being blamed despite their painful pangs of delayed labor! But then again, it was two down and two of us to go.

As the droning, expressionless announcer continued his "Happy Birthday" litany with each successive ball, I began to do some feverish mental statistical calculations trying to calculate how the "factorials" changed with each number drawn; however, I never really did well with those statistical functions, maybe because I could never grasp the concept of a number with an exclamation point after it. Okay, I know you're dying to know what a factorial is – it's the product of all positive integers of the number in front of the exclamation point, for example, 4! is simply 4x3x2x1 or 24. I can't remember specifically what factorials had to do with calculating my draft odds, but I knew at the time that it had everything to do with how many ways there were to arrange the order of the number of balls in the barrel.

Remember, this was long before the advent of personal computers or even hand-held calculators, so trying to work out a 300+ factorial was daunting even for a skilled, sober statistician. I was certainly not the former and the inhibiting effects of Old Bohemian were taking care of the latter. In any event, my brain was still non-stop sprinting through the math while continually coming up with what I felt were mathematically-induced and seemingly logical questions. Was it better to be faced with a greater odds for being chosen due to fewer balls being in the barrel? If so, how much did my odds change with each draw? What was the possible effect of having a "near-miss", like one day before or after my birthday?

How much wood could a woodchuck chuck if a woodchuck could chuck wood…?

As I struggled with the intricate statistical calculations being processed in a not-quite-so well-oiled mental quagmire of tension and beer and the lottery numbers went into the thirties, I suddenly heard the third of our group shout out, "Son of a ___!" He was chosen as number 36. Ken and the two of them all toasted, sang, and then talked about possibly enlisting together, hoping for a "group discount", I guess. Incidentally, to the best of my knowledge, the U. S. Army never showed any inclination to be very keen on the yet-undeveloped concept of "bundling".

I tried to participate in the frivolities (or the wake, if you will) but my mind was busy doing additional calculations and pondering new statistical complications. Let's see now, I asked myself, 4 guys in the same room, three of which had their birthdays drawn in the first 36 of 365 balls, that's GOT to improve my odds somehow, right? But, no, wait a minute…having the four of us in the same room doesn't have anything to do with the actual odds generated in an independently conducted drawing, right? But, no, my odds HAVE to be improved…they HAVE to be. I knew that this was fundamentally wrong but it sounded reassuring to me at that time. As it turned out, sounding good was about the best thing to be said for my musings. Then again, I think I got a C in Statistics the year before. Stupid factorials!

My beer-chilled brain was unable to resolve the conundrum at the time. Still, I reasoned that somewhere the "odds gods" must be smiling on me. It just felt right – three out of four early, one very late, gosh, you just HAD to love math, right? "The Queen of Science", she's called! Or perhaps, just perhaps, something else?

As the drawn numbers passed 50 I began to allow myself the luxury of a hint of relief. Sure, I said to myself, I'm going to be number 365… Think positive! And besides, green never was your color! The TV announcer's monotone pronouncements along with the generous flow of Old Bohemian were together slowly dulling my senses and diminishing my concerns. Looking back on it now,

I was oblivious to the wicked tendency of Life to lull you to sleep, sweetly singing a tender lullaby and gently rocking you - right before suddenly dropping you squarely on your head while laughing fiendishly?

Apparently, I didn't take enough statistical training (or I had been staring at the not-so-smiling odds gods while landing on my head) because somewhere in the 50's numbers, November 7 popped out of the barrel. I remember thinking, "Nah, he didn't say 'November'; it must have been December, or September, or maybe even October..." But, at that time I still had reasonably good hearing and the television flashed the current birthday digits in very plain, stark white letters like the garish signs of a side-street Las Vegas casino and, yes, it was indeed November 7. The now-neon-looking television lettering seemed to leap off of the screen, flashing on and off, proclaiming – "November 7, November 7, all aboard for a fast, direct, and not necessarily round-trip to fabulous, exotic, adventure-filled Viet Nam. Ooh, la-la!"

Funny thing, my first thought was, I guess having four guys in the same room really DOESN'T affect the statistical odds of an independent drawing after all. Typical Engineer thought process, I guess? Then, I was helping my three friends toast myself, joining in the now-familiar repeat rendition of, "*You're in the Army now...*" sung, this time, with more fervent conviction and less mirth.

Interestingly, now 40+ years later, I've uncovered some actual statistical data regarding that first draft lottery in 1969. Realizing that, at first glance, this will seem to matter to no one but me as a true Statistical weenie, I'll present the Reader's Digest version.

You see, with 365 days in the year (okay, so I'm forgetting February 29 for Leap Year), if you put a ball with each date in a barrel, assuming all of the balls are "the same", except for the date written on each one, mix them all thoroughly, and then draw out each one, numbering the order drawn with the corresponding dates from 1 to 365, a statistical review (actually, a graphical plot of the 365 dates versus the order in which they were drawn) would be expected to yield what is called a "Random Correlation". In other words, the graph would exhibit a "shotgun-pattern", e.g., no particular defined pattern, simply a random cluster of datum-dots.

However upon closer review, the actual plot of the data from the 1969 draft lottery DOES show a very slight correlation, technically, -0.39, which is not very "strong" but far from random. This is highly unexpected given the assumption that this lottery was supposedly random and unbiased.

This "negative-correlation" of -0.39 actually suggests some bias was present, not necessarily intentional, but a bias nonetheless. It now appears likely that the balls were initially loaded into the barrel but subsequently not mixed thoroughly, or at least not enough to guarantee a fully random outcome. The result (that's where that minus sign comes in) was that the birth dates in the latter part of the calendar year, from July to December, were more likely to be pulled out first (FYI – the first number pulled was September 14). Perhaps they were added last to the barrel, as if someone had started tossing the balls in beginning with the one for January 1. Whatever the advent of that "non-homogeneity", those of us conceived in the end-of-year Holidays (or perhaps near Valentine's Day, or early Spring Fever) were rewarded for their parents' red-hot passion with Military green-and-brown camouflage.

So, I guess the odds WERE indeed "stacked against me"? Hence, an interesting statistical anomaly that ultimately had little relative importance except to a few young men in 1969 with birthdays from July to December. However, for this statistically ill-fated "band of brothers", as the old saying laments, "For want of a nail, the shoe was lost; for want of the shoe, the horse was lost; for want of the horse, the rider was lost, for want of the rider…the kingdom was lost." In my specific case, for want of a thorough mixing, seven years of being in Army green…at the time though, a scary thought.

But you know, despite the overall bad statistical luck that evening, I honestly remember shrugging, taking the "Scarlett O'Hara" approach ("I'll think about it tomorrow…"), having another Old Bohemian, and mentally shelving the whole experience. After all, it wasn't even 1970 yet and I still had another 2+ trimesters to go at Pitt. I was 21 years old, I had a nice, cream-colored 1967 Chevrolet Chevelle convertible with black-leather "Strato-Bucket Seats", and life in general was very, very good at that time. After all, I reasoned, a lot could happen in the next year or so, what, I wasn't exactly sure nor what I would do if it DID happen…. That night, though, for the very first time I dreamed of being in uniform, and the climate was very warm and humid. The next morning, I found my "mental shelf" looking a bit crooked, but once again I figured, "Tomorrow – I'll worry about it tomorrow." Fiddle-dee-dee.

Looking back now on the following year, it seems as if I had simply blinked my eyes and suddenly it was December 1970 and I was opening the mail confirming my achievement of a Bachelor of Science degree in Metallurgical Engineering. Also in my hot little hand was a job offer which I subsequently and quickly accepted (to start the day after New Year's) as well. Still, I could hear the somewhat faint, yet mournful strains of, *"You're In the Army Now"* echoing in my brain. But then again, I reasoned, I had a job and an engineering degree, and 1971 was dawning…

Now let me admit, it wasn't as if I had suddenly awakened in December of 1970 to the shifting of possibility to probability of Military Service. In fact, in the summer of 1970, I had sat down with my Uncle Bill (101'st Airborne, 506'th Parachute Regiment), a decorated WWII veteran living in Johnstown, PA, and discussed my likely options for Military Service. We had talked direct enlistment (Corps of Engineers), Reserves (long waiting list but an opportunity to serve part-time over the long-haul – 6 years), and of course, simply waiting for the Draft (two years, with the likely choices of ending up in the Infantry, Infantry, or…).

Those were THE options; in my Family, with proud and valiant military service back to the Civil War (both "Gray and Blue Teams"), then World War I, II, and Korea, I wouldn't even have conceived of "other non-conventional options", such as beating feet to Canada, a not only popular but even lauded alternative being touted at the time. Simply put, if you were called to Serve your Country, my Family expected that you would answer that call promptly and without hesitation, just as your ancestors had done years before. Personal philosophies, dislikes, and particular current politics were non-issues.

Clearly, our Family believed that as a citizen of the United States of America, a male served when called and as an extension of the Government's policies, not as the creator of those same policies. If you fervently disagreed with the Government's direction, you were advised to become a lawyer or a political adviser – but to get that specific education on the GI Bill after you had completed your service to your Country.

I remember reading some heart-felt Civil War letters written by one of my Great-Great-Uncles, two weeks before his death in The Battle of Mechanicsville. In it, he said something to the effect of, "We marched today and I could see our Flag fluttering overhead…" Funny, what seeing your Country's flag fluttering in the breeze does for a soldier. It's that lump in the back of your throat that forms when you think of what that rectangle of cloth with bright stars and broad stripes really stands for. It's that chill you get as the bugler sounds "Retreat", when the flag is lowered at the end of the day, and your First Sergeant says to no one in particular, "Another day of proud service for "the Good Guys." There's always a special, ageless feeling when standing at attention and saluting The Flag for any American veteran.

Besides that intense love and pride you feel for America, you also never feel alone, because in truth you aren't. There's a long, dusty line of U. S. soldiers, stretching back into the distant past of a brash, young Country through over two centuries of phenomenal growth mixed with too-brief periods of peace and nation-threatening war. Starting with the Minutemen militia, literally the first "National Guard", standing against arguably the finest professional army in the world at that time, these early American soldiers blazed the trail for every young man or woman who today puts on their Country's uniform. Once you do, you're forever in a very special and exclusive "club", its fraternity and bonds unexplainable to anyone who has never pulled on Army or Marine green/camouflage, Navy white, or Air Force blue.

Even today, when I struggle into my "khaki's" on Memorial Day Sunday at Church, I still feel the warm, intense pride of wearing my Country's uniform and the honor I was given to have been a United States soldier. I can recall while we were traveling on our way from Basic Combat Training in Ft. Lewis, WA down to Ft. Polk, at one point we endured the abuse of some anti-war-protesters just outside the Seattle airport. Ft. Lewis was a staging point for Army troops both going to or coming back from Viet Nam; therefore, those protesting the war found it a choice "target of opportunity" for making soldiers coming or going feel extra "special." There was a measure of guilt flung at those returning and added misery and humiliation for those just beginning their combat journey.

As we exited our obviously military-green bus and began our walk to the airport terminal, we were greeted by the catcalls and shouts of "baby killers!" Heck, I thought to myself, we've only finished Basic Training; we're not even officially would-be "killers" yet. My young, at that time still-controlled blood pressure, quickly spiked. Then, one of our Drill Sergeants calmly said, "Men, you're doing what you're doing so that these people will always have the right to do what they're doing."

I never have forgotten that and I always try to remember that statement when someone tells me how "naively" America-proud or politically "incorrect" I am. After all, I've personally helped insure that they have the open and free right to do just that.

Having said all of this, as I literally walked off of the Pitt campus and almost directly into the Military, the Army was beyond a doubt an altogether different experience compared to anything else in my life up to that time. As was to be expected, I quickly ended up being called for Military Duty, although it was via the call and enlistment into the Army Reserve National Guard (ARNG) in March, 1971. The famous and dreaded letter starting with

"Greetings" arrived shortly thereafter and C Company, 145th Infantry responded, "Sorry, we've already got him!" Then, and almost as quickly, I had gone to Basic Combat Training at Ft. Lewis, WA, just outside Seattle, on the 6th of July.

I remember being up at my Grandparents' home in rural south-central Pennsylvania for the traditional July 4th Family picnic. That evening, as I prepared to return home to Pittsburgh, bag already packed in preparation for departure the next day (not much inside, really; just a few pair of under-shorts, soap, shaving cream and razor, toothbrush and toothpaste, and a small pocket Bible), I was saying my goodbyes. My Grandmother hugged me tightly, saying nothing, tears forming in her eyes.

My Grandfather, a World War I combat veteran, shook my hand firmly, and simply said, "Do it right, Slim." I remember nodding and wondering just how I would measure up to a man I so completely idolized?

The subsequent transition from citizen to soldier was intense, rapid, and thorough. One of the first things I learned to appreciate was the Army's special attention paid to "looking military", starting with haircuts. Today, this doesn't sound like such a big deal; in 1971, though, it most decidedly was. Long hair had become almost a "badge of protesting youth"; short hair, on the other hand, was viewed, particularly by young ladies, as indicative of "the establishment", unpopular and also very "un-sexy". Ask me which of these two reasons – political correctness vs. attracting girls – was likely the most important in regard to a guy's hair length, and you will greatly disappoint me.

The pre-Army length of my hair, at the time, was short, at least relatively speaking, mainly due to the fact that if you lived in the Lauer household, you were always groomed "as a proper gentleman". Your hair was expected to be clean, neatly combed, and always "indicative of your upbringing and personal pride." There was no debate on the subject. I remember during the advent of young men wearing ear-rings, at least in a normal, social manner, my Father once commented, "The only men in my era that wore ear-rings were pirates." So, unless the first words out of your mouth were, "Ahoy, Matey," or you were indeed a member of the opposite sex, men in our household never wore ear-rings.

As we stood in the haircut line for our first U. S. Army ear-lowering, probably resembling a ragged flock of forlorn sheep waiting to be sheared, some trainees (note, at this point in the program, we were simply "trainees", in no way worthy of even the hint of the still-to-be-earned title, "soldier") were decidedly nervous, particularly those with shoulder-length locks. One guy in front of me turned and said, "I haven't had a haircut for two years! Katie will never speak to me again!" I thought to myself at the time, "This could be a near-religious experience for you and for Katie!"

But in truly democratic tradition (unusual for the U. S. Army, by the way) you had a "choice" in haircut styles: the "short" and the "long". "The short" was, well, short – essentially a scalp-hugging buzz cut. No one asked concerning "the long"; in fact, most of the guys figured it had to be "a trap." And no one was, at this stage of the game, ready to "stand out" in any way, shape, or form.

Call it my engineer-bred curiosity which got the better of my concern for being called-attention-to. When my name was called I was the first to request "the long"; after all, I could see what "short" was and, hey, I just kinda had to know. There was a brief moment of silence in the room, as I remember, and then the Army barber smiled and said, "Sure, one 'long' haircut coming up!" Not surprisingly, in about 20 seconds I had been given "the long" haircut which of course looked exactly the same as the "short" haircut. Out of the corner of my eye I could see our Drill Sergeant making a notation in his olive-drab notepad and I could almost imagine him thinking, "Lemme see, is there one or two "R's in Lauer?" But you see at least I had been given a choice, right? And I had immediately seen that personal choice was certainly in short supply when it came to Basic Training existence.

Then the days had rolled into weeks and months of PT, physical training including running to all classes/ranges and also to and from chow, basic weapon familiarization (to this day, I can still field-strip an M-16 rifle without a rational thought), and all manner of basic soldier information, instruction, and warnings. I guess that's why they call it "Basic Training"? Plus, you learned to look and act like "a Soldier" – marching, uniform maintenance, and, yes, most importantly, following orders – all instantaneously upon command.

Most of all, you learned to perform vital tasks without having to waste time thinking. For example, performing "Immediate" and/or "Remedial Action" on a balky M16 without having to mentally go through the procedure step-by-step was a skill that could easily make the difference between going home standing and breathing and going home lying on your back, stiff and dead.

For me, the civilian-to-solider transition was not terribly difficult. I had grown up with responsibilities and respect for those who were older and, to my thinking, longer on life-experience than me. For other new recruits, the changeover was a major mental and physical shock. I saw young men who had never really been forced to do anything they didn't specifically want to do learn to perform just about any required task almost instantly given the appropriate and proper command. The "learn" part was quicker for some than for others.

For example, I was amazed at the number of young men who had no clue how to make up a bunk. As one guy told me early in Basic, right after I advised him that the sheet probably went under the blanket, "Heck, Mom always did this for me." He was one of the many trainees who found the adjustment to Army life challenging. You see, the U. S. Army is not big on allowing Mom to accompany Junior to Basic Training.

Part of it too, I learned, was simply the realization that, in civilian life you could be a "loner", truly "do your own thing." Once you joined the U. S. Army and went from life as a civilian to becoming a Soldier, you eventually discovered that you were now part of a larger whole, not a collection of independent entities with separate goals, desires, and motives. The quest for a common objective is the ultimate job of a soldier – any soldier at any time. If you're a stubborn, me-first type of individual, you will probably have a difficult time adjusting to the military.

Of course, there's a difference between being persevering and just plain obstinate. The Army will subsequently reward the former and punish/purge the latter. There are always some people who cannot understand the difference; they end up either being lousy soldiers or permanently unhappy "short-timers", leaving the military altogether as soon as their enlistment is up.

More importantly, in Basic Training I found that learning to operate as an integral part of an Infantry squad also helped you potentially avoid dying in a particularly ugly manner in combat which is obviously a very valuable skill to acquire. As was mentioned before, sometimes, particularly in the Infantry, doing what you've been trained to do without having to spend a significant (or even insignificant) amount of time contemplating the action is the difference between staying alive and experiencing a quick and/or really unpleasant death.

The recognition of the distinct possibility of being sent into armed combat in Viet Nam was also part of a growing realization that my life had changed significantly starting in July of 1971. I was now fully part of the great, wide, forever-flowing "River of Life." I had left the small feeder-stream of college life in Pittsburgh, PA and was sailing down-stream into a much larger river with tremendously strong and fickle currents.

As a reminder of that fact, every evening I would lay on my top-bunk, gaze out my battered green-trimmed barracks window, and contemplate Mt. Rainer off in the distance 50 miles away, its snow-crested top contrasting starkly with the deep-blue of the summer Seattle evening sky. As the sun sank lower in the west, I would watch the shadows slowly climb Mt. Rainer until they would eventually extinguish the sun-reflected snow glare. Then, for a short period afterwards, the still-white peak would be vaguely visible against the rapidly blackening sky.

Each night I would watch that majestic, repeat performance with the same wonder accompanied by the realization of how small I really was in the overall scheme of things. The mountain had been putting on that magnificent performance for thousands of years and would continue to do so for thousands more unless, as some volcano experts predict today, it finally blows its top, wiping out Seattle along with a good bit of the State of Washington and ushering in a new, global and life-altering Ice Age. On the other hand, I realized that I might live at best another sixty or seventy years – or perhaps far fewer, depending on my near-term destination. Either way, Mt. Rainer would likely remain, along with much of the rest of the big wide world, long after I had returned to dust.

As September 1971 approached along with the end of Basic Training, I received my orders assigning me to Ft. Polk, LA. I remember my first thought was, "That's the state where they hold the Mardi Gras, right?" Plus, it was in the South and, I figured, spending the fall further south couldn't be all that bad. And so, I approached my move to Advanced Individual Training (or AIT) with some reasonably positive anticipation along with a new-found mixture of caution and skepticism born of Army Basic Training. Truly, I had found, military life had a habit of not being like civilian living in either environment or predictability, regardless of the locale. And, as I quickly found, Ft. Polk, Louisiana, was not quite the same as festive New Orleans, Louisiana, not by a long shot.

Given that comment, let me say a word about Louisiana and, particularly, the West-Central region. It's reportedly a lovely portion of a beautiful section of the United States and I'm sure that Louisiana-natives cherish their native soil, just as I do the mountains of south-central Pennsylvania. But you've got to understand that good old PA doesn't have mean, vicious, exceptionally bad-attitude (e.g., the Water Moccasin), and highly venomous snakes (e.g., the Coral Snake), crabby scorpions (they object vehemently to being sat upon, even unintentionally), dangerous spiders (like the Brown Recluse, who love to curl up in dark places like combat boots and are loathe to share the cramped space with unsuspecting toes), all of whom also love the warmth of a sleeping bag (occupied or not) placed on the cold November ground.

One Louisiana native told me that you could tell a Brown Recluse (he called them "brown fiddlers") by looking for a violin-shaped black mark on their backs and by the fact that they have six eyes versus eight for other spiders. I immediately remember thinking, "Sure, I'll just get on down eyeball-to-eyeball with a poisonous spider and start to count." Of course by comparison, the wild pigs and alligators (again, not native to Pennsylvania) lurking in the tall, marshy grasses and bayous are mere "porch-pets" – that is, to Louisiana natives. Count their eyes…sheesh!

As for me, though, I particularly hated the wild pigs. Until coming to Louisiana, my country-boy Pennsylvania experience with a pig being reportedly "wild" had consisted of one of my Grandfather's neighbors whose pet pig, Porky (of course), had gotten a snout full of cayenne pepper. I often wondered whether the eventual bacon had retained any of the fiery hot seasoning.

But these particular porkers, or Razorbacks as some of the Arkansas boys called them, made Porky look like Mickey Mouse (or is that simply a figment of "mixed-animation"?). The males sported upper and lower tusks anywhere from two to four inches in length, the upper ones menacingly curving upwards. As if that wasn't sufficient, wild pigs like to use the lower tusks to keep a nice, sharp edge on the upper ones. And when they're really irritated, they charge like a Front-Four and use those tusks like flailing machetes. In the high marsh grasses, you can hear them coming but can't see them until they are right on top of you. Have the misfortune to run into one during mating season, and your day can turn decidedly ugly very quickly, just like the pigs they are, that is unless you're a girl-pig, I guess. Wild pigs are nothing to take lightly and, as I mentioned earlier, I'd rather deal with an alligator. Then again, I guess it's like saying you'd rather get hit by a Chevy than a Greyhound bus. I really hated those pigs.

Secondly, I thought that they were sending me to the Tropics for training, or at least preparing me for a similar environment as found in Southeast Asia. Indeed, when I had arrived in September, the heat was still stifling, the humidity dripping-wet, and the remnants of a late-September hurricane had left behind a tree-branch littered landscape which by itself was a reminiscent of a war zone. Even by the beginning of October which had mercifully yielded a slight drop in the day-time temperature from full kitchen oven-hot to toaster-oven warm, the fatigues-soaking mugginess continued with little respite. So far, yep, there seemed to be definite tropical similarities.

But then, there's November in Louisiana, which can sometimes be wonderful as long as the sun is up. At night, however, let's just say that it wasn't pixie dust that coated my sleeping bag and made my teeth chatter. Well, you might comment, that's what sleeping bags are for, right? Quite true; however, as the song says, *"This Is The Army…"* and as such there are no "luggage handlers" except yourself. You might stay warm overnight but then you had to carry the stupid, bulky thing the next morning as the temperature got back into the 70's…but wait, I'm getting ahead of myself.

AIT was sort of an intense, advanced version of Basic Training, except that we all knew that after AIT we were one step closer to the jungles in Viet Nam. Therefore, we all paid a bit more attention to the more in-depth training as the days and weeks passed, became a bit more serious regarding our outlook on the future, and the Base churches I'm sure saw an up-tick in attendance at Services on Sunday morning as the various Brigades' Infantry Companies progressed through their AIT schedules.

We learned to fire the single-shot LAW-72 (light-antitank weapon), which was essentially a modern Bazooka. It's definitely a rush the first time you see that fiery rocket leap out of the light alloy tube perched atop your puny shoulder accompanied by a deafening "WHOOSH" as it powers off to pulverize a thoroughly junked deuce-and-a-half (a two and one-half ton Army truck) downrange. Similarly, watching the every-fourth-round red tracers from the heavy .50-caliber machine gun pound other wrecked target trucks 1100 yards away makes a lasting impression as to the lethal effects of modern weaponry firepower.

But my absolute favorites were the various plastic explosives (C-4), blasting caps, and other related "boom-stuff." It always amazed me that you could burn C-4, whack it with a hammer, or similarly abuse the stuff – as long as you didn't burn AND whack at the same time. Flame plus concussion, which is where the blasting caps came in, could be both friend and enemy, depending on if you were setting the explosives or encountering them unawares. I used to volunteer for the post-class detail assigned to dispose of the remaining explosives from the day's class. Like the character in that golf movie, I'd sometimes fashion "Mr. Squirrel" and "Mr. Hawk" and then have them "dual to the death", accompanied by the appropriate blasting-caps. Ah, where was a camera when I could have used it? Then again, I had been a fireworks fanatic since I was four, after watching a lit-Snake pellet explode in front of my Grandmother – the look on her face, the not-so-loud "boom", and I was hooked - and the Fourth of July was always my favorite holiday.

Of course there were the unrelenting "Squad Maneuvers" classes where we learned how to move, signal, "sneaky-Pete patrol", come on-line, and generally function effectively as an Infantry Rifle Squad or Platoon. It was emphasized again and again how important battlefield communications were. I'm sure each and every military unit stretching back to the first battles with rocks and clubs felt that they had good battlefield coordination and communications, only to discover how difficult it can be to maintain formation discipline and effective combat tactics as life and death are flashing in front of your eyes (or, more recently, just beyond your field of vision).

Even as an Infantryman's weapons had advanced from bows and arrows to cross-bows to primitive flint-sparked muskets to repeating carbines and finally to M-16's (standard U.S. issue, 5.56 mm semi-automatic/automatic rifle; it replaced the M-14 as standard U. S. Army issue in 1967) and AK-47's (a Soviet-bloc assault rifle, 7.62 caliber, also known as the Kalashnikov AK-47), communications among infantrymen (and now women) became more important and the need for speed even more imperative. It was true in 1971; it remains just as true today, and every Infantry soldier learns that fact, sometimes (and still) the hard way.

That's why a good Infantry team gets to know each member's tendencies, habits - good and bad - and also their individual capabilities. You develop an unspoken cohesiveness that lets one person look in one direction while you are covering a slightly different view and the person behind you is covering yet another region, giving the team full 360-degree vision, all without uttering a word. In fact, whether it's in the woods or jungle, sound can have an uncanny knack of carrying surprisingly great distances. So, you learn to tie/tape everything you carry to avoid clinking and clacking, keep your mouth shut for hours – sometimes days - at a time, and pay particular and close attention to what your next step will be, not only for nasty booby-traps/trip-wires but also to maintain complete silence during movement. Hand-signals substitute for vocal commands. After all, you're not out for a pleasant stroll in the park, where the most dangerous things around you are squirrels busy gathering acorns unless, I suppose, you're in Central Park. A combat patrol is literally a life-and-death hike, not a casual pleasure-walk. You learn to take it very, very seriously, and remain supremely focused, as if your life depends on it – because it actually does.

In short, it's intense and often dangerous training simply because War is, well, inherently dangerous to a soldier. Looking back on it now, where I'm afraid to get up on my own roof to clean leaf-clogged gutters in the fall or (sometimes) even light the gas-barbecue grill, it's a good thing I was only 22 years old and therefore didn't know better regarding the lethal power I once held in my grimy but youthful hands. Then again, when you're 22, you feel immortal – nothing's going to jump up and get you, even a bullet, a "LAWs rocket", a rocket-propelled grenade (RPG), or a hidden booby trap packed with plastic explosives.

Today I try to light a firecracker while covering both ears. At 22, you're going to live forever and even if you know deep down that you won't, death is not even remotely on your radar screen of thoughts let alone feelings in regard to your own mortality. I maintain that, truly, War is for the young, where Life is still (apparently) playing "by the rules" and has not yet revealed her notoriously cruel, ugly side. Candidly, that's the only way you could get sane human beings to face some of the things a soldier must confront.

And so, as we watched the Louisiana foliage turn from greenish-brown to mostly brown and as Halloween came and went (for us GI's, however, all of our costumes were the same – olive-drab in color for "standard duty" with "tiger-striped" dark-green-and-black jungle fatigues for night patrols), we all began to anticipate the culmination of AIT - Peson Ridge, the "final exam" for Infantry personnel, or per the designation, 11-Bravo, "Light-Weapons Infantry". In essence, Peson Ridge was both the Final Exam and also a dress-rehearsal for Southeast Asia.

Now, you might question just why we would have been so anxious to go from Louisiana to Viet Nam; after all, they usually aren't shooting at you in particular in any one of the United States of America. Well, part of the reason for our casualness was just described in a previous paragraph regarding youth. On the other hand, I think that it was also a mentality that simply said, "Hey, I don't know what's around the next corner in my military life but I want to move on from this "garden spot" and get the next part over with as quickly as possible so that I can get back to my own real, personal life." Left largely unspoken was the caveat: "and hopefully I will exit the adventure in one single living personal and cohesive body unit." But again, we all KNEW that we would each not only live to return home but ultimately live forever so, "Bring it on!"

Looking at it in another, more analytical way, "The Ridge" was the final, practical test for the Infantryman. He (by the way, there weren't any "she's" back then in 11-Bravo, at least that I knew of, and I figure something like that would have become obvious after 3 months of group-showering together, but, hey...) had to learn to eat, sleep, and fight outdoors anywhere in the world. Remember, this was long before high-tech electronic combat-situation simulators, video-recording to help critique and analyze group and individual performance, and instantaneous and precise-to-the-nearest-foot global-positioning equipment. The possibility of on-hand computing and even simple video-games had not yet been contemplated, even by two brilliant guys working in a garage; heck, it would be another decade or so before we would even have "Pong"!

In 1971, the best and most realistic assessment of a brand new Infantryman's skills consisted of placement in a simulated Viet Nam combat environment, calling into practice all of the accumulated lessons learned both in Infantry Basic Training and, lately, Infantry AIT. In essence, we had received a crash course in the fundamentals of Armed Combat - Infantry. Now it was time to see if any of it had taken, and Heaven help you if it had not.

As an aside, Peson Ridge was reportedly scheduled to be closed in November of 1971 as by then the Viet Nam war appeared to be winding down. In fact, my Training Company (Delta 4-3 – our Company motto: "We're rough, we're tough, we sleep in caves and ditches..." the rest is mostly unprintable and rhymes with "ditches" preceded by "sons-of...") was reported to be among the last Groups scheduled to be processed through the area. I later heard that the next 10 Training Companies were also told the same thing. Heck, for all I know they're still patrolling through those deep forests, slogging across muddy bayous (by the way, I found that it's best not to contemplate too closely who/what else is in that water alongside you; sometimes, as they say, "ignorance is bliss"), and, oh yes, "taking the Hill."

As the "old man" of the Company, I had learned to take the various Basic and AIT experiences with a certain degree of "philosophical contemplation" along with the usual and unavoidable physical pain. Even after exiting the "gas chamber", the final session of our day of "CBR Training" (Chemical, Biological, Radiological), where we unlucky trainees, standing at attention in a tightly-sealed non-descript black tarpaper shack, were ordered to remove our gas masks to "experience the reality of a noxious-gas environment" (actually tear-gas), I admittedly found "experiential enlightenment."

For the half-second after I had removed my gas mask, I remember thinking to myself, "Well, this isn't so baaaaaaa…" It was as if someone had tossed a bowl of black-pepper into my eyes, then reached down my throat and yanked my lungs out through my nose. However, after hacking, drooling, and snorking for what seemed like an hour, I had to admit that they had made their point very well – namely, it's best to get your gas mask on (and quickly) in the event of a gas attack, particularly when it would likely not be pepper attacking your lungs and eyes.

Indeed, very early on in my military career, I found that a pragmatic, relatively simple, philosophical approach was useful in coping with certain events in my military service without having to spend copious amounts of time in deep introspection. First, relying on complex, time-consuming reasoning rather than your Infantry training could get you seriously killed. Secondly, adopting a simple approach to military life seemed to save wasted effort in regard to attempting to comprehend the non-comprehendible.

For example, I recall taking a battery of aptitude tests two weeks after arriving for Basic Training at Ft. Lewis, WA. Having a college degree and an Engineering background gave me an obvious advantage on these exams, although I hadn't quite figured out what that advantage really amounted to. Regardless, I breezed through most of them. After all, once you've taken your SAT's plus college Physics, Calculus, and Chemistry finals a few times, general-subject aptitude testing becomes pretty non-threatening.

Shortly afterwards, I received orders to report for a "personal interview" with a young, gung-ho-looking First Lieutenant, resplendent in razor-sharp starched fatigues and mirror-shine jump boots. As I stood at ramrod-straight attention facing his very plain oak desk, the Lieutenant closely studied the test papers in front of him, gazed up at me over top of chrome-rimmed/dark glasses and said, "Private, these scores are certainly outstanding." My first thought was, "Yes!" My next thought was, "Uh-oh…" He continued, shaking his head enthusiastically, "I'm sure that the United States Army will have an appropriate and positive use for your obvious skills and aptitude." After I had saluted smartly, about-faced, and exited the office, I could feel a little candle-flame of optimism flickering into existence somewhere deep in the secret recesses of my new military brain.

"Well," I thought, "Maybe this won't be so bad after all....'positive use', the man had said!" Visions of duty in a quiet office with air-conditioning, daily tasks where the most strenuous and dangerous work would be possible eyestrain from reviewing engineering drawings, or perhaps analyzing information in Army Intelligence flashed briefly before my eyes. After all, I WAS a college graduate, right? The Lieutenant and others had obviously taken note of my capabilities. And I would eventually be put to some "positive use", right? I mean, that's what "The Army" had just said. My personal "candle" was beginning to bravely shine out into the sea of military storm-tossed waves.

Never let it be said that the U. S. Army lacked a subtle, if morbidly twisted sense of humor nor that it was above dumping a full ocean of ice-cold water onto a tiny flicker of candle-flame. Two days later, our assignments (known as MOS – Military Occupation Skill) were posted on the barrack's bulletin board where our Drill Sergeant had unceremoniously tacked up several 8-1/2" x 11" single-spaced typed sheets. With uncharacteristic confidence I marched up to the bulletin board, joining the crowd of men-in-green jockeying for position, and looked for the sheet with the "L's" on it.

Slowly I tracked the by now well-known names down the list thinking, "Wow, lots of poor slobs are being posted for...." And then I stopped at: Lauer, Barry A. – 11Bravo – Light Weapons Infantry. Me? – a "ground-pounder, a "grunt", CANNON FODDER?? "But...but..." I mentally stammered, "I scored good. I scored very good." Yes indeed, they had apparently found the "right place" for me! That is, in the good ol' Infantry!

Adding to the experience of the moment, as I stood there rechecking to see if there was perhaps a second Lauer, Barry A. listed, a full "Bird" Colonel was, unknown to me, standing behind me peering over my shoulder, following my finger's movement to the 11Bravo designation. Normally, someone would have called "Attention!" with an officer in the area, but I guess a soldier becomes single-minded when searching a list for his potential fate. Quietly, the Colonel moved up beside me, then put his arm warmly around my left shoulder, and said in a hearty voice, "It's just gonna be you and me in Viet Nam, son!" He gave me one more shoulder-squeeze, wheeled about, and strolled confidently out the barracks door.

I vividly remember walking back to my bunk, mumbling to myself, "But I'm a college graduate. A college graduate…" Plus somehow I also doubted that it was going to be "me and the Colonel" shoulder-to-shoulder on patrol in the lush and deadly jungles of Viet Nam. After a few seconds I found myself starting to smile, then actually chuckle. It indeed occurred to me that the Army did have a sense of humor, albeit wicked, after all.

Still, you'd have thought that, by now, I would have at least begun to understand that college graduates were being routinely placed in positions requiring non-office (outdoor) activities. This situation had not just begun in the fall of 1971. Yet I still wrestled with the whole concept of "The Infantry." Although I was a "casual outdoorsman", meaning I liked to be out in the south-central Pennsylvania mountains bagging an occasional rabbit or grouse, feeling the crisp autumn air, providing my Grandfather had stocked up on "Iron City" beer, Kraft Extra-Sharp cheddar cheese, Italian pepperoni, and Ritz crackers which we always ended the day with while seated next to the electric resistance-heater, this Army back-to-nature routine was not what I had imagined almost a year after graduation.

To wit - earlier at Ft. Polk, on a late-September night-patrol exercise, as I had led a rifle-squad on a "mission somewhere", wading through some swamp/bayou (not sure I ever figured out the difference), M-16 held overhead in one hand, and straining to read the lensatic compass clutched in the other in the 2:00AM darkness, I said to myself, "It doesn't get any worse than this!" Just then I heard something swishing nearby in the water and found myself hoping, praying that it was an alligator and not a water moccasin, a particularly ornery snake with a very sour and aggressive disposition. Put the face of the actor Jack Palance – "Curly" in "*City Slickers*" or the extraordinarily-evil bad-guy in the old Bible movie, "*Barabbas*" - on the head of a really, really mean snake with an exceptionally bad attitude and you get a water moccasin. I had found myself once again muttering to no one in particular, "But I'm a college graduate, a college graduate..." I'm sure that, regardless, the U. S. Army did care about that fact. Really. I mean it. Okay, not in the least.

At that particular time, and many times after, I found myself asking, "Why me?" Today, my wife would simply reply, "Why not?" But back then, I still expected a more complete answer to unfold or at least, that someday I would understand.

In the back of my mind, though, in fact all through the prior 5 months, the training had really been more or less "clinical", I guess, almost detached. True, I was continually reminded that Army National Guard troops had been called up for every American conflict, sometimes as in Korea, during the very early stages of the conflict. Acting as a buffer and buying time for the Regulars to get geared up, National Guard soldiers had at times taken horrendous casualties, outmanned and outgunned due to the unfortunate lag in re-armament from peace-time. Therefore, I recognized that the training was, although perhaps not felt with the same intensity as the 2-year draftees, still not exactly a hypothetical, "this will never happen" exercise.

However, I figured that, barring a serious escalation and/or setback in Viet Nam, I would likely be released from active duty and returned to my home Army Reserve National Guard unit back in Akron, Ohio. Therefore, it was sometimes difficult to take everything that had occurred in Basic or Advanced THAT seriously. Sure, we were using live ammunition and explosives and it really IS amazing what a hand grenade can actually do or, as the jingle said, "When the pin is pulled, Mr. Grenade is NOT our friend!" But the dummy targets always fell obediently when our rounds struck them on the live-fire ranges; there was always a decided disconnect between training and real-life interaction with an enemy. After all, the cardboard silhouette targets weren't shooting back. Maybe it was the lack of blood?

I confess, though, that all of my "this just isn't for real" thoughts changed permanently one day in late-October when we experienced "The Ambush Trail". This devilish little path through the Louisiana woods was thoughtfully and viciously laced with a large and select number of inert but still dirty little tricks, most of which had been learned through hard experience in Viet Nam courtesy of the Communist Viet Cong. Things like booby-trapped souvenirs (don't just walk over and pick up that apparently discarded Chi-Com weapon); or what appeared to be "obvious sites" for an explosive device which, it turned out, only led you to step to the side where the REAL device was set up to do you harm even as your gaze was fixed on "the obvious." Or, trip-wires, those almost invisible lines just waiting for a careless GI's boot to step through and trigger a particularly nasty explosive charge; or the wickedly-staked log that swung out of the tree and pinned you to another tree. Well, I think you get my drift – this was not like skipping down the "bunny trail".

After our Platoon had been briefed, then processed through the Ambush Trail exercise, the Site Instructor studied the papers on his clipboard, then called out, "Private Lauer!" I stood and snapped to attention.

"Private, you have achieved the best score in this Platoon." I couldn't help but smile inwardly, feeling once more grateful for the obvious benefits of a college education as well as the keen combat-savvy of a trained Infantry soldier. "The best score…" the man had said!

"You, Private, were only killed or maimed three times." Actually, this WAS pretty "good", as one soldier was scored to have been killed/maimed a total of 12 times. Then again, it was kind of like back in Physics class where you ended up with a 58 on the exam and the class average was a 38; hooray! However, the professor graded strictly by percentage, not "curving" the scores; therefore, you still failed the exam.

So, I had done "well" on the exam compared to my comrades. Great! Unfortunately for me, I had still "failed" the exam. In truth, I had failed the exam the first time I had been killed; as in my college Physics tests, there was no "partial-credit" given. And, in this particular genre of trials, you had potentially more to worry about than explaining a failing class-grade to your Parents. An "F" on the next "test" could cost you your life or, perhaps worse, permanent existence in a wheelchair, and it wouldn't matter how many college degrees you possessed.

I wondered which of those little "dirty tricks" had been the first to terminate my in-training mortal existence – a trip-wire, an off-trail "bounding-Betty"? Then again, I concluded after further contemplation, it really wouldn't have mattered. As Tennessee Ernie Ford once sang in *"Sixteen Tons"*, "…if the right one don't get you, then the left one will!"

"Now," the instructor continued, "None of you seemed to catch on to some of the other obvious signs left by the enemy." What signs, I wondered, was he talking about? "For example: that bamboo table in that bunker; anyone notice that dab of cooked rice? Was it soft to the touch? Think maybe Charlie might have been there recently? What about the trees nearby? Any of you notice the marks from hammock hooks? How about flattened grass and leaves – or none – where they might lie down? Think, people! Think about how you would be bivouacked if you were the enemy! Think LIKE your enemy! These kinds of clues could save your lives!" On the march back from the range I was rapidly coming to the conclusion that, as a "jungle fighter", I still had much to learn.

But later that evening as I continued to reflect on the day's lesson while sipping on a chilled Black Label, I began to also come to grips with the fact that it was difficult to remain philosophical about being "only" killed or maimed three times (which still sounded like 3-times too often to me). Plus, I had never really considered the "maimed" part – having a leg or an arm blown off and then fearing NOT dying, having to live the rest of your life with a stump for a leg or arm – or worse. Talk about turning a corner and having life smack you up-side of the head with a brick!

As I thought about what had happened that afternoon along that wooded trail, so quiet, innocent, and green-looking, and thought about losing my life suddenly and horribly, it occurred to me that concentrating a bit harder on what we had learned so far might just save our lives, and especially my own, if worse came to worst. It struck me as dead-serious that a roughly 12 hour airplane flight could take a soldier from the Land of "baseball, hot dogs, apple pie, and Chevrolet" and land him in the live war zone called Viet Nam. Then and very suddenly, the make-believe could become a deadly reality, or even a life-time reality of dealing with things worse than death.

From that time on, I admit, I tried to approach any training with a heightened sense of urgency and attention which, I guess, is not surprising when you're thinking of the possibility of having your legs blown off. After all, despite what the entertainment industry might present in their graphic visual enhancements, actual combat is not make-believe. It's loud, dirty, thoroughly confusing, and utterly horrible. And, if you're unlucky, there's also no "Take 2." Mistakes have permanent and profound consequences.

Decades before Hollywood decided to try to show the actual carnage on a battlefield in minute and grisly detail, I was introduced to it, on film as well. In this case, I was undergoing cross-training as a combat-medic and learning to treat "traumatic battlefield casualties", specifically, "battlefield amputations." As we sat at a long folding table watching this training film, the best thing I can possibly say about that short 20 minutes of instruction is that I was the last of ten men viewing to put his head down on his arms. It was absolutely the most horrible, gruesome thing I had ever seen. I remember being in Driver's Education as a sixteen-year-old high school student and having to watch the Ohio Highway Patrol "Signal Thirty" films in which deadly automobile accidents were shown. By comparison, they were "Mickey Mouse" cartoons compared to that 20 minute sequence. To this day, I wonder how I would have reacted in such horrific situations; hopefully, I would have done my job and dealt with the personal aftermath.

At the end of that late-October day in 1971, I knew for sure that I was involved in deadly-serious business. It was the day my life and thinking as a soldier changed.

Now, less than a week later, as we sat huddled in the back of an open 2-1/2 ton truck that early-November afternoon with the driving rain dripping off of the lip of our steel pots (that's helmets), waiting to head for "The Ridge", I was drawn to thoughts of a family trip to Florida back in November of 1955 – sunshine, warm, friendly ocean surf, the opportunity to "See the USA in a Chevrolet", specifically our 1955 yellow-and white Bel Air coupe. I was only seven years old at the time, but for me, that was my on-going image of "the South." In particular, the South meant warmth in the winter months, including November for people born in the Pennsylvania Mountains. And this WAS Louisiana, right? And the last time I had looked on a map, it appeared as if both Florida and Louisiana were in the South, correct? So, I wondered, what was I missing?

The temperature at game time was 50°F and the low scudding stratus clouds added to the gloom, although it was only a few minutes after high-noon. Thoughts of pitching a pup-tent in the mud and me, as usual, with an air-mattress full of more holes than a factory of doughnuts, were already helping me to adopt the proper attitude for the upcoming festivities. Rain, a slight chill, gloom – yep, that about summed up how I felt.

Now, I have dear friends who just enjoy the blazes out of packing the tent and sleeping bags and heading up to the mountains for a weekend of "back to nature". God bless them! In the past 35-plus years I have consistently made it a point to sleep under a roof each night. To this day, my idea of roughing it is a Holiday Inn with no swimming pool and/or room service. To be fair, though, camping and military bivouacking are, after all, fundamentally dissimilar, as in the former there's usually no one shooting at you unless, of course, you hear banjo music.

Now, concerning just exactly what Peson Ridge was geographically all about, I'm not entirely sure. Yes, there WAS a ridge-line located in the area and I remember to the south and southwest was supposedly a live artillery range which we were encouraged to avoid transgressing into or upon. I took particular note of that fact. Frankly, though, Peson Ridge looked like most of the rest of the area around Ft. Polk, LA, except for the sign over the incoming road saying, "Welcome to Peson Ridge". Welcome, indeed…

As we pulled into the disembarking area at the top of Peson Ridge, the rain began to slacken to a semi-torrent and, yes, it actually was - the sun began to filter haltingly through the overcast. My hopes began to grudgingly rise along with the ambient light level. And immediately began to sink back down as the sweet, melodious voice of my Drill Sergeant shrieked, "Fall in, you @#$%! Hustle it up! You guys really @#$% me off!"

I'm blanking some words out, of course, but you see, no one can truly tell a "military story" without including or alluding-to the swearing, cussing, abusive and derogatory language and coarse sentiments. Now I'm admittedly and unashamedly a "Born-Again Christian" and was raised in a household where if my Mom or Dad said, "Damn!", the Tribulation and Final Apocalypse were commencing simultaneously.

I confess, however, that even after the crude and ever-more vulgar and descriptive verbiage of High School and College, I found "military swearing" to be almost a verbal art-form, firmly rooted in ultimate vulgarity, insult-ation, and steeped in creative genealogy/personal intimate behavior degradation, or insinuations of such. I admit that, if one of the Drill Sergeants had ever said to me, "Lauer, you're making me angry!" I'd have collapsed into a fetal position, cowering in abject terror. Somehow, being demeaned linguistically seemed to make us feel, well, more secure.

Maybe because we all felt like @#$%'s together? Or maybe it was simply that after a while, you learned to ignore what was being said other than what was, at least to you, important. Perhaps it's something like a husband listening to his wife?

I saw a similar situation occur in a Pittsburgh, PA plant of Jones & Laughlin Steel, where the Head-Melter, an hourly (union) guy who was in charge of the Open-Hearth steelmaking furnace, got into a heated disagreement with the Works Chief Metallurgist. John, the melter, and Charlie, the WCM, were in each other's faces, shouting torrents of abuse using terms that would have dropped a "person of the cloth" in absolute shock in a heart-beat. It was perversely fascinating to listen to each combatant weave a series of personal degradations deeper and more personal than the last one. It was almost like listening to a heated debate in a language that you can't really understand, with inventive prose and perverse imagery mixed with a crescendo of white-hot emotions. It was like watching the indicator on the steam-pressure meter crossing the threshold of the red-area on the dial; you knew that something or someone had to give.

The explosion happened with a whimper as opposed to a roar. Charlie began to turn away and simply said, "Aw ___, John, you're just being childish." Now these two guys had just insulted each other's lineages back ¾ of the way to Adam and Eve but now the final, camel's back-breaking straw was an accusation of "being childish".

Instantly John was on top of Charlie, swinging wildly, in an incoherent rage. He wasn't swearing, cursing, or otherwise coherently verbalizing – simply roaring. As we all leaped in to try and disentangle the two gladiators, Charlie managed to crawl away from the war zone. As for John, he just kept on roaring and swinging. I've never seen anything like that before or since.

From then on I've always been respectful of the hidden power of spoken language as well as the utter lack of civility, sanity, and sometimes personal-ness when it comes to swearing or other coarse, foul, and vulgar language. I've also never forgotten that words that can make one man shrug can also make another into a raving lunatic. Just to be on the safe side, though, I've never used the word "childish" in casual conversation since then.

And while on the subject of coarseness, let me take a minute and address, yes, our Drill Sergeants. These were the non-commissioned soldiers provided by the U. S. Army to specifically mold us into lean, mean, combat-ready Infantry troops. I'd call them, charitably, an "eclectic" group. In truth, most of them were indeed Viet Nam veterans and very good soldiers. It's just that they all seemed to have subscribed to the "iron-fist in a velvet glove but without the velvet glove" theory. A Drill Sergeant held an all-powerful position over his Training Platoon (4 Squads – 10 men per Squad). Like a Roman Emperor, he could imperiously pronounce severe penalties for any and all actions that displeased him, and these penalties usually took the form of some physically punitive test of endurance and degradation in the dirt/dust/mud/whatever.

By the way, it's amazing how much saw-dust you can involuntarily scoop up in your pockets while low-crawling back and forth in "the pit" (think of a small parking lot-sized area bounded by railroad ties and filled with, yes, saw-dust), one of the all-time Drill Sergeant favorites for communicating dissatisfaction with any aspect of a trainee's performance and/or attitude and the corresponding dispensation of "corrective reinforcement." Then again, if the Fates frowned upon us, sometimes we would be invited to plow our way through "the pit" just because we had finished our training early and it was deemed too soon to hit the showers. Regardless, you needed one after a session in "the pit."

Once, our entire platoon had failed to properly execute a column-right during a road-march. Our Drill Sergeant was most highly displeased. First, we squad leaders were forced to get down on our bellies and "low-crawl" through a conveniently-placed sawdust pit (not our "home pit", which made actually made no difference at all; after all, sawdust is sawdust). By the way, it's also amazing where you will still find sawdust lodged months later; I actually found some particles almost a full year later wedged inside one of the links of my Timex watch's Twist-O-Flex watchband.

We squad leaders had been singled-out specifically as the perpetrators of the mass transgression. This was because we were responsible for communicating the column-right orders to our squad. Therefore, if the squads failed to perform as required, it was obviously the fault of the squad leaders; simple logic, really. So as we pulled ourselves out of the far end of the pit and began the futile attempt to dislodge sawdust from our teeth, noses, and other bodily crevices, each individual member of the squad began the low-crawl exercise back and forth, back and forth, the length of the sawdust pit.

A more miserable, dusty (particularly when you were covered with sweat to start with) experience one could hardly describe. I would have preferred to run 10 miles than do a half-dozen circuits in "the pit." Not surprisingly, any session in the pit was accompanied by torrents of verbal abuse but at that point, you didn't really care since, with all of the sawdust dust, nobody was clearly visible; therefore, you couldn't actually take it personally.

You see, the U. S. Army also believed that implementing immediate corrective action of a physical nature would stick with us longer than a torrent of invectives (see the explanation above). Lord, I hated low-crawling. You were scraping along on elbows and knees with a choking cloud of sawdust enveloping your face. You're already hot and sweaty; and then having to perform in front of your squad. I don't know that I ever felt so thoroughly filthy and humiliated. Admittedly, though, after that experience we always executed a column-right in a precisely correct and completely military manner.

Now again, maybe because I was 22 years old at the time and the oldest man in the Platoon, I was a bit more philosophical or at least somewhat less stressed about serving under "the Antichrist" (aka, our Drill Sergeant). Clearly you did your best not to screw-up and also to stay out of his way as much as possible. But with the wisdom of (some) age, I really did understand that, "This too shall pass." On the other hand, sometimes time seemed to stand still and events conspired against me. For example…

I remember one particularly steamy afternoon out on an M-16 Marksmanship Range, standing in formation, while Senior Drill Sergeant Grabozwski (I'm sure I'm missing a "z" or "h" or some other consonant in there where I have placed a vowel) was raging, concerning what, I had/have no clue, I slipped up. In an unguarded and utterly foolish moment, I recklessly let a benign smile creep across my face as I became absorbed by the exquisite linguistic splendor of the Drill Sergeant's diatribe. I happened to be wearing a pair of military glasses, a very plain collection of lenses (the frames were not, shall we say, Dior) with a slight distance correction, which I only used for shooting.

Drill Sergeant Grabozwski, on the other hand, wore huge, Coke-bottle-bottom thickness glasses with massive steel-gray frames that made his eyes appear to be popping out from behind massive boat portholes. In fact, we called him "the BEB", short for "bug-eyed b___", thoroughly and exclusively behind his back, of course.

Suddenly he stopped in mid-tirade, paused for what seemed like approximately two years, walked in a straight-line quick-step up in front of me, squared his body exactly to mine, shoved his face a few millimeters from my nose, his "Smokey the Bear" hat pressed against my forehead, and screamed, "You find this funny, 'four-eyes'?!" I swear that I could see the veins in his eyes thickening, the eye-whites taking on the look of golf balls ready to pop out of his eye-sockets. His nose flared in short, noisy blasts which heaved his heavy glasses up, then down, and he was standing on his toes, towering above me. I couldn't help but picture Daffy Duck in one of his hysterical cartoon-rages with Elmer Fudd. And, wow, Drill Sergeant G. could really have used a Cert! Maybe two!

Well, the original situation had been admittedly mildly amusing and was now all but forgotten, but THIS…. Standing eyeglasses-to-eyeglasses, brim of a Smokey the Bear hat pressed against my forehead, foul-breath to whatever – and suddenly, it was simply THE funniest thing that I had ever experienced. Deep down in my diaphragm, like the growling of a muscle-car V-8 engine revving up, I could feel the humor gaining massive volumes of inertia, surging like a tidal bore, straining to leap up my throat and expel itself in torrential sheets of insane, maniacal laughter.

While this tidal swell of mirth was initiating itself, another part of my being prayed, deeply, fervently, with great urgency, "Please, please, DON'T let me...", knowing that if I failed, I would likely spend the next week consigned to exploring the intimate details of "the pit." I tried to think of horrible, deep-depressing thoughts, holding my breath, anything but – LAUGHING! But there he was, standing and staring in front of me on his tip-toes in a Daffy Duck-stance with those telescope-lens spectacles barely touching mine. I suppose that you could have paid serious coin for this kind of entertainment but I didn't even want to consider the probable consequences of losing my composure at that moment.

It was truly the longest 10 seconds of my life. I held it in; in perhaps the greatest effort of self-control yet displayed in my young life I managed to "maintain an even presence." The guy next to me told me later that he could see me twitching in my forearms, my lips triple-folded over, as I did my absolute very best to remain grim-faced. Inside, my vitals simply shook in hopeless spasms of mirth. To this day, I think about that face, those glasses, the stance, the hat, and I begin to cackle. And twitch. Also, forever, Daffy is Sgt. G. Woohoo!

Day 1

But today, on The Ridge, it was Drill Sgt. Tyrone that paced in front of us, a not unusual look of disgust on his face as if he had just spotted a slimy, half-eaten disgrace of a worm. And, in fact, it was us he was eying. "Gentlemens, today we is gonna get you "soldiers", the tone conveying obvious doubt and considerable condescension, in better condition and familiarize yuz with what we in the Army call, 'Search and Destroy Operations'. Has I got any questions?" Of course, we all knew that it was wise NOT to have any questions at that point, because then you would take abuse for not already knowing the answer to a question that you should have known already but also for having the temerity to actually ASK one, which always cracked me up; then again, maybe my soldiering cracked him up too. Actually, Sgt. Tyrone was a very good soldier.

Three hours and twelve miles later, I felt like searching out and destroying something – anything wearing brass or stripes. Since I was loaded down with my bulky field pack, M-16 weapon, ammo clips, two M-60 machine gun belts, and two 4.2 mortar rounds, even my by-now well-muscled legs were leaden and aching. My shoulders chafed, and my forearms trembled slightly from fatigue, as I held my M-16 in the ready position. And it was only 3:00PM. Then again, it occurred to me that maybe actual warfare doesn't make accommodations or considerations for time-outs and/or rest-breaks. "So, quit complaining and just march," I growled to myself.

Fortunately for me, I had gotten a tip from a two-tours-in-Nam Infantry sergeant back at the base Rod and Gun Club the weekend before. He had advised me that on a "long-walk" it was best to leave some of the pack-buckles and straps unhooked so that the weight would naturally redistribute over my body. Of course too, he had reminded me, make sure to tape and pad anything that might generate metal-to-metal contact. After all, metallic clinking-sounds are not indigenous to Mother Nature; and the Enemy knows that all too well.

A half-of-a lifetime (actually, a short time) later, I heard the sweetest words in our Language: "We'z gonna set up our night defensive perimeter here. Secure your position!" With renewed strength and a semblance of inner joy, I began to hollow-out my defensive foxhole and run-off trench outside of the tent area. My tent-mate, John, 17 years old, a native of Los Angeles, and definitely not an outdoorsman, struggled repeatedly to secure his side of the tent. Actually his shelter-half had a broken tether rope and John ended up tying one end to a thin willow tree, which wasn't all that surprising as he had never truly grasped the concept of anchoring a tent using a tent-spike anyway. With each gust of wind, our tent took on a lop-sided, grinning look. Then again, I guess you didn't do much tent-pitching in downtown Los Angeles.

Of course, and not totally unexpectedly, ten minutes later we were given orders to gather our gear and move to another defensive perimeter. Again, I had half-expected it. You see, the Army has always had a philosophy that "practice makes perfect" so they like you to keep doing things over and over…and then again. Also, I suspect that they felt that it added to the general morale of the troops, in this case making us meaner, more ornery – the ultimate "Fighting GI." Possibly, though, it was a continuation of the mindset that preached, "Doing the correct thing immediately upon ordered without having to think about it can promote longer-living habits in a combat environment."

After the third move, around 4:30PM (that's 16:30 MST – Military Standard Time), I expected that we were potentially set for the night. So, time for a break for supper? Sure! Maybe a little snooze after chow – yeah, that would be perfect. So, out came a C-Ration container with the "swill du jour" - a can of Turkey (actually not too bad, the first time or two; after that, uh, well…). Then came canned peaches, long considered a real delicacy in the C-Ration lineup; you'd always try to trade your ham and potatoes for peaches, mainly because you never were really certain as to what form of dubious origination and/or edibility the ham and potatoes actually were, let alone which war they had originally been canned for; and finally, the after-dinner crackers, washed down with a mouthful or two of lukewarm, plastic-tasting canteen water. Ah, check please, monsieur?

As an aside to comments regarding military cuisine, the Army also started me on a life-long addiction to, believe it or not, Tabasco sauce. Call it whatever you like – Louisiana Hot Sauce, Texas Pete Hot Sauce, or what I consider "the best" – McIlhenney Co. Tabasco Sauce (Original) – I literally "don't leave home without it." I have two bottles at work, three at home, plus Teriyaki, Chipotle, and Habanéro varieties, and two small bottles that I carry in my work briefcase just for emergencies. I always use it on meat of any kind, eggs, salads, and just about anything other than ice cream, and I've even considered that once or twice. I can only hope that someday medical science comes up with proof that using the stuff in copious quantities prolongs life and cures the common cold. If they do, I'll live forever sneeze-free.

Now you might ask, assuming you're the real curious kind: How did this life-long addiction to Tabasco sauce come about? Well, in about our second week of AIT, a Special Forces (aka "Green Beret") recruiter came to look for volunteers. Along with three other soldiers from our platoon, I had stepped forward. The Sgt. Barry Sadler song "*Ballad of the Green Berets*" had been ringing in my ears and I had read the Robin Moore book "*The Green Berets*" (per the book jacket: "A new kind of soldier for a new kind of war!"). Simply stated, the Green Beret Special Forces soldiers were, and still are "the best." And I admit to having been captured by the song lyrics: "Silver wings upon their chests; these are men, America's best…" Plus, I had seen pictures of my Uncle Bill (Merle) with his "Screaming Eagle" 101st Airborne shoulder patch and Airborne jump wings. As the song also said, "Fighting soldiers from the sky, these are men who jump and die…"

What I deeply feared would be a potentially major negative to achieving my dream of wearing that elite Green Beret was the simple fact that Special Forces troops routinely jumped (parachuted) out of perfectly good airplanes. And, I was afraid of heights; really, really afraid. When the recruiting Green Beret Captain had asked me that question directly regarding heights, without thinking I had truthfully blurted out, "Yes Sir! Perhaps excessively so!" He had smiled, then simply said, "We'll teach you to control that fear, Private."

To this day, I still dislike high places. I never have been able to get over that fear. Years after the Captain's comment, however, I came to understand what he meant: you may always be afraid of heights but you can learn to function despite the fear, to actually train and learn to control it. Part of the key is to simply concentrate on the mission rather than spending an inordinate amount of time looking down. I've done it many times since; it works.

The Special Forces qualifying test included a long list of physical challenges – a 15 mile run, a survival swim with a full pack, and a number of other exercises to test the physical and mental mettle of each candidate. They were not necessarily looking for the biggest and strongest; just the most persevering. The song had claimed "…one hundred men will test today, but only three win the Green Beret." Actually, when all of the training and testing were completed, the number was actually around 15, so I heard. Still, that has to qualify as an "elite group."

One of the guys from our platoon had talked of nothing but winning the Green Beret. He kept claiming, "I don't feel pain. Here, take my knife and slice my finger! I may bleed to death but I won't feel it!" I figured that if the Green Berets were looking for mental cases, then this guy had to be a shoo-in. Unfortunately (depending on your point of view), Private Painless washed-out early, so to speak; it seemed that he couldn't swim – not a bit - and finally had to be fished out of the survival swim from the bottom of the pool with a shepherd's crook. Afterwards, his only comment was, "I wasn't planning on qualifying for the Navy."

My own brief flash as a Special Forces candidate ended fairly abruptly and without high drama, not because of a lack of physical stamina nor even my intense dislike of high places, but rather because my right eye was "only 20-30". Apparently, you couldn't "jump and die" without excellent eyesight in both eyes. As a result, I became one of the 97 "others."

Now, getting back to the original subject of Tabasco sauce…in one of the "here's what it's like to be in a Special Forces outfit" bull-sessions, a Sergeant McGowan had mentioned that Tabasco sauce had found its way into the Viet Nam soldiers' diet. Apparently, the word was that it helped a trooper cope with the intense heat and humidity of Southeast-Asia; plus, it added some much-needed spice to a usually bland Vietnamese diet, including C-rations. McGowan had claimed that just about every Green Beret carried small bottles of Tabasco sauce and that if we were really "serious", we should begin adding it to our daily diets. Consequently, I did and I have ever since. Strange, quiet, subtle, and lasting are the habits and influences of the military…

Back on Peson Ridge and with a semi-contented grunt mingled with a slight Tabasco-laden burp, I settled back on my irregularly lumpy pack, rolled up my sleeves, and let the warm late-afternoon November sun begin to aid digestion. 75 degrees, quiet, wow was it nice. This Peson Ridge thing would be a cake-walk if all we had to do was march, set up a defense, eat, and sleep. Ah yes, "…we sleep in caves and ditches…" sounded softly in my ears as consciousness faded, albeit quite temporarily.

A sharp poke in the side woke me up. John was mumbling something about a night patrol. Night? "John," I muttered, "You know I'm scared of the dark, and besides…"

"Yeah, but Sgt. Tyrone says you're leading the patrol anyway!" he half-spit at me. I started to protest again when he added, "Aw, Barry, all we have to do is go out the main road, turn left, go a few hundred yards to a clump of trees, and set up an ambush." Great, I thought. This guy hadn't even seen a tree until he started Basic Training, and now he actually KNOWS where some are?

Besides, that bit about being 'afraid of the dark' – not really; however, I WAS definitely afraid of the biting, ferocious, venomous critters hiding out there in the dark, all with short-tempers about being stepped on by clumsy soldiers in combat boots thrashing around the bushes in the dark. Heck, it was relatively easy to accidentally stomp on something mean and dangerous in the daylight.

I'd heard the tales of rattlers curling up to share a nice, warm sleeping bag, Black Widow spiders climbing into vacant combat boots for a night's snooze (along with the previously-mentioned Brown Recluse spiders), Coral Snakes fastening onto the webbing between fingers or ears and injecting their nerve toxin. As a college graduate, an engineer, and a snake-hater I had asked Drill Sergeant Tyrone what the correct and best procedure was in the event of the bite of a Coral Snake.

His answer was not particularly helpful, although pointed: "Gentlemens, if yuz guys ever get bit by one of them Co-rall snakes, yuz just better go down in the woods somewheres so that yuz don' bother the rest of us with your cryin' and moanin' whiles you die.". For about a week after hearing that explanation, I had gone into the woods with my fingers held tightly together and my neck tucked down low like a snapping turtle to protect my ears. I was bound and determined that if that "Co-rall" snake was going to get me, he was going to have to work for it!

Of course, too, we had been told about Southeast-Asia snakes that reportedly made our Rattlers, Water Moccasins, and Coral Snakes seem like Garters. The infamous pit viper was only mentioned in hushed-tones. It was nicknamed the "two step" – because that's about how far you supposedly got before you died. Then again, it seemed that everything in Southeast Asia was said to be bigger, meaner, and more lethal – kind of like Texas. It made me wonder why anyone would want to go there, let alone live there.

"Well," I said, "Okay, if it's gotta be then it's gotta be." Besides, I always liked being the "ambusher" rather than the "-ee". And, maybe after that, they would let us alone, I thought. Somehow, though, the last 6 months had taught me never to put much stock in a rash assumption such as being cut a break of any kind in training. Then again, I was becoming equally sure that, in the "real thing", an enemy wouldn't either.

You know, it's really interesting how quickly it gets dark in November the further south you are. Kind of like, you can read one minute and the next, where'd the book go? The sun was just dropping below the trees as I began collecting my combat gear – M-16, five magazines of blank-ammo, the belts of M-60 (light-machine gun) ammo, and most importantly, three full-size Baby Ruth's. By the time the candy bars were tucked away, it was truly "Who turned out the lights!" dark.

We proceeded to march down that still-muddy side-road (I couldn't see it was muddy, mind you, just feel it refusing to completely let go of my combat boot soles with each step, adding another element of thrills and adventure in the dark) with the PRC 25 (radio) directing us from our position to the main road. Stumbling onto the paved road without significant casualties (it's not as funny as it sounds, this moving at night, my friend), we tramped up the pavement a few hundred yards, looked deep into the gloom and 'voila', there indeed stood a clump of trees. This HAD to be the target area! After all, trees were trees, right? It was just that, there seemed to be lots of other of them there trees as well.

"Delta 1 this is Delta 5, over?" Now I was just being absolutely sure here; unfortunately for me, Sergeant Tyrone was not in an exceptionally approving or confirming mood. "Delta 5, what the ___ do you want?" Well, I wanted to be sure, that's all. "Uh, Delta 1, I'm about 2 klicks (kilometers) up the hardtop; is this the right clump of trees...?" The interruption was crisp and clear: "Private, didn't you study the ___ map?! Get that ___ position set up NOW!" So, okay, now I was sure.

Stepping off a good field of fire about 100 yards down the road and clearing some vision-interfering loose brush in between (yes, after a while, your eyes DO adjust to the dark), I began to carefully position each squad member appropriately for their predatory ambush. Now, I can admit it - John said, quite appropriately, "Barry, do you think they maybe wanted us to set up down the road further? This doesn't seem like '2 klicks' to me?" True, it didn't seem far enough to me either.

On the one hand, I never could understand why the Army didn't like to use simple Christian units such as inches, feet, yards, miles, quarts, and gallons; on the other hand as I said before, thanks to Sgt. Tyrone's gentle admonition, I was now sure and told John so, adding that if he still had questions, he could personally contact Delta 1. And besides, what was I going to do – ask Sgt. Tyrone AGAIN? John thought for a second and then, ultimately and also unfortunately, chose not to confirm his suspicions.

"Just go out and check the positions, John, and let us know if you see anyone coming." Besides, it would give him something to do, plus, he'd stay warm. You see, after the sun went down, the temperature was already dropping like a beat-up penny-stock. For us, miserable but thoroughly hidden in the Louisiana night, staying warm was now as important to us as stalking the enemy. I admit to thinking, however, that in a live-combat situation, our priorities might probably be reversed.

Eventually, everyone was relatively quiet and concealed, I thought, as I surveyed my TAOR (Tactical Area of Responsibility), unfortunately except for one guy, Jensen, from Cheektowaga, NY, who had fallen asleep on top of a sand dune, pile of dirt, or whatever the hump-in-the-dark was. He said that he was playing the role of a dead soldier to add realism to the exercise. I told him that we didn't want to report any casualties on our side and after a minute or so of half-hearted protests, he reluctantly crawled back behind a tree. I swear, 30 seconds later I could hear the rasping snores commencing their evening concert once more.

After about 30 minutes as indicated by my $10 Post-Exchange Timex with the marvelously luminous numbers (you know, I've often wondered just how much radium was on those glowing letters, as this was still back in the good old days of "radiation is our friend – usually"), sure enough, there came two squads of troops noisily clunking along the road – from the right. I found that strange, as I had expected things to come from up the way to the left where the main road was. Plus, for a night combat patrol, these guys were awfully casual regarding noise discipline and movement.

But, I reasoned, who else would be out here in the dark but our foes and, as I thought had been confirmed by Sergeant Tyrone, THESE were clearly our "clump of trees". "The dumb enemy," I thought, "Go figure. Well, he'll pay." After all, they probably didn't want to be out here in the dark and cold any more than we did, so they had probably gotten their directions mixed up or something. Looking back on the incident, you've got to understand, it sounded semi-reasonable at the time to a green Infantryman.

Smoothly and silently, I flipped the safety lever off on the M-16 and noiselessly patted the ammo magazine to make sure it was fully seated. Yep, blanks ready for firing. As I heard the almost imperceptible snick of safeties being released, I reached for a grenade simulator (a really, really loud firecracker). It would go nicely, I felt, when the M-60 machine gun opened up. The command Evaluators (roughly equivalent to the "umpires" for our final exam) would love the extra sound intensity and "site-realism" additions to us "achieving and maintaining fire superiority", I figured. It would show them that we were, indeed, "rough, tough, ...sleeping in caves and ditches..."

It's strange. Even though we knew this was a simulation/training exercise, I could feel a trickle of sweat run down my back. Regardless of that training knowledge, I wondered to myself what it must be like to be in the real thing, sitting ready to spring a lethal trap of fire and steel. All you had to do was gently squeeze the trigger to spit out a killing stream of high-velocity metal. Life or death laid in your cold little fingers, an instant dose of mortality for some unlucky soul. I knew that, right now, for here, we were ready, a skillful, stealthy, lethal killing machine, fully prepared to heap mayhem, ruin, and utter destruction upon the unsuspecting "enemy".

Unfortunately and fairly quickly, the wheels began to fall off of the well-hone killing machine. Jensen, the sleeping "Rip Van Winkle", had positioned himself too close to the side of the road and, therefore, directly in line with the enemy's flank (on either side) security. We were to be given a signal (hello, Jensen?) on when to open-up and spring the ambush to enable us to catch the whole contingent in an effective "killing zone", so I held my breath as they kept coming in the dark. Gosh, I muttered, they sound awfully close. Where's that signal, I wondered?

When their flank security tripped and fell over Jensen, cursing in the dark, I figured it was a good time to "light 'em up". Oh, and man, did we cut loose. The M-60 began its thud-thudding, spitting a tiny sheet of orange flame, I was tossing grenade simulators like confetti, and bursts of M-16 automatic weapon fire added to the barrage of noise and fireworks. "The enemy" just about jumped out of their boots, screaming and hollering. Wow, what a righteous ambush, I was thinking, as we were having our jollies rock-and-rolling on automatic fire selector settings. I could feel a sly smile growing across my face. "Like mice in a roomful of fire-spouting mousetraps," I muttered.

As I paused to eject an empty ammo clip from my smoking M-16, I heard a voice screaming out of the radio, "Lauer, you ____, that's Parker and 2nd and 3rd Squad!" OH! "Cease fire," I shouted hoarsely, trying not to sound as dumb as I felt.

The post-mortem showed that we had set up our ambush just about 200 yards down the road from where 2nd and 3rd Squads had been told to set up an ambush about an hour later. Apparently, I hadn't paced off more than about one klick (now be fair: it was dark, there are no "mile-markers" in the boonies, and therefore nothing "klicked" in my embryonic-Infantryman's brain). Mental note – learn to carefully judge distances, as if your life – and a lot of other soldiers' lives – depended on it.

Unfortunately, that had not been my only mistake. We had assumed that, despite coming from the opposite direction, they must still be the enemy. In truth, I hadn't stopped to check on "friendly unit operations" for that evening, a stupid, rookie mistake. So, we essentially chopped them up by mistake. It could happen to anybody, I figured, that is, anyone who was fatally careless. Parker, to his credit, laughed about it. "You just lopped off 10 years of my life back there. I thought Armageddon had started!" Yeah, I guess it was funny, after the fact, depending on your point of view. Somehow, though, I wasn't laughing.

Headquarters, and particularly Sergeant Tyrone, didn't quite find any humor in the incident either – not even remotely. Did you ever get your tail chewed out over a PRC 25 radio? "Lauer, you screw up one more !@#$ time and I'm sending you straight to Viet Nam.

They'll just shove your sorry !@#$ out the door into Charlie's lap and you can sorry-!@#$ ambush them to pieces. You're the dumbest…" After a while, you just learned to turn it off, as the Sergeant and Lieutenant took turns tag-team abusing me. Finally, although I had fully deserved the butt-chewing, I said, "Sir, you're breaking up…." as I whacked the mike against a log, over and over again. All I could think of was whether there was one or a pair of "s-es" in LOSER.

As I sat all by myself in the dark, feeling lower than whale dung, a solitary figure walked over and stood off to my side. "Nice ambush," he said, "Except for the part where you ended up killing a whole mess of the good guys." I was about to reply, in a not-so-friendly manner, "Thanks a whole heckuva lot!" Then, despite the darkness, I noticed the outline of Airborne jump wings above his breast pocket along with the unmistakable form of the CIB (Combat Infantryman's Badge). I quickly stood up, trying to stammer out some sort of apology.

He half-waved me quiet and then calmly asked, "So, what did you do wrong?"

"Well, sir, to begin with I set up at the wrong ambush-site coordinates."

"And did you have the correct coordinates?"

"I assumed I did, sir. Everything looked right."

"Next time, don't assume. Confirm it; and by the way, a "clump of trees" isn't good confirmation. You've got a map, you know how to use it; so, use it. Also, in night combat operations you have to know who else is going to be in the vicinity. That's a Squad Leader's responsibility too." He paused, reached into his fatigue-shirt pocket for a pack of Camels, offered me one, then a moment later continued. "On the plus side, you caught 'em all in a righteous killing zone." I guessed that was supposed to make me feel better; it didn't.

"Another bit of advice; don't ever put up with someone doping-off on a patrol, especially at night. That's your responsibility as well. I've seen an entire Recon-team wiped out because people couldn't stay awake. Charlie walked right over the snoring LP (listening post) and greased everyone. It can and does happen, even to soldiers who should know better." He offered me another Camel, but I was smoked-out.

"One more thing; you're a squad leader. So lead. If you don't want that responsibility, let someone lead who does. It's your choice, son." I was amazed at his calm, quiet demeanor about the whole thing, almost matter-of-fact but clearly deadly-serious as well.

Let me say here that for the next 7 years of my Army Reserve National Guard (ARNG) experience, in whatever Non-Commissioned Officer role I was in, I always made doubly sure that I had my communications straight, my mission objectives perfectly clear, and my coordination with other friendly units defined, precise, yet fluid. My LPs were always set up with soldiers who were good at, yes, actually listening and not sleeping, smoking, or doing anything else but what I had them out there for: to be the first soldiers to detect the enemy.

Maybe the most important lesson, though, that I learned that night was not to be intimidated into failing to ask a question on any part of an operation that wasn't crystal-clear. From that time on, I never failed to ask for clarification until I and everyone else on the combat team was sure that we truly understood what it was that we had been unclear about. Sometimes it would cause an officer irritation; that was perfectly okay, assuming I hadn't carelessly forgotten something that I had already been told. And, even then, okay, so you take a little abuse. Better that than end up with dead American soldiers because you were both lazy and stupid.

The fact is, in combat, "friendly fire" kills just as surely as that of the enemy. I vowed never to have that guilt on my head – ever. Gradually too, I was beginning to see why the Army practices. And practices. Then practices some more. Fortunately for me and the ambushees that night, Death doesn't usually count in practice, unless you REALLY screw up....

About 45 minutes later, "the real enemy" showed up and we sprung our "official" ambush. Somehow though, it just wasn't as good – no looks of surprise and terror, no screaming in fear, no rush of adrenalin with the thud-thudding of the M-60 and the slam-bang of the grenade simulators. For us ambush veterans, it was thoroughly anti-climactic. On the positive side, they didn't step on Jensen. He and I had a down-by-the-river, heart-to-heart dialogue and at least one of us, I'm sure, came away with a deeper understanding of the responsibilities of a Combat Infantryman. Also on the bright side, this time our victims were indeed "the enemy". Still, I admit, it didn't provide quite the same adrenaline rush as the first time.

Tired, cold, and thoroughly humiliated, I trudged the squad back to our defensive perimeter, there to face a thorough troop-to-officer blistering, I figured. This, I knew I deserved. But, at least I also expected to be able, at some point, to possibly sack-out and get warm, right? A logical assumption for reasonable people, I felt. Then again, I should have known better.

I watched my hopes flutter away like Chinese confetti in a Kansas tornado as we were quickly informed that a 100% alert was in progress with everyone and I mean EVERYONE manning their positions. "The Aggressors" were reportedly close by.

The Aggressors were actually another group of trainees who had been hand-picked to generally harass and bug us, all with the incentive that if they penetrated our perimeter, they would get the next day off. We, on the other hand, would have to move our defensive position – immediately, in the dark. Now this was serious business; we were cold and tired and not in the kind of mood to put up with what we perceived were butt-kissing jerks even if they wore the same color uniforms. If they decided to pay us a visit, someone would pay. After all, a grumpy, tired, cold soldier is not known particularly for an attitude of Christian charity. In short, we weren't about to have to move and we vowed that the Aggressors would not be able to realize their hopes regarding their planned activities for a day off.

I had my barbed wire effectively strung-out, and then set up some good fresh tree-branch camouflage. A few weeks earlier we had been out on a platoon problem and I had noticed how long-dead foliage failed as an effective camouflage compared to the surrounding greenery. Mine, on the contrary, was now nice and fresh; too bad it was pitch-dark.

Confident, prepared, and more than a little aggravated, we waiting for "the dreaded enemy" to attack. He did, too. We suffered an estimated 80% casualty rate, which is decidedly undesirable. The sneaky rats really pulled a fast one. Did they use Viet Cong guerilla tactics to get under our wire, probe for a lack of over-lapping defensive fire, or overwhelm a careless lookout post? No, they simply walked up the road and shot the bejeebers out of the place. Yes, the road guards (from First Squad, of course!) had fallen asleep.

Amazingly, it had all gone down just like my recent adviser-in-the-dark had predicted. One or two soldiers doping-off had gotten the whole outfit hypothetically massacred. Another lesson learned – thankfully bloodlessly and, better yet, not the result of a slip-up by my squad. Nevertheless, after a stumbling trek in the dark to our new home, we spent the remainder of the night spread out (without tents) in a field of two-foot tall field grass, shivering in the dark. Again, on the positive side, you had to be alive to shiver.

As I lay there that night looking up at the night sky, the words of the Airborne evaluator kept re-playing inside my chilled head: "It can and does happen, even to soldiers who should know better." I realized that "over there", in a real combat situation where fatigue, heat, and sheer mental tension grinds a soldier down, the full check could be handed to us for immediate payment if we were not consistently stealthy, cunning, and otherwise good soldiers. But even "good soldiers" like that Recon team could screw up. The difference was that in their case the Grim Reaper ended up being "the Evaluator", not an officer with a clip-board and checklist. I didn't sleep well that night, and it wasn't just because of the cold.

Day 2

Next morning, the Company Commander was, shall we say, exceptionally displeased with everyone. However, there is a subtle difference in being chewed-out by an officer versus a non-commissioned officer. You see, an officer is trained to rant and rave in a completely different manner; same meaning, just more creative, polished insults. The gist of the tirade was that we clearly needed more patrolling to "sharpen our obviously weak and deficient Combat Infantrymen skills".

Subsequently, for the rest of the morning, we sought out and attacked "the feared enemy", an imaginary defensive force, at the cost of two men. Actually, they were eventually caught racking-out up in a tree and counted as casualties. It's amazing – give a GI a chance to catch some "z's" and he'll take it, although I'll bet if "Charlie" were actually around, there would be some seriously intense thought before sacking out, particularly when the result could be a permanent, cold, deep sleep. I was clearly beginning to understand that in real-life combat, one guy doping off can get the entire team greased.

Complicating matters, though, and adding to my dismay, in this particular instance they were attached to my own squad and I didn't know what had become of those two sleeping clowns. We had been bobbing and weaving through some heavy brush and I had been trying to keep everyone in visual contact with about the same success as attempting to corral 10 Siamese kitty-cats. The Turkey C-rations from early morning (basted in Tabasco, of course) were flip-flopping in my stomach as the PRC 25 did its usual job of bawling us out – "Either confirm your Combat Strength or give me a !@#$ body-count!". My "exec", John, was beginning to get a little frayed around the edges with all of this. "What if something happened to them?" he asked.

"Something had better have happened to those idiots or I WILL kill them," I muttered back. And so, after a semi-thorough search of the area and, as a last futile gesture, I resorted to the best comfort I could think of – lunch. Unfortunately, the luck of the draw was matching my overall string of lousy fortune and netted – chicken ala king, the C-Ration scourge. We always figured that whatever was left over on the ground after the rest of the C-Ration cans were stuffed was finally raked together and labeled Chicken ala King, basically inedible even when generously marinated with Tabasco sauce. But then again, everything in a dark green can was beginning to get a bit "old" now.

Actually, some of the C-rations we were issued WERE well-aged; I never got one but the stories were told about Korean War-era rations finding their way into our Training C-rations. And, as I mindlessly stuffed the can's contents into my dry mouth, I kept telling myself, "Well, chicken is kinda like turkey, right? Isn't it? They're both birds." Or was it that turkey supposedly tasted like chicken?

Luckily for me, the two AWOL's showed up around 13:00 hours thanks to our Airborne evaluator. Now they would probably have gotten off with a severe tongue-lashing by the Company Commander, had they not played the "smart-a__". When the CO (Commanding Officer) had asked them where in the sam-hill they had been, one replied that he was narcoleptic, which might have been semi-believable, had not his partner begun to snicker and cackle, obviously amused at the utterly lame excuse.

An officer may be more polished, but I guess it's like a brightly-shined, beautifully decorated sword – don't mistake its looks for a lack of potential lethality. When last I saw them, those two jokers were crawling on their bellies in a saw-dust pit, holding their arms upright with buckets of paint and brushes, working on painting two 4-foot posts situated about 100 yards apart. Paint one, crawl to the other, paint that one, crawl back to the other….. I had no sympathy – feeling sleepy NOW, fellas?

After chow, the second-day afternoon was taken up by a class on Defensive Positions and preparation for a movement that night on a fortified hill manned once more by hand-picked swine looking to earn a day off As sunset approached, I dug into another carton of C-rations to find – you guessed it, chicken ala king. Now seriously, I might not have minded the cold-chicken along with the congealed sauce/gravy/whatever which I always thoroughly mellowed with Tabasco, of course, particularly if I had been able to get my can of Sterno lit. With all respects to its manufacturer, as a Metallurgical Engineer and thoroughly familiar with the principles of a blast furnace, I found it decidedly humiliating not to be able to get a crummy can of the stuff to light. I dug holes, made a grating, everything, and eventually ended up throwing the Sterno can as far as I could heave it. Chow was cold that evening, although I wasn't sure if it would have really made a difference. "Guess I should have been an Eagle Scout, or Campfire girl, uh, or something like that," I muttered to no one in particular.

At 18:00 hrs. (that's 6:00PM), we began the move-out for the hill assault, with the assignment of reinforcing the Advance Squads as soon as they made contact with "the enemy" upon the hill. Typical of combat operations, they made contact alright; unfortunately, we were still about a half-mile away at the time. There's a wise military adage that states, "no battle plan survives fully intact the first contact with the enemy" or something like that. Case in point here – "the enemy" refused to perform the scene according to the script. They had moved just down-hill from the crest. Thoughts of shivering again throughout the night in the frigid November air suddenly leaped into my mental worry zone.

But more than that, something probably buried deep inside the embryonic "makings of a soldier" region in my gut yelled, "Focus! Concentrate on what you need to do to complete your Mission!" Clearly, we needed more firepower to make a strong, combined assault and that meant the Advance Squads needed more troops quickly. So, I made a mini-command decision – move quickly and bring the Squad on line to the left to concentrate fire power in support of the Advance Squads, then sweep right in an oblique flanking move. Did you ever run the better part of a mile uphill, at night, with a full pack, a belt of M-60 ammo, an M-16 with five ammo clips, and all this right after supper? I could feel king-chicken in my stomach attempting to crow.

But amazingly, the quick movement worked; as we added our strength to the other Squads "the enemy" began to fall back (either that or their chicken was squawking back at them too). Our flanking movement also pushed them off the side of the hill and down into a swampy valley where we hoped they would thoroughly mix along with the other snakes and vermin.

"Good thinking on your feet, soldier," Sgt. Tyrone's voice sounded somewhere behind me in the dark. Almost immediately, the chicken began to settle flaccidly back down as I found a small, satisfied smile creeping up my face. The words "good" and "soldier" being used together to describe "me"! It felt, well, good! I kept mentally repeating the words over and over again. Somehow "good" and "soldier" placed together were sweet music to my ears, kind of like "true" and "love."

The after-glow of success faded quickly, crowded out by the feel of the November night air permeating my still sweat-soaked fatigues. As we began to prepare our night positions on top of the hill sans tents, I found myself fumbling in my pack for my heavy field jacket. The temperature had already tumbled below freezing (someone had said it was 25°F). And then it occurred to me – we had decided earlier that we didn't want to carry the extra weight and bulk so we had left our jackets to be taken back to the barracks. Okay, I figured, time to improvise.

Today, they advertise an "As Seen On TV" snuggle-sack with holes for your arms and legs; that night, I had beaten them in product-development by about 3 decades. I figured I could stay reasonably warm by sitting semi-zipped in my down-filled sleeping bag with a tent-half spread over my hands and M-16 to keep the cold and frost from permeating both flesh and steel. I hurriedly finished my rough foxhole and quickly climbed into my sleeping bag, zipped it up snugly against my armpits, leaned back against a pine tree, and sat on guard while John slept, a 50% alert – later he took a shift, then me again, throughout the night.

Around 03:00 hours (that's 3:00 AM), I quietly brushed the frost off of my bag cover. Amazing how still the woods can be in the middle of the night; apparently, even the usual night critters had turned in early in order to nestle into a warm place. But then I heard something; well, actually "sensed" something not quite right. At first I gloried in my growing combat skills, discerning from the non-nature-like sounds that the enemy was near. In truth, it was the slam of a truck tailgate about 400 yards away that sort of gave me a further hint. However, a new lesson learned – noise sure can travel a long ways, particularly in a quiet night – and you can hear it provided you're darn quiet! Later in my military career, I heard more than a few stories of bad things happening because soldiers – not just "friendlies" - were yakking instead of staying quiet and listening. Apparently, even the vaunted Viet Cong had its share of marginal soldiers.

Now, with a new feeling of "I've done this before", I quietly snapped the M-16 selector switch from safe to automatic as I tensed and listened. Slowly, I raised the weapon to my shoulder, peering down the blackened sights. The full moon now silhouetted the entire hill and it was almost comical to see five "enemy" soldiers apparently sneaking across the field below and approaching the foot of the hill. Did they actually believe that they were moving unseen and/or that we were all asleep? Actually, I found out afterwards, they did, on both counts; another lesson regarding assumptions and how they can get you and your buddies killed. I squinted down the dull-black length of the M-16 and let them approach closer, closer, gradually filling the sight-picture…

When they were roughly 20 yards away I cut loose on automatic. It's amazing how big human eyes can get, even at night, when totally startled, particularly when the combination of flame from the barrel and the sharp concussion of M-16 rounds erupt in your face. Within seconds, the M-60 behind me starting its thud-thudding, and quickly it did indeed sound like a war. Those five "enemy" high-tailed it back down the hill and across the field and the last sound I heard a few minutes later was the slam of a truck tailgate and the sound of a motor fading into the distance. But I was still remembering those eyes, that look, and the benefits and rewards of staying quiet, concealed, awake, and above all at the end, alive.

My Grandfather, James R. Kimmel, had once told me that it was always "the eyes" that he remembered as he vaulted into the German trenches in World War I. For the first time, I think I began to understand what he had meant.

Before you assume that I was being "Sgt. Rock" single handedly, John did eventually join the battle. He sat up in his sleeping bag, fired three quick shots, and lay back down. I was duly impressed with his apparent confidence in me and his firm dedication to duty.

The rest of the night would have gone well for my squad except for a slight screw-up by Jensen, who was supposed to be manning our forward LP. Yes, I had sworn that I would never do that again, but somehow, I was determined to make him into a decent or at least half-ways competent soldier; however, there's an old adage about not being able to "make chicken-salad out of chicken-something". It seems that Sgt. Rodriguez had taken a small security patrol out to make sure the perimeter was secure following the evening's "action". As he approached the LP, I heard, "Halt, who goes there?" Okay, Jensen, I thought, correct procedure.

"Sgt. Rodriguez," said the voice.

"Advance and be recognized," Jensen said. Correct again, I thought – perfect military procedure. Now all he had to do was give the first part of the password.

"Blue", whispered Jensen.

"Moon," answered the Sergeant. Now from a technical standpoint, everything was going correctly. Recognition from sighting to passwords was being executed properly and in a soldierly manner.

All seemed well, which should have given me my first hint of trouble.

There was, however, one tiny glitch. It seems that Jensen had only remembered yesterday's response to the password – "Cheese." We had gone over the day's Operation Orders earlier including the password, and I actually had considered writing it down for Jensen, not that it would likely have mattered. So, in order to be sure rather than sorry, he ripped off a burst of blank automatic weapon fire directly in front of Sgt. Rodriguez.

I could make out the faint outline of the Sarge almost jumping out of his boots as the M-16 racket contrasted with the dead-quiet 3:00 AM night. "Whazamatta you! I give you the right word and you shoot me! You crazy, man, you!@#$%." I laid there and just died laughing as the cascade of profanities/obscenities continued to rain down on poor Jensen. Deep down though, it was another lesson as to how simple it was to get killed in a combat situation, particularly at night, unless you're on top of your "A-Game". Seemingly minor, careless slips could be lethal.

As I turned over the watch duties to John and curled up in my sleeping bag, I also reminded myself that if I got sent to Viet Nam and they partnered me with Jensen, I was going to respectfully request assignment to the Foreign Legion (there IS still one, I'm told). But more than that, if Southeast Asia ended up being my destination or wherever else I found myself, I vowed to give it my very best to always be on my "A-Game". After all, it was becoming crystal-clear that there were a multitude of stupid ways to get oneself killed including, as I had just witnessed, poor memory.

Day 3

Sunrise of the third day on Peson Ridge found me chewing on chicken again, running perilously low on Tabasco sauce, and preparing to move out for the day's adventures. I shaved, dry, of course, as they apparently didn't market a combat-gear-ready

"Gillette Foamy"; also, all we had were those single-blade/two-edged Gillette "Blue-Blade" razor blades and a safety razor, the kind where you turned the knob on the bottom of the handle to open the inverted bomb-bay doors that secured the twin-edged blade. BIC disposable razors were still awaiting invention at the time, as were double, triple, and quadruple multi-blade razors. Together, this combination of dull-axe sharpness and no soapy lubricant made for, shall we say, a miserable start to a morning.

In keeping with my mood, I then began to attempt to pack my now-soaked (remember, there was frost the night before) sleeping bag into my pack along with my formerly-dry spare fatigues. So by move-out time, I was in a particularly non-Christian mood; not surprisingly, this mattered to absolutely nobody but me, as everyone else was essentially in the same boat. Then again, I think that down through history, it's been a soldier's duty – no, make that his legacy, responsibility, and heritage - to complain. Somehow it always seemed to me that complaining took your mind off of the potentially really serious matters ahead for the day. But if "War is hell", then dry-shaving and permanently-soaked fatigues are at least deserving of a ranking or level of discomfort equal to purgatory.

We road-marched down to an intersection of two nondescript dirt roads just as the military-green deuce-and-a-half trucks appeared. Truck after truck came lumbering by, stirring up great clouds of dust until nobody could see farther than an arm's-length. Out of one of these dust-storms, I suddenly saw a 2-1/2 ton truck skidding sideways towards us. As I began to bolt away from the road, I saw Jensen calmly sitting there thoroughly enjoying his breakfast (Spaghetti! How had he gotten THAT?). I shouted a warning but he barely turned his head towards me. Fortunately, the truck stopped about 3" (no exaggeration) from his head. I complemented the driver on his sense of the dramatic and filed the experience away under, "Pay attention around a road with military traffic!" I also couldn't help wondering just how in the heck that stupid Jensen had gotten spaghetti, the "haute cuisine" of C-rations.

Now they hadn't sent us trucks just to make life a bit easier for us, not that the thought would have even crossed my mind. No, we were going to practice truck convoy tactics next, another bit of education developed through hard experience in Viet Nam along the Ho Chi Minh Trail. Somewhere up ahead, an aggressor force was waiting to do us grievous harm. I found myself watching, observing the terrain, trying to figure where I would plan a good ambush if I were the enemy.

At the time, it occurred to me that this kind of thinking was probably a very good thing to cultivate in order to stay alive in Southeast Asia, or any of the various and sundry dangerous places in the world that the United States Army might be called to serve. Unknown to me at the time, as it turned out, good combat convoy tactics would still be vital even thirty years later.

One key thing I learned continually throughout my military career was that a soldier could end up paying dearly for carelessness. Inattention, whether due to fatigue or just boredom, could quickly get you and your buddies killed. In dangerous situations, you HAD to remain focused, and I was beginning to realize that this included paying attention in training.

I remember being appointed to NCO (Non-Commissioned Officer) School two years later and applying myself studiously to the lectures and tactical exercises. Others in the class were more interested in having two weeks away from home, which was okay by me; that was entirely their own personal business. Mine was to become a good and better Non-Commissioned Officer.

In one particular class, the Instructor became aggravated by most of the class's obvious lack of preparation the previous night. Finally, I stood up and provided the appropriate, correct answers to the questions asked, earning a "Good work, sergeant," from the Instructor and afterwards some serious abuse from several fellow candidates. "Lighten up, General; it's only practice," they growled after class. I remember replying, "Yeah, but maybe someday it'll be the real thing." The response was, "After Viet Nam, the United States will never send armed troops into combat again!"

I've often picked up the newspaper in the following decades and asked myself, "I wonder how accurate THAT prediction turned out to be?" Even in the 21st Century danger still rides along the path of military convoys, booby traps and concealed roadside explosives still kill and maim, and carelessness continues to reward the recipient with unpleasant surprises. Take away the mechanisms and modern firepower and I'll bet that "the eternal soldier" would agree whatever the age and weaponry. Yet, we seem to think that we're too smart, too sophisticated to have war continue. My sad guess is that the soldier of the 3000 AD's will be thinking the exact same thing.

Sure, it was sometimes tedious and, just like in math class, you often wondered why you needed to know how to do something or when in your life you might need THAT bit of information. Interestingly, it often ended up that those little bits of combat intelligence and passed-along experience came together to help you, the soldier, anticipate and prepare for a variety of dangers and situations. But the key to me, always, was to pay attention; even as a young optimist, I just couldn't visualize a future with no bad guys operating somewhere in the world, at least until Christ's Second Coming.

We came to a blind curve in the road where our truck down-shifted into second gear and slowed to negotiate the sharp left turn. Nice place for an ambush, I thought to myself. Catch the trucks as they slowed down and presented a nice, plump full-side target – yeah, that's where I'd hold the surprise party if I were planning the ambush. Almost in answer to my thoughts, artillery simulators detonated left and right as the aggressor force struck our left-flank. I scrambled out of the truck, slamming my knee against a rock as I stumbled and hit the ground.

As I massaged my throbbing leg, an artillery simulator landed about three feet away. I was consistently amazed at the self-healing powers of the human body in certain critical situations. I began to do the cartoon-figure movement – you know, where the guy leaps, turns in midair, and begins to run 180 degrees in the other direction. The thundering "BOOM" and hot blast of air from the exploding charge helped propel me even faster. Still, after the initial thundering noise had stopped, we had semi-miraculously deployed almost correctly, assaulted the aggressors' positions, achieved and maintained fire superiority, and had even mildly anticipated where a dangerous situation might develop. I think Sergeant Tyrone almost had a smile on his face.

As a reward for our "reasonable" response to this tactical test (I took that comment to be indicative of having achieved a holy-cow flaming success), we gathered our gear and marched along a ragged wood line and into a particularly disgusting-smelling swampy area. Some reward! Finding a single small patch of dry-looking ground and feeling my stomach calling, I signaled for a halt and began rummaging through my pack for some C-rations. Chicken again, of course. Where the heck was the "Jensen's Spaghetti", I asked myself, shaking the last precious drops out of the Tabasco bottle?

Clouds of chiggers (not plain gnats; these little buggers loved to bite) instantly appeared, almost as if someone threw a switch, challenging us for ownership of our meals. I eventually found that it was best to save the energy expended in swatting and simply proceed with eating – chiggers and all. Actually, you couldn't really taste the difference as long as you didn't dwell on the situation too long or, if you will, let it "bug you."

I had just pried open a nice can of gooey pineapples, one of the better C-treats, when a thudding explosion shot up to my left.

"Get moving, you !@#$%s, they're after us!" Sgt. Tyrone shouted. Now, I was bound and determined that I wasn't going to leave my sweet pineapples, regardless of the tactical situation, so I absently jammed the ¾-opened can into one of my empty ammo pouches and promptly forgot about them as I crawled under a barbed-wire fence, dodged around several huge Cypress-looking-trees and raced across a slimy stretch of swamp grass just about as fast as a human being could run with a loaded pack, weaponry, and wearing heavy combat boots.

As I plopped down on a rotted tree stump to catch my breath, a felt a slow, sticky sensation edging up my left fatigue-shirt sleeve. Any idea of how sticky pineapple juice can be (and this was before "pre-packaged moist-wipe days")? I finally ended up taking my shirt completely off, turning it inside-out, and licking the globs of juice up ¾ to the armpits (ugh!). Then I looked at my left ammo pouch. I imagined what the next guy that ended up drawing that ammo pouch might find. It made me feel very guilty, for about 30 seconds. But there was no time to analyze and deal with the feelings of contrition. I stuffed a tattered Kleenex inside and trusted to "the legendary healing power of facial tissue" to make the sticky goo disappear; by the way, it didn't. Another urban myth exposed. In the meantime, we were moving again.

After traipsing through roughly 4 kilometers of heavy pine forest for what seemed to be about 95 hours, and passing close enough to see two very small towns nearby along with two very nice-looking young ladies out in the back yard hanging wash – sheesh, soldiers, you know…, we came to a heavily-wooded hill overlooking a shallow, pine-forested valley. This, we were told, would become our night defensive position.

John and I chose a spot with a particularly sensational drop over about a 15 foot cliff right outside our tent. To demonstrate our inventiveness, we hauled rocks up the hill and placed them at the cliff edge with the idea that we could roll them down if we were attacked that night, all in fun, of course; hopefully it would be those clowns that had forced us to move our tents the other night who would find our work equally hilarious and be ground to a fine powder under our barrage of boulders. Sometimes, I admit, one had to remind oneself that, after the contest, we were all on the same side. At the time, however, I was not thinking real hard about forgiveness and camaraderie but rather of ways to smite the heathen, even if they wore the same color uniforms. I guess you had to be there.

I think that John actually had a bit of "Tarzan" and Hollywood in him. He tied down two little trees near the edge of the cliff so that when the attack came that night, the trees would spring up. And do what, I wasn't sure, but I had to admit that it sure looked cool. We hadn't figured out how someone would scale the escarpment in front of us only to come face to face with John's tension-loaded "sapling-swatter" but, again, you had to be sharing the experience to understand why this gave both of us a great if somewhat weird feeling of satisfaction.

So, as darkness began to fall once again upon Peson Ridge, I fished a C-Ration out of my pack (yes, Chicken again), got as comfortable as possible leaning back against my pack, and listened to the evening silence blend with the growing Louisiana darkness. Not too bad, I thought. We're getting there. By gosh, things were actually looking up.

As the minutes, half-hours, and hours drug along, the temperature headed south again, so we crawled inside of our tent, peeled the flaps back, and propped ourselves up in our sleeping bags to stand guard (another 100% alert). I always had my bag zipped all the way up out of deference to that ubiquitous story of the chilled timber-rattler crawling inside a warm sleeping bag to curl up beside a sleeping soldier. Yeah, if that slithering little creature (the snake, not the soldier) wanted inside my sleeping bag, he was going to have to go through my ear, I thought to myself, not through a half-zipped zipper. Earlier in AIT this had been a challenge in the hot and humid September nights but by early November those warm nights were only a memory. The temperature quickly slid below freezing again by 23:00 or 11:00PM in Civilian Time.

The moon had not risen yet and as the minutes continued to creep by along with the pleasant warmth of my sleeping bag, I could feel my eyelids fighting the seductive urge to succumb to gravity. I had told John to prop himself up to be 100% alert but I knew that he would probably try to catch a little shut-eye while I kept a lookout. However, as the minutes crawled on I was beginning to catch myself nodding, head dropping down, and suddenly waking myself, and snapping my head back up. Gosh, it was cold, the bag warm...

The footsteps behind me gave me a start. Sgt. Streck whispered hoarsely, "Where's Simmons?"

"Uh, I think he went on a detail carrying the PRC 25, Sarge," I stammered.

"So, he's with the radio, huh?" Just then a muffled snore sounded from within a mound of sleeping bag. Streck reached in, grabbed the edge of the bag, and with a ferocious yank pulled bag and John out of the tent and right to the edge of the cliff. A muted, "What the heck…" came from the bag, followed by a whispered torrent of a profanity/obscenity.

"Aw, c'mon, Sarge, "I started, "The kid just nodded off. Besides, I'll stay awake and.."

"Are you giving me !@#$ lip," Streck snarled.

"Me? Oh no, Sergeant. Not me."

"I want every !@#$ in this !@#$ platoon awake. If I catch either of you two !@#$% s asleep again, I'll pitch you and your gear over the cliff." Then, as he turned to walk away, he stopped, paused a few seconds, and said almost matter-of-factly, "Real combat won't care if the kid's tired or not. He'll still likely be dead, and maybe you along with him. Now stay the !@#$% awake!"

"Yes, Sergeant," I said solemnly. John and I both cracked up afterwards, but as we laughed, I know at least one of us was thinking, "Another lesson learned." We both stayed awake from that point on.

I know that, at this point, you probably think that I was becoming obsessed with "lessons" – screw-ups, carelessness, or the consequences of just doping-off. The fact is, I probably was, and I think that's what the Army was trying to accomplish. A soldier can sit in a class, then go through the motions afterwards in practice, and still get greased in the "real world." The Army was doing its very best to try to shake some awareness into us before we found ourselves somewhere dangerous such as Southeast Asia.

I learned that just before we started the Peson Ridge exercise. We were practicing a squad combat patrol through a heavily wooded area, then walked out into a slight clearing. Our flank security had closed in to avoid the clusters of briars lining the wooded trail, so when we broke out into even a slightly-open area, we were bunched together.

That's when the ambush was sprung. As the aggressors opened up on us I found myself, just like most everyone else, frozen. I had been trained to immediately bring the squad's firepower to bear and attempt to assault the position. Since I had allowed my flank security to move in, thus eliminating the option of flanking the aggressor's position, a direct assault was our only real course of action. Yes, we could have tried to dive back into the cover of brush on the opposite side of the ambush, also an incorrect action, but we were all so stunned that even this option was academic.

Once the fire died down, the class evaluator stepped forward and tapped first me, then virtually every member of the squad on the shoulder, simply saying, "You're dead." Believe me, that got my attention.

You see, I had been taught what to do and how to do it; I simply had not paid close enough attention. When it came time to actually perform accordingly, particularly when you didn't have time to think, remember, and then act, I had frozen. It would have been a fatal mistake.

By the way, the aggressors had actually hoped we would scramble back into the cover of the brush on the opposite side; apparently, they had rigged some neat booby-traps for those GI's who might have perhaps not frozen but incorrectly chose to dive for cover. The Army, I'm sure, was hoping that the lessons we were learning, particularly those where you, the soldier, were pronounced "dead", would finally sink in. As for me, I can assure you that, by the end of AIT, I was "sunk."

Shortly after 02:00 hours, "the attack" began. Earlier that evening I had sent an LP out a couple of hundred yards over on one of the ridge fingers hopefully to interdict the attackers and maybe precipitate a little preliminary rumble in the bushes. You see, after 3 days in the field, we weren't feeling very civil. I could only imagine how those LRP/LRRP's (Long-Range Patrol/Long-Range Reconnaissance Patrol) Rangers and Special Forces soldiers must have felt after 10 days or so out in the boonies with Charlie/Charles/Chuck looking diligently to do them mortal harm. Somehow, upon retrospection, 3 days seemed pretty brief and tame.

Not long afterwards, the LP crawled back in, having spotted "the enemy." Then, we all lit up the very early morning darkness with M-16 and M-60 bursts plus we proceeded to send our string of rocks plunging off of the cliff and rolling down the hill. I don't think that our little avalanche hurt anyone, really, but it was neat to hear those voices in the dark swearing and snarling along with the crashing of the stones through the underbrush. Ah yes, I thought, Mr. Gravity is not their friend tonight!

After successfully repulsing the attack, we curled back up in our sleeping bags and, somehow around 04:00, found ourselves completely asleep. I guess we figured that in practice, attacks only happened once a night. But, in reality, we both understood that the "real enemy", although probably cold and tired just like us (although admittedly unlikely in the steamy jungles of Viet Nam), could be expected to attack without paying close attention to the training schedule.

Day 4

Our final morning on Peson Ridge began as usual – a cold, dry shave, with the same Gillette "Blue Blade", and a Chicken C-Ration, unfortunately, sans Tabasco. But I wasn't really upset about that. Chow was now simply, well, chow – food for body fuel. My taste buds had gone into hibernation about 3 days earlier.

Instead, I was already dreading the upcoming "E&E", Escape and Evasion, scheduled for that night.

E&E is where you are considered captured, placed in a group of four other motley POW soldiers at night, tied together, with no map or flashlight (after all, the U. S. Army doubted that POW's would be provided those items by the capturing enemy, probably not a bad assumption), and "allowed" to escape into the woods. From there, you attempted to find your way back to friendly lines un-captured through about 3 miles of forest, swamp, and jungle.

Just to make things more interesting, there were genuine incentives for POWs to avoid being re-captured, if for no other reason than if you were, they would take you back to the starting point where you could begin your "thrill-packed adventure" one more time. Rumor had it that they messed around with you as well.

None of us had really given capture much thought despite our training. The U.S. Army didn't really talk much about that possibility, other than it was a soldier's duty to not surrender. I had assumed that it was mostly macho, that the mottos such as "Surrender is not in our creed" were just Special Forces hype. However, the longer I was in uniform the more I began to see that it was not just the act of surrender that was the issue.

Rather, it was the rationale of what or who considered the situation to be "hopeless", let alone when did "the needs of the many outweigh the needs of the few." Part of being a good military leader is understanding the difference between what is difficult and what is without hope, when courage and devotion to duty transition to obstinate stupidity, when the concerns for one's men reach beyond a situation and conversely when the situation is far more important than the lives of people you respect and even love, and even your own.

Sometimes surrender is impossible to avoid; the human body is, after all, vulnerable. But I think the U.S. Army wanted to draw the distinction between "things are tough" and "I've done everything I humanly can." Not any two soldiers would agree on whether the difference between the two conditions is mile-wide or millimeter-thin.

But for me, I was also highly impressed with the fact that not every enemy subscribes to the Geneva Code. Then again, a "code of warfare" always seemed like an oxymoron to me, sort of like saying that "humane slaughter" was preferable and tolerated compared to non-approved forms of killing. Apparently, though, this little exercise would serve as an additional, not-so-subtle reminder of the fact that surrendering was not as easy as just "quitting the war." You don't just call a time-out in the middle of a to-the-death firefight. If you could, I'm sure that smart soldiers such as George Armstrong Custer would have tried it.

Subsequent stories including "the Hanoi Hilton" and POW survivor stories of mindless brutality at the hands of the Japanese in World War II have reinforced my belief and understanding that "rules for warfare" are exceedingly difficult to enforce as a prisoner and very often utterly ignored by the captor. You are powerless as a prisoner; the enemy has complete control. That fact always seemed to indicate to me that exceptionally bad things could very easily happen to captives; therefore, if humanly possible, don't get caught.

In November of 1971 I had not even begun to consider the possibility of capture. All I knew was that once "free", I was not going to be caught. Pondering the reasons and possibilities as to how I could get caught in the first place would wait until years later. Again, when you're young not only will you live forever but you'll never be taken prisoner either. No soldier ever figures it will happen to him (or her).

My thoughts regarding the evening's festivities were quickly brought back to the immediate situation at hand – a simulated Vietnamese village which we were to surprise with a lightning-fast raid. I guess our lightning was a bit slow, as "the enemy" quickly scattered just as we approached the first hut. It seems that, although we thought we were well hidden and stealthy in our approach, Jensen had decided to light up a cigarette. Apparently, the smoke cloud billowing over the top of the thick brush along with the aroma of burning tobacco sort of gave a slight, tiny indication to "the enemy" that something "non-indigenous" was close by. It's similar to soldiers who never seemed to understand that those big antennae on the back of a jeep or truck were possibly conspicuous, even given that flagpole-straight "flyswatters" aren't known to grow on trees.

Once again I was being given a lesson in combat-discipline. Noise suppression, good, fresh camouflage, an understanding that straight lines are unnatural in nature, and the avoidance of anything that would indicate the presence of anything other than God's natural creation and animal creatures were the keys to being a good Infantryman. I was also coming to the conclusion that, just like any other human skill, some people seemed to be born either with or without a combat-sense. Jensen was obviously in the latter group.

Although I was sure we would have clobbered them otherwise, my squad was very unhappy to see "the enemy" slip away. By this time, our combat blood was really up. We wanted to "Get Charlie!" So, we did the next best thing – we pulled an ambush on a civilian, beat-up red Ford F-150 pickup truck. Really cool – 10 guys yelling and shooting blanks at a poor, terrified, unarmed (we think) farmer. Fortunately for us, he was a pretty good sport about the whole thing, particularly when we gave him some blank shell-casings for him to set on the dashboard. Looking for positive takeaways from the exercise, at least I was somewhat confident that Jensen could have probably handled the situation, assuming the farmer didn't manage to run over him multiple times.

As the afternoon wore on, I found myself with some time for contemplation while performing a little preventive maintenance on my M16. Keeping the small-caliber weapon reasonably clean was essential to avoiding stoppages in firing. The M16 had developed an unfortunate reputation for developing stoppages – various failures to feed, chamber, lock, extract, or eject. With our training-weary weapons and subsequent loose-clearances, it didn't take much to encounter a stoppage; in fact, I can probably still pull both "Immediate" and "Remedial" action on an M16 even today.

Somewhat sloppy tolerances on moving and sliding parts, mixed with dirt and debris can confound even a well-built piece of equipment. In truth, you learned to live with that fact. But, just like any other piece of equipment subjected to rough and hostile environmental conditions, it had been drummed into our heads that keeping an M16 well-maintained was good insurance for having a functioning weapon when it was needed. And, having to pull "Remedial action" repeatedly in a close-in firefight is never desirable.

Personally, I always liked the M16. People have blubbered ecstatically over the AK-47 for its ruggedness, which is in fact probably deserved. However, I think it developed an undeserved aura similar to the Viet Cong – better than it/they actually were. I can still tell when an AK-47 is being fired, even today. Whenever I hear one, I find myself instinctively reaching for my M16 selector lever to flip it on Automatic, always prepared, though, to perform Immediate or Remedial action.

As evening began to close in, I didn't even notice the Chicken C-Ration sitting by my pack. All I could think about was E&E. Sgt. Tyrone interrupted my solitude with a half-snarled "Here," and handed me a slip of paper. On it was my name followed by John, "the String", and Gary. My partners on our dash to freedom had been chosen and not necessarily to my advantage. On the other hand, I didn't have to be tied to Jensen.

Of course, I knew about John and his previous utter lack of familiarity with trees. "The String" (don't ask, but it had something to do with "Señorita Rita, the Couhilla Bandita") was a city boy from Akron, OH, who had once gotten lost on his way back from the PX at Ft. Lewis, and Gary from Virginia, who had done some hunting but I think it was on horseback with somebody shouting, "Tally-Ho!" And then there was me – a mountain-born boy from Pennsylvania who had lived most of his life in Pittsburgh.

Not that I was necessarily lacking in casual outdoor skills, but once hunting up on Bald Knob Mountain I got lost so badly that they darn near called out the State Police to try to find me. Fortunately, I had possessed the sense to follow a small mountain stream downhill and walked out onto a road right at sunset, cold but relieved. But on that occasion, no one was out both chasing and hoping to FIND me.

In retrospect, things could have actually been worse. Four of my Hispanic buddies were grouped together and none of them had ever been out of the Rio Grande Valley. They had gotten lost in Leesville, LA's Town Square, a small town near Ft. Polk with a reputation sort of like a cross between Tombstone, AZ and Las Vegas without any of the few good features of either place, and there were only three, count-em, three trees in the entire town.

While I was pondering this not-to-promising chain of events, we were summarily rousted onto our feet and marched double-time for roughly four kilometers. My evening chicken-meal was trying to decide which way to go – up or down. I never was able to eat and then immediately exert myself. I remember a church-league basketball game on a Monday evening years earlier. Mom had made spaghetti for supper and I had asked to be excused due to the upcoming game. Permission had been denied – no dinner, no basketball. So, I ate and then played the first half of the game, incidentally scoring 15 points. Subsequently during half-time, I had retired to the locker room and worshipped before "the porcelain idol" with an offering of regurgitated spaghetti. Then, I went out and played the second half (and scored another 12 points).

Unfortunately, the Army had never consulted with me on this particular piece of my personal physiology, nor had they ever indicated a willingness to arrange training around this personal physical reality. Slowly, though, I had learned to "eat and run" – literally, ignoring the gastric complaints. But then again, I eventually had come to the conclusion that in all likelihood an enemy wouldn't care either, nor would they arrange their attack schedule to allow me time for my food to digest.

Almost abruptly, as we marched around a sharp road bend, a forlorn-looking arch appeared overhead with crude "E&E" lettering scribed on a rough, weathered plank. Thoughts of the "OK Corral" drifted through my brain as I muttered tensely, "Nothing like a warm welcome…"

As we dropped off our gear and weapons (you see, the Army figured that POW's were NOT likely going to be permitted to remain armed), I could feel the tension rising. The briefing which followed did nothing in the least to ease those feelings. There would be 75 "enemy aggressors" flanking the road and another 50 combing the woods, searching for us escapees. I was waiting to hear the number of rabid dogs, snake handlers, and main battle tanks. The only instructions we were given were, "Run when you see the chance. And don't get caught." I've often thought about those brief instructions; then again, it has occurred to me that there really wasn't much more to be said. I kept repeating that mantra over and over in my mind, "Run…don't get caught…"

The "POW Commandant" was dressed in black "VC pajamas", had a thin mustache, and a shaved head, all of which seemed to scream, "I am NOT your friend." Then, the real screaming and shouting started. We were forced into a "duck-walk" position and herded into a circle where we "waddled" around and around. Occasionally, some unlucky soldier was singled out for abuse-aided pushups. All of this was done under the auspices of "The Commandant" and his shrieking "guards." I kept muttering to myself, "Remember, Barry, we're all on the same side…" Then again, I wondered how magnanimous an actual enemy would be. All the same, my thigh-muscles protested.

I think every person has, at some time in their life, wondered just how they would react under extreme physical duress, e.g., torture. Most guys, I'll bet, have macho visions inspired by movies, particularly of *Rambo* being bound tightly, the electrodes hooked up, and watching him take about a million volts of electricity, all without spilling his guts and telling his tormentors everything he knows. I had always figured, hey, if HE could do it, so could I.

It's funny how life can give you a bit of a glimpse of reality even while you're still convinced regarding your own inner strength and general invincibility. Around 15 years ago I had encountered my first experience with chronic pain. I had been placing some heavy boxes into the attic after Christmas, the kind where you're determined to use every square millimeter of space available in the container, only to find that the infinitely-densely-packed box is really, really heavy. Anyway, in the process of lifting and turning while trying my best not to fall off the flimsy fold-down attic ladder steps, I did something to my left shoulder.

At first, I figured that it was just a muscle strain; however, after about two weeks, the pain had become miserable, unrelenting, throbbing like a toothache. I began the trek from aspirin to ibuprofen to Janet's gall-bladder operation 600 milligram Motrin, all without any real relief (the Motrin maybe knocked just the tip of the pain-peak off). Sleeping became a struggle to avoid moving the left side of my body. Even the slightest twitch would ratchet up the agony to a sleep-robbing level.

The seemingly unending, merciless pain became a constant uninvited invader into my life. Added to my loss of sleep, it was making me miserable; but it also was giving me some insight and empathy with those poor human beings who really do suffer daily with severe, chronic pain. I can understand why, eventually, even the strongest-willed individual would begin to contemplate drastic steps to be able to escape the ever-present agony, even if only for a few moments – or forever.

After almost a month of trying to tough it out, I had finally gone to my PCP (Personal Care Physician, in HMO terms) who referred me to an orthopedics doctor. There, the pronouncement was: shoulder impingement. The cure: physical therapy and exercises (welcome to the red- and green-rubber tubes – nice, stretchy hoses for strengthening the surrounding shoulder muscles; don't laugh – they actually work).

Physical therapy – that shouldn't be too bad, I figured. I mean, therapists are there to help people, I reasoned. However, I hadn't counted on my therapist being "Iris the Iranian." Reportedly, Iris and her family had come to the United States roughly two years after the 1980 Iranian revolution that overthrew the Shah of Iran and installed an Islamic state under the Ayatollah Khomeini. Apparently, members of Iris' family had been part of the Shah's entourage and, therefore, had not fared well after the change in political regimes. After a period of incarceration mixed with several incidents of torture, the family had been allowed to leave Iran. Iris was, not surprisingly, lacking in warmth. Obviously, when I heard the story, I felt sorry for her and vowed silently to do my best to be a model therapy patient. Somewhere, I had the feeling that I could hear Life snickering.

I had just taken my seat in the waiting room for my first physical therapy session when a voice like a Drill Sergeant called out, "Meester Lauer, please come!" Instantly, I did as I was told.

"You vill seet down here and I will begin zee therapy!" Okay, I said to myself, sounds relatively harmless. On the table beside me sat a breadbox-sized white-cased box with a few dials and two cable leads ending in what looked like waffle-pads. Again, I wasn't terribly concerned; after all, this was supposed to be physical therapy, and I was confident that it would help me. At least that was my preconception. Little did I know that it was my turn to play *Rambo*.

Iris fastened the waffle-pads to my left shoulder, turned the white-cased gizmo on, then slowly began to turn the main dial knob clockwise, red LED numbers beginning their ascent on the meter dials. Almost instantly, I felt as if an electric eel had wrapped itself around my shoulder and decided to drain off excessive electric charge directly into the ball-and-joint socket in my shoulder.

The pain was excruciating. My already tender shoulder was screaming for mercy, while I attempted to grind my teeth down to the nubs. I wanted to shout out, "Wait! Enough!" But, in true manly fashion, I simply sat there, pain and sweat seeming to mingle together, while the seconds crept along.

After about ten minutes (or maybe it was ten years?), Iris returned. "Have you had enuff of zees? Iz zees too much for you?" she asked. I wanted to scream out, "Oh, please, don't hurt me anymore!"

Would I have "talked"? Heck, I'd have told that woman the President's social-security number, if I had known it! However…thoughts of being in uniform, standing under the Flag of my Country, carrying my shield or on it…all raced through my mind.

So, through teeth firmly clenched, I croaked, "No, I'm okay." For the first time, I thought I could detect a hint of a smile from Iris, almost as I would expect to see from a thoroughly delighted POW Commandant.

"Excellent! Zen I vill dial in a beet more!" she half-hissed. And then, she cranked the control knob further clockwise. What happened after that is kind of a foggy memory, the kind that I'm told occurs when the brain tries to shut down to avoid permanent psychological damage. Somehow and sometime later, Iris returned, cut the power, looked me squarely in the eyes, and simply said, "Vee are done!"

I was scheduled for more physical therapy the following week; I was definitely not looking forward to it. I called first, to see what days Iris was NOT working. When I arrived for my next session, the kind young lady that day, Stacey, walked me over to the dreaded white-cased instrument of torment. I cringed, feeling the sweat beginning to trickle down my back. My left shoulder began to twitch involuntarily. In half-desperation, I timidly told her the story of my previous visit.

"Where did she have the machine set?" Stacey asked, obviously concerned. I indicated the spot on the dial, praying that I had not somehow had the misfortune to draw Iris' super-best friend.

The young woman, who I will forever refer to as "Saint Stacey", looked where I was pointing, put her hand to her mouth, and simply said, "Oh, my!" She then placed the waffle-pads on my left shoulder and began a gentle, tingling current that stimulated but also soothed my injured wing. As I sat there, relief instead of sweat dripping off of me, I remember thinking, "Well, so much for resistance to torture, tough guy!"

But this was all in my future; squatting there in the dark of the Louisiana night, I was beginning to understand that being a prisoner was not a good thing and that "giving up" wasn't as simple as throwing in your poker hand and saying, "I fold." Falling into the enemy's hands was and is a leap into the unknown. After all, you COULD just end up surrendering to one of Iris' brothers!

After what was probably about a half-hour of this mock-abuse, we were ordered onto our feet. Then, watching the dusk deepen into dark Louisiana night, we were summarily grouped, tied at the wrists, and then marched by-fours to the road, holding onto each other's pistol belts to try and stay together. Yes, we were TIED together, but we didn't want each other going tails-over-tin-cups when we made our "big break". As our guards were doing their persistent trash-talking, I was trying to survey the woods beside the road, looking for a not-too-wide opening through which we could dash and disappear quickly. But all I could make out were dense scrub-brush and utter pitch blackness.

As the road twisted into a left bend, the guards fumbled to light cigarettes in the dark while continuing to heap insults and threats upon their "prisoners". I heard one Guard call out, "Hey Smitty, you got a Marlboro? These Salems are 'girl' smokes".

"Yeah, somewhere in my pack. Why do you keep buying those !@#$ things anyway?"

"Aw, Jeannie likes 'em." And I could hear the crackle of cellophane cigarette wrappers as our guards decided to dope-off for a few seconds.

That was good enough for me. I knew that it was time and we were ready; or at least I was. With a harder-than-planned yank on the ropes and belts, I headed for the trees off of the right side of the road, dragging an obviously startled mob behind me. I could hear the cursing and fumbling from the guards as we all stumbled, trampled, and generally barreled our way helter-skelter for about 200 yards through whatever brush was in our way.

The first briar patch we tore through hurt like blazes but I didn't care. The adrenalin was pumping full-bore and I was not stopping, no-way, no-how. After running, tripping, and lurching for what seemed about 3 hours (maybe 3 minutes?) I stopped, bent over my knees, panting, listening for the sounds of hot pursuit. Apparently, our guards had lost interest when they hit that first patch of 1"-long briars, and had returned to the road to get flashlights.

After a minute or so, my lungs pushed themselves back down out of my throat, and I looked through the haze of brush overhead trying to find a familiar starry constellation for guidance. But the tree canopy was too dense. We really WERE on our own now, but then again we were "on the loose", unshackled, "free" (thank God Almighty). And the one thing I knew was that we would stay that way, regardless of who we might possibly run into.

What I didn't know, though, was that we had actually royally spoiled the guards' plans. They were planning to routinely tap a group of four on the shoulder, give them a few seconds head-start, and then quickly follow them into the brush, probably rounding up everyone before they could get untied and deeper into the forest. Then, they could prolong the fun by marching their captives back to the assembly area, drop about half of the prisoners for pushups, and generally continue to mess with them. We were missing all of that "fun".

So, as we panted and fumbled to free ourselves from each other, the guards were just now beginning to sweep into the underbrush, loaded with flashlights and even meaner dispositions. Eventually, despite cold fingers and pitch-black darkness, we were all untied. That was a moral victory if nothing else. I knew then - we were not going to get caught.

But first, I had to check on my personal "gang of four". Gary was okay. John was still there. And The String? Well, I thought I could hear a slight muted whimper. And me? I don't know how to describe it. I was cold, disoriented, puffing, and generally physically uncomfortable in the extreme. But somewhere, a smoldering embryonic confidence was smoking to life. We were going to find our way through this – somehow, I knew. All we had to do was stick together, use our heads, maintain good noise discipline, and not walk in circles. We CAN do this! I knew it.

Through occasional breaks in the forest canopy, I located two reasonably-high-latitude stars and fixed them over my left shoulder. Keep 'em right there, I thought, as we twisted and turned, all the while attempting to avoid walking in circles. The road we had broken away from, I remembered from the briefing, had been essentially East-West and I knew we needed to head south. If we did this successfully, we should eventually walk out onto the paralleling "safe" road – cross it, and officially be "free". The trick was going to be finding it while staying as silent as possible, not wandering around aimlessly, stumbling noisily in the dark, and thereby decreasing the chance of being found by the now frantically-searching guards.

Doing my best to keep my sky-guides over my left shoulder, I herded my little group along, using the best noise-suppression tactics I could muster (walking on the balls and not heels of my feet, avoiding digging my toes into the underbrush but rather letting my feet "feel" their way along). Amazing, I thought, I'm really using the Training – again. Occasionally, I would halt everyone and just listen. Once in a while we could hear someone crashing through the brush, stumbling, cursing, followed shortly thereafter by a triumphant shout announcing "a capture". Clearly, the guards were out there in these same woods too.

It's really interesting how the small ravines and shallow bayous can seem to wander aimlessly, without purpose, but actually following a course carved by eons of flowing water and gravity while defying a straight-line, as-the-crow-flies route. It was clear to me that mindlessly blundering through the woods in the dark would increase the chances of getting lost, hopelessly disoriented, and eventually walking smack-dab into a group of ticked-off guards. And as the seemingly endless expanses of brush stretched out ahead, I could feel my own anxiety growing, fueled also by fatigue. Suddenly, I snapped back to full attention. Time to tighten up and pay attention, stay heads-up, I repeatedly told myself.

"Barry, you know where we're at, right?" The String asked in a trembling voice. Well, I thought to myself, aside from the fact that we're lost in the dark somewhere in Louisiana, yes, I suppose we're all right; at least, we haven't been captured.

"Yeah, we're doing okay," I lied, gradually realizing that, indeed, like it or not, desire it or not, these guys were counting on me – my skills, regardless of how limited, and also my character - as an individual, a leader, and a soldier. And it was something that, despite my being a four-year engineering school graduate, I had never learned in College.

As I once more checked my celestial "friends" to insure that at least we weren't walking in circles, I caught several intense, almost instantaneous flashes poking through the trees ahead. Instantly it hit me – the artillery range, in the Southwest corner of Ft. Polk! I had overheard some officers a week or two before talking about a group of South Vietnamese pilots being scheduled to practice their fighter-bomber ground support tactics on the South Artillery Range at night during our Ridge week. That HAD to be them, I figured. If that was the case, all we had to do was steer a bit to the left and we should be heading directly and steady south! Thank the Lord I had been paying attention to the map at the briefing earlier! I could feel a slight glimmer of confidence sputtering to life and, yes, building.

One hundred yards further on and I froze. A small glimmer of light appeared off to the left. Guards? Then again, it wasn't a flashlight beam; more like a match-light. I didn't know, but the sense and longing for human companionship began to overwhelm my fears of capture. We crept as quietly as possible through the brush in the direction of the now-extinguished light. Then, I heard a small stick crackle under foot. For what seemed like an hour, I stopped in mid-stride, contemplating our next steps. Then, as quietly, silently as possible, I whispered, "Who goes there?"

Instantly, a voice rasped, "Parker! Where are you?" Good ol' Parker!

"Hey, it's Lauer – off to your right!" Quickly, our four became eight, feeding off of each other's presence, dripping relief. In the dark of the Louisiana night, there was plenty of quiet but very animated back-slapping and hand-shaking.

"We've been wandering around for the past two hours walking into trees," said Parker with disgust, rubbing an obviously sore right leg, twisted courtesy of some nasty half-buried tree roots (obviously not buried deep enough to allow heavy combat boots to glide over top of them). "Plus, we heard snorts and growls in some high grass and we hoped it was a wild pig and not those !@#$ guards!" Funny, I thought, a wild pig hidden in the lush marsh grasses, let alone at night, was not a critter to be trifled with. As mentioned previously, I would certainly rather tangle with a 150-pound human than a roughly 100-pound hunk of ornery wild bacon with razor-sharp tusks. I didn't want to get captured but after all, menacing guards were one thing; a wild, life-threatening animal was something much scarier, at least to me.

"Well, I think that the moon should be coming up soon. That should help us some," I said, trying to sound certain. "Besides, I think we've been heading south all along." I could see Parker nod, his silhouette barely visible against the brush background.

Several of the guys were complaining about scrapes, the cold, and other generally uncomfortable facts-of-life found in the outdoors at night. But by this time all I could think was: this is still "make-believe". It will eventually end. Even the "Guards" wouldn't kill us if we were caught. Imagine having to execute E&E in "the real thing". There, the guards carried weapons loaded with non-imaginary bullets and a much nastier, thoroughly lethal disposition.

Once again I was reminded of our indoctrination regarding surrender, that it was "inadvisable". Also, I recalled that one Ranger tenet is, "Rangers don't leave Rangers behind." Again, I had reasoned that this was all simply military bravado, the old "never surrender" mindset. Death before dishonor! But now, in addition to the risks involved in personal surrender, I could see that having to try to escape from captivity and evade unarmed put a soldier at a serious disadvantage. If you were lucky enough to escape, you now had zero weapons to defend yourself other than bare hands or, if you were lucky, a crude wooden club.

Plus, the elements themselves could do you in just as surely as an enemy bullet. At least we had our fatigue uniforms and combat boots on; yet, we were still cold and physically worn. All the more reason to avoid capture in the first place, I concluded, pretend-escape or not. And, a key part of helping to insure that surrender was not necessary to consider appeared to be grounded in once again, yes, being a "good soldier" – staying focused, paying attention, and practicing – which is exactly what all of the prior months' training had been trying to accomplish. The light bulb in my brain had snapped on and the filament was at full brilliance.

As we crested another low hill, I decided to shinny up a tree for a look. Climbing a tree in almost pitch blackness is an interesting experience involving tactile coordination, as you feel your way up the trunk, and muscular control. The good news is – you don't get scared looking down. Was that a slight glow on what I guessed was the eastern horizon? Pulling myself up to another limb, I could see a whitish line, then a barely perceptible rounded disk-top. The moon!

"Okay," I whispered after sliding down what felt like about 200 feet and leaping down what I hoped was about 4-feet, "I think we're definitely heading due south now." As I rubbed my skinned shins I could feel the renewed energy in our little party and a return of, dare I say, some swagger?

As we reached another brushy hilltop, we literally bumped into eight more "escapees". Shortly after that, eight more joined our "POW Parade." Now I knew that we would not in any way, shape, or form, be captured. This had become a large, determined group - we were tired, cold, battered and bruised, and without question we were also not about to play by "gentlemen's' rules". If we met up with guards, I felt certain that there would be a rumble in the dark! After all, I remembered, "We sleep in caves and ditches...."

About 30 minutes later, I scrambled through a particularly nasty briar patch ("How in the heck did rabbits EVER get through these !@#$ things?" I muttered to myself) and literally stumbled onto a paved road. At first, it felt good to feel hard ground underfoot; but, just as quickly I could feel my muscles tense. Now the question: The "safe road" or one of the twisting, enemy-held side roads? As I halted our now-merry band, or rather, tired, evilly-disposed mob, I caught a glimpse of a figure off to our right.

"Back into the woods!" I hissed, diving back into the fiendish briars.

I lay there motionless, my rasping breath muffled against my left arm. "Not this close to the end?" I found myself praying. Then I heard the sweetest voice ever, yelling, "The finish check point is 100 yards up the road to the left. Get your !@#$ sorry !@#$'s on down there!" Sgt. Tyrone! Hallelujah, Brother! Twenty-four screaming maniacs suddenly leaped out of the brush and sprinted off down the road to the left. It was sheer, joyful pandemonium. I think Sgt. Tyrone was even surprised.

Subsequently, we stood in a ragged line illuminated by a jeep's feeble headlights, as a much-too-clean-looking PFC clerk checked our names off of the Exercise List. "Yes," I thought, "Put that P-for Pass" notation right there beside Lauer, Barry A. PV1."

After that, my memory is blurred. Perhaps it was the adrenalin-withdrawal, or the cold, or the sheer fatigue, I don't know. But I seem to recall wandering over to a nearby oak tree (big, massive roots, and scorpions? I didn't care), dropping to my knees, and pulling my fatigue shirt closer around my neck against the Louisiana night air. Somewhere in the distance, I knew, there were trucks rolling our way to take us back to warm, shower-equipped barracks.

"Well, Lauer, you made it. And your group," Sgt. Tyrone's voice awoke me from my brief contemplation.

"Yes Sergeant," I replied wearily. "I suppose we did."

"You know, the purpose of all of this ain't just to harass you troops. Hopefully, yuz learned from your mistakes – communications, signaling, and just being a better soldier. Good luck to you. Even if you end up in 'Nam, I know that you're a !@#$-of-a lot smarter now than when yuz started 10 weeks ago."

I sat there for a moment, looking up at that face which I had sworn I would for all Eternity hold in a special, particularly spite-filled place in my heart reserved for people who had mightily abused me in life. Now, for the first time, I saw the face of a soldier, and (almost) a human being. I was stunned. Then again, I thought, I'm also very, very tired.

After a long silence, I simply said, "I guess I DO understand it better now. Thanks, Sergeant." He turned away, then glanced back over his shoulder, smiled, and said, "See you around, soldier." For some strange reason, that sounded very good.

Just then The String shuffled over and dropped beside me. "Barry, we never could have made that without you." Without me - the dumb college guy? Six months ago I was simply a cocky engineering-school graduate; now, maybe, starting to be a soldier?

I smiled to myself, then laughed and tried to look cool. No, I didn't tell him that I was also sometimes scared, tired, and unsure. And maybe this time, lucky. But I admit that now I DID feel like a soldier.

"String," I whispered, "We're going home. Next Friday we'll be home!" And two weeks after that, Thanksgiving at my Grandparents' house in south-central Pennsylvania – real chow, turkey, gravy, pumpkin pie, and NO chicken. We both settled back against that tree, silent, relieved, contented.

But deep inside, I knew I had changed. I was still a college graduate, but now – albeit still greener than fresh spring grass - also a Soldier. Closing my eyes I could almost visualize my Great-Great-Grandfather, blue Union Army shirt catching the afternoon sun at The Battle of Cedar Creek, attempting to rally his regiment to withstand a savage attack on their left-flank by Confederate General Jubal Early and subsequently falling, mortally wounded. I could see my Grandpa Jim as a Doughboy soldier serving under General Pershing in World War I, over-the-top five times at Meuse-Argonne (The Battle of the Argonne Forest) to face the German trenches and heavy machine guns. Similarly, Uncle Bill with the 101st Airborne, fighting to hang on by their fingernails against constant German onslaughts in the snows of Bastogne (The Battle of The Bulge), exclaiming "Nuts!" at the thought of surrender, and Uncle Jim with the Army Rangers across the Remagen (Ludendorff) Bridge into Nazi Germany and then to Korea just in time to cover a fighting retreat against North Korean and Chinese Communist human-wave assaults at bitterly freezing Chosin Reservoir. All of this to serve a Flag with red-and-white stripes and a cluster of white stars on a blue field; all because they had apparently loved those "purple mountains, fruited plains, and sea to shining sea".

It had taken some time – about six months – to comprehend. But, gradually, I had begun to understand why. Being a United States Soldier will do that. And that's exactly what I had become.

In the dim jeep-lit night, I fingered the "U. S. Army" patch above my fatigue-shirt's left breast pocket. "Now, a Soldier…" As I shivered in the growing cold, I turned over on my stomach, curled up, smiled slightly, and let the sounds of the November Louisiana nighttime gently and thoroughly lull me to sleep.

*I've changed the names of my comrades not only to "protect the innocent" but also because I've forgotten some of their actual names.

PVI Barry A. Lauer – July, 1971 – Ft. Lewis, WA

Intervening Years' Service

For all my groaning and complaining regarding MOS 11-Bravo, Light-Weapons - Infantry, I spent most of my service time involved in that MOS starting as a PFC (Private First Class) squad member, then gradually moving to Squad Leader and then Platoon Sergeant. I served with C-Company, 1st Battalion, 145th Infantry out of Akron, OH until moving back to Pittsburgh in 1973. While there, however, I had the privilege to serve under the finest commanding officer in my career: Captain Charles Santos. He was a Viet Nam veteran, Airborne Ranger, and wore the LRRPs patch. To give you an idea of how I felt serving under him, if he had told me to jump off the roof of the Armory, my only question would have been, "Where do you want me to land?"

Captain Santos was a no-nonsense CO but also kept the baloney to a minimum. He expected his command to perform in a consistently outstanding manner while being pragmatic enough to understand the distinction between outstanding and flaming impossible and/or reckless. One night during a week's maneuvers in the field at Camp Grayling, Michigan, he led our platoon on a night-attack problem. Starting at about 04:00 (that's 4:00AM), he guided us through thick northern-Michigan pine forests, stealthily past "the enemy" (actually Battalion Headquarters) LPs, and we literally walked right into the sleeping camp, capturing the Battalion Commander who was standing there in his green skivvies. It was a glorious sight.

The Colonel, however, was not amused; he took his immediate and official wrath out on his own men. But, I don't know that he ever really forgave Captain Santos or C Company. Later in the week, we conducted a rather difficult platoon fire-movement (more on that below) and, per Captain Santos, the Battalion CO grudgingly made the comment, "Your men appear to be as well-trained in the daylight as they are at night." The Captain took me aside later that day and simply said, "Thanks, Sarge; that helped get my a__ out of a sling."

Looking out for his men was nothing new for Charles Santos, particularly when it came to insisting on respect. One evening, Sergeant Nicodemus and I had been attending an evening Non-Com meeting at Battalion Headquarters. As we walked back to the Company area, we saw two Warrant Officers approaching. Now, Warrant Officers are kind of an odd breed to start with. Appointed for particular skills and knowledge, they share the same status and privileges as other Officers, other than not having specific command status. Apparently, though, adherence to standard military protocols is not at the top of their list of concerns, or at least it wasn't for these two guys.

Regardless, proper and appropriately, we two Sergeants both saluted. The two officers smiled and proceeded to give us a casual waist-high finger-wave as they walked by. Obviously, this was neither proper military courtesy nor was it particularly intentional, merely inconsiderate. Sergeant Nicodemus and I watched them pass, looked at each other, shrugged, mutually thinking, "Warrant Officers – go figure." And that normally would have been the end of it.

Except that, apparently, someone had witnessed the incident and casually mentioned it to Captain Santos. The next morning, Sergeant Nicodemus and I were told to report to Company Headquarters. Not being aware of any particular and/or recent screw-up, we dutifully presented ourselves at the Captain's tent. "Come in, men," he said, through the open tent flap. As we stepped inside, standing at strict attention were our two Warrant Officers.

"Gentlemen?" the Captain firmly directed to the Officers. Immediately, we received two crisp, militarily-correct salutes; we rendered crisp salutes in return. "When two of my non-commissioned officers present military courtesies, I expect that you both, as officers in the United States Army, will willingly and respectfully return those courtesies. That's all."

After our two "guests" had left, I guess Sergeant Nicodemus and I both had dumbfounded looks on our face. The Captain turned to us and said, "As an officer, I apologize." I started to say something, but he continued, "Some things don't and shouldn't change. Proper military courtesy is one of those things."

As we walked back to our tents, I can't speak for Nicodemus but I know I felt genuine respect for the Captain. Here was a CO who demanded the best from his non-coms, but also would insist that they be accorded appropriate respect by others outside his command. It was another lesson in leadership and I've never forgotten it.

One last comment regarding the Captain: shortly before I was to return to Pittsburgh and my new unit, we were going out on a 3-day exercise. It was October, chilly and damp, and I had decided that C-rations weren't going to be quite enough. While our back-packs were packed "right and tight", I had managed to stick two small bags of Fritos inside two of my ammo pouches (since I was going to be carrying the 4.2 mortar rounds and two M-60 machine-gun belts, I felt that I only needed to be carrying 6 clips of M-16 blank ammunition). As we stood in our initial formation, the Battalion Commander ranted and raved concerning "extraneous, non-issue items" being taken into the field. Subsequently, he instructed the Company Commanders to inspect all troops for the same.

Standing at attention in front of my platoon, I could feel the sweat running down my back as transistor radios, candy, and even a sitz-bath (one of the mortar-men had them really, really bad) were eventually exposed to the light of day and subsequently deposited on the armory floor. As Captain Santos stopped in front of me, he smiled, seeing my freshly-starched fatigues, spit-polished combat boots, close haircut, and clean, well-taped web-gear.

"Looking sharp, Sergeant Lauer," he said. Then I saw him look down at my web-belt. Attached there were two very "well-developed" ammo pouches, next to two very skinny ones. The Captain reached out, opened both full ones, saw the Fritos, smiled, and said, "Outstanding choice there, Sergeant." Without another word he snapped both ammo pouches shut, then turned and walked on by me. Later, I found out that he actually worked for Frito-Lay in Akron. But I don't think that fact was his reason for cutting me some slack. Hopefully, he knew that I was trying to be a good soldier and that I knew the difference between "mission" and "trivial", and he wasn't going to make a big deal out of "the trivial."

It was also under his command that I experienced my only real "under-fire" experience several months earlier. The "enemy", unfortunately, was a U. S. Naval Reserve sailor. We had been assigned to Camp Grayling, MI for our two-week annual Active Duty stint in August of 1973. (Grayling is situated far enough north, by the way, to have very chilly nights even in August.)

During the late-1960's and early-1970's the Army found itself with some very serious issues in regard to the quality of recruits. In retrospect, this shouldn't have been a surprise, given the fact that draftees were non-volunteers and that the military draft was still going on. Subsequently there were two distinct sides to the coin. On the one hand, the Army found – both as draftees and Reservists – that many soldiers were college graduates, just like me. As a result, some units including many Reserve and Army National Guard organizations performed very well in most military exercises. I know that in C-Company, my squad had eight-of-ten men that were college graduates.

That doesn't mean that educated people necessarily make good (or bad) soldiers; however, it usually helps simply because the men are generally older and have dealt with the need for academic (as well as personal) maturity and discipline. Of course, not every college guy exhibited a high degree of maturity. But at the very least, the college boys usually scored well on the Army aptitude tests and, similar to pursuing a degree, they realized that sometimes you just have to endure certain situations if nothing else.

Of course the draft also brought in the average 18-year old high school graduate, the average or better student who had no desire (or means) for college and just wanted to get his commitment to serving his Country completed. They were often excellent soldiers with a good work ethic, but sometimes simply boys who were now being forced to grow up in under six months.

In short, it was a diverse group of young men that served in the military in the those times, and most did their duty to the best of their individual abilities. However, the draft also brought in other men who were certainly "marginal" as soldiers, occasionally serving in the Army where the "or" part (directed by a court) meant going to jail. The offenses usually were relatively minor – drug possession, petty theft – and sometimes, I'm sure, the Army gave these guys the second chance that they needed. Occasionally, though, the military ended up with a marginal soldier at best, and usually every man in the platoon knew who and what they were.

We just accepted that, sometimes, a draftee could be a liability to serve with. After all, passing the draft physical in a time of war was not very difficult (I think that the doctor's form had one question on it: Breathing – Yes/No) and as a result the path from civilian to military life was often very short, or at least not long enough for people to leave certain bad habits behind.

Also reflecting Society at the time, drug abuse was a problem in the military. I remember a number of surprise inspections during Basic and AIT, usually conducted in the middle of the night. All soldiers were ordered out of the barracks (in one case we were ordered to sit in the middle of the barracks aisle-way while a special team of "contraband military police" conducted a search of our personal gear). While the premise of the searches was to look for stolen ordinance (once in AIT, we were told that a hand grenade was unaccounted for" from the day's training), the real purpose was to search for drugs and associated paraphernalia. Some nights the MP's found what they were looking for; the offending trainee was escorted from the company area and not seen again, at least with our unit.

As a squad leader, I knew each man and their task and I also knew what they did in civilian life. To the best of my knowledge, everyone was "straight" in my squad, or at least very circumspect if they did anything at all including marijuana. (Alcohol, on the other hand was used liberally – I did mention that eight of my men were college guys, right?) All I ever expected was that when we fell-in for duty, I had all hands on-deck and ready to do their jobs.

This was one of the major reasons that I disliked the two-week Active Duty stint: fill-in soldiers could be assigned to your unit, and not necessarily with an Infantry MOS. This could make any Infantry squad exercise more difficult as the usual integrity and functionality of the group would be disrupted. Still, it was a not uncommon fact of military life. In my case, the guy was a Naval Reservist assigned to do his annual duty with us. I suspected that he must have really messed-up to have merited a two-week vacation with the Infantry. But, in fairness, he pretty much kept to himself and was no particular problem as far as discipline went. Then again, he took little or no interest in our assignments and squad tactical problems.

I suppose that I should have noted some of the warning signs – a lack of attentiveness, absence from squad meetings in the evenings (in fairness to myself though, he WAS a Navy guy and I didn't expect him to immediately relish being an Infantryman), and a general look of "vacancy". The guy just didn't seem to be "with it." I didn't put two-and-two together, probably because none of my immediate friends were anything other than beer-junkies. Still, it almost cost me my life.

Towards the end of the second week at Grayling we were assigned the left flank of a platoon live-fire exercise. The plan of action would include a platoon on-line assault up a fairly steep hill with all four squads moving forward in a single line and with the objective of "achieving and maintaining fire-superiority." This called for every man to exercise proper move-discipline and, particularly, that the squad leaders control their individual squads so that no individual unit either fell behind or surged ahead of the rest of the platoon. This all sounds very simple, except for the fact that we were using live ammunition that becomes friendless once it leaves the gun barrel and that maintaining uniform movement while trying to move quickly, aim, and fire a weapon is not inherently easy. I could only imagine having to do that when, in addition, an enemy was firing back!

Our Platoon Leader, a very green Second Lieutenant fresh out of a college ROTC program, had done his best to go over the essentials of the live-fire exercise. However, just before we assembled prior to moving out, Captain Santos came over to me and took me aside.

"Stay close to 'the Swabbee', Sergeant," he said quietly. "He's not with it today."

"Do you want me to pull him out, sir?" I asked.

"No, the Colonel was ordered to include this guy in the exercise. I told the "old-man" that I would put him in your squad so that you could keep an eye on him." Then he paused, looked around for a second and added, "Sorry, Lauer. I'll be following close behind you if you need help."

As I mentioned before, as long as Captain Santos gave the order, I would obey it; I might not necessarily like it – and I didn't like this one at all – but I would carry it out. As my squad lined up, I personally inspected each man's gear to insure that nothing dangling would come loose and create a distraction. Soldiers, particularly of the part-time variety, sometimes forget where they are pointing the business-end of an M-16 – even good ones. I also checked each man's ammo pouches to make sure that the exercise-directed four 20-round clips were present. (Actually, you never loaded a full twenty rounds; the darn clips had a nasty tendency to jam unless you had a very good, tight weapon, and none of us Reservists did.)

As an aside, the M-16 (we carried the M16A-1) had gotten a great deal of bad press early in its deployment to combat units. It was reportedly prone to jamming and not very robust in operating in the grungy conditions often experienced in warfare. These complaints were true; early teething problems due to corrosion (remedied by adding a chrome-lined chamber and bore) and the ammunition originally developed to yield higher rates of fire (it left a residue in the chamber which could lead to "failure to extract", where a spent cartridge case remained lodged in the chamber), were not myths. Solutions were developed (e.g., chrome-linings, "forward assist" with which one could quickly clear a weapon jam). Still, we had all heard the horror stories of dead GIs found with their disassembled M-16's, killed while trying to un-jam their weapons.

Early in Basic Training we had been issued some of the early, previously-used XM16E1 models. We quickly learned that the weapons had to be kept scrupulously clean to prevent the buildup of ammunition residue and, yes, the weapons had a tendency to jam. However, this was more the result of wear and tear resulting in loose tolerances more than anything else. Still, it taught us all the necessity of really maintaining the heck out of the M-16.

Personally, I always like the weapon. It was light and had virtually zero recoil. In fact, in Basic Training, our introductory training in the M-16 included the instructor placing the stock-butt of the weapon against his forehead (and then even more sensitive regions of his body) and firing the weapon on Automatic. Plus, the M-16 could really throw the rounds out. I could field-strip the M-16 in seconds and had complete confidence in my ability to keep the thing firing. It had gotten an early bum rap, as far as I was concerned.

Anyway, I assembled my squad on-line and dressed-right on Sergeant Nicodemus' second squad while positioning myself three steps behind and just to the right of the Navy guy. As the Lieutenant shouted, "Move out!", I steadied my men forward in a uniform but rapid movement. While occasionally striding forward to urge ahead or slow a man slightly (and keeping the second squad's line in the corner of my eye), my squad moved very smoothly for the first half of the assault.

Suddenly, and without any warning, the Navy guy stumbled. I was moving towards him to straighten him up with a firm grasp on his left lower pack-strap when he suddenly began to turn towards me.

The problem was, his finger was still on the M-16's trigger and he was locked on Automatic. I saw the muzzle-flashes as the gun barrel swung first left, then right. My first thought was, "One of my guys is going to get killed by this guy!"

Instinctively, I grabbed his right pack shoulder strap, still holding onto his lower pack strap with my left hand and jerked him upright. I guess it was the momentum from my high right hand grab, but slowly he turned directly towards me. (The Lieutenant said it happened in an instant but for me it was all in slow-motion.)

It's amazing – an M-16 round is only really a "super-22 size" (actually 5.56mm; the round itself is 45mm in length or about 1.8"); the round simply has a really, really high muzzle velocity, around 3,100 ft./sec. As such, the barrel is actually quite small in diameter but you don't want to be anywhere near its business end. However, to me in that instant, I thought I was looking down a large-diameter sewer pipe. I could almost imagine seeing the chrome-lined rifling inside the barrel. Fortunately for me (literally, "The Hand of God"), the Navy guy had momentarily released the trigger.

As I spun him around and kicked his left leg out from under him with a reverse left-leg shin-kick, he let loose with another burst of M-16 fire. I heard the distinct "Crack!" of the rounds going over my left shoulder and felt the heat of the muzzle blast. Then, as I drove him face-first into the ground I could almost immediately feel two MP's piling on top of me.

I heard Captain Santos shouting, "Get that man out of my company area!" The MP's secured the Navy guy's weapon, slapped a pair of hand-cuffs on him, and the last I saw of him he was in a jeep heading off of the live-fire range. The report back later that day simply stated that the man had been high on cocaine at the time.

It all happened so rapidly that I never had a chance to think about any of it. I had been simply doing what a squad leader does; something happened and I dealt with it to the best of my ability. It wasn't until that evening that it all began to sink in. And, today, almost 40 years later, I can still see the barrel of that M-16, and it's still a really BIG sucker!

Captain Santos didn't forget about that incident. In December of 1973, the Letter of Commendation he wrote for me stated:

"Sergeant E-5 Barry A. Lauer, RA _____ (back then your Social Security number was your military/Regular Army number), is awarded this letter of commendation for excellent leadership of his squad in various situations. As a good fighting leader, he sets the example for his men by displaying personal integrity, military bearing, and constant professionalism in all aspects of his duties."

"Sergeant E-5 Lauer is a credit to himself, his unit, and the Ohio Army National Guard."

Captain Santos was, indeed, a "leader of men."

Then too, I suppose, leadership is not just about leading. There's also an added element beyond just directing traffic; a leader needs to also be preparing others to lead, effectively establishing a chain of responsibility that ideally never ends. That was something extra that Captain Santos and other good Army officers passed along to me as a non-commissioned officer.

I too recognized that preparing the next generation of Infantry leaders was also part of my job and responsibilities. Most of the time, this took the form of small nudges, a timely "Why don't you consider...", or simply taking the initiative and leading by example. Occasionally, the leadership lessons involved small matters with large implications, the kinds of things that can make a difference between an individual simply carrying a gun and a disciplined, motivated soldier prepared for armed combat. Sometimes, you find yourself fortunate to be in a position to drive the point home, to make a difference, albeit small.

At the end of a four-day field exercise in the Grayling, MI woods, a hungry Infantry platoon had gathered for their first hot meal since arriving. It's always amazing what reasonably fresh, hot chow does for a soldier – mostly good. Maybe it's the reminder of "regular living", or simply a break in the monotony of cold, canned food. Hot chow has many great things to recommend it. However, it can also make a soldier forgetful, and forgetfulness is always a dangerous attribute for a soldier.

My green-as-grass Second Lieutenant had just brought the platoon up to the assembly area and released us for chow. Release, though, is a complex word in military jargon with a number of non-civilian subtleties, including "Release does not mean you are not still first and foremost a soldier." There are some things you are best never to forget, specifically, the weather, the terrain, the immediate tactical situation, and equally important, the current location and disposition of "the military love of your life", aka your weapon, in our case, the M16-A1.

Essentially, you as an Infantryman have your M16 attached to you just as you would one of your arms or legs. In the field, you learn to function at all times while in contact with your M16. Even the most basic bodily functions are accomplished while adjoined to that piece of blackened, machined steel and impact-resistant black plastic. You can get into trouble through many and various actions of stupidity and negligence as a soldier and an Infantryman, all with varying degrees of severity and penalties assessed.

However, THE worst sin for an Infantryman, with very few real exceptions – treason, disobeying a direct order come to mind – is losing your weapon, or in an only somewhat-milder form, not having it immediately within reach. Securing the weapon is an Infantryman's personal, no excuses acceptable responsibility. In short, if you're holding your best girl tight, your M16 had best be close beside you, only held tighter.

This is Infantry 101, and more than a few historical but also careless Infantrymen have slept for 30 days or more curled up next to a musket, carbine, Springfield, M-1, or, yes, M16. I am confident that those forgetful few never made that mistake again and likely went on to be good soldiers. Secure your weapon – to an Infantryman, it's the same as taking the next breath. Apparently, ROTC Officer's Basic Training in 1973 did not emphasize this fact heavily enough. Either that or new green-as-grass Second Lieutenants on their initial assignments as Infantry Platoon Leaders are somehow prone to forgetfulness.

Sergeant Nicodemus and I had just placed our respective squads in the line for chow, then joined the end for our own portion of the feast, M16s slung over our respective shoulders. In a few minutes, with a plate of roast pork and brown gravy, mashed potatoes, steamed green beans, dinner roll, butter, and a slice of apple pie we staked out our respective spots underneath a clump of scrub-pines.

Normally, my focus would have been fixed solely on the choice hot food before me (anything would have been "choice" after days of C-rations). But for some reason, I detected the proverbial "disturbance in the Force". Somewhere, there was a barely imperceptible lack of balance in the military universe, call it a Sergeant's nose for naught. Then I saw it! Leaning up against one of the pine trees, looking forlorn and shockingly forgotten, was a lonely M16-A1. For a few seconds I just stared, overwhelmed by the gravity and heinous nature of the offense. This was akin to spitting on the Cross!

Then, again with an Infantry Sergeant's innate ability to put two and two together (and either get four or look for a green Lieutenant as the source of all evil), I immediately turned and looked at the chow line. There was my Second Lieutenant, regaled in his officer-ly splendor, topographical maps wrapped in Saran-wrap at his side, aluminum mess-gear in hand, all sans M16. I turned back, looked at the single, unmanned M16, said to no one in particular, "Hmmmm…", and nudged Sergeant Nicodemus who was in mid mashed-potatoes bite.

"Sergeant Nicodemus," I said, pointing toward the pine tree, "Do you happen to see what I see?"

He looked, mashed-potatoes frozen in mid-bite, blinked, then turned to me and said, "Sergeant Lauer, that appears to me to be an unsecured M16 weapon." For a few seconds more, we two Sergeants stared at the decidedly unholy sight. Then, without ceremony or further comment, I got to my feet, walked over to the tree, retrieved the M16, placed it across my left shoulder next to my own weapon (so it wouldn't feel lonely), sat back down, and continued placing pork, potatoes, green beans, roll, etc. into my mouth.

A minute later, my Second Lieutenant came over, mess-gear resplendent and overflowing with hot chow, obviously consumed (no pun intended) with the prospect of his own personal feast. He sat down and settled back against the pine tree while Sergeant Nicodemus and I slowly turned to face him, patiently waiting.

It's always interesting to see that moment of full recognition reach an individual's face. The Lieutenant's mashed-potatoes fork was three-quarters to his mouth when it hit him. He quickly grabbed with his left hand to the exact spot where his M16 had been deposited only a minute before, but felt only empty air and rough pine-bark. Then came the look of panic. Where…Maybe it had fallen over and was lying behind the tree? Maybe…?

Sergeant Nicodemus and I gave him another ten seconds to fully experience the fear and horror of his Infantry-transgression. Then, holding his lost-M16 over my head I called out, "Lieutenant?"

His desperate, panic-stricken face turned, his eyes focused on the object held over my head like Moses' serpent in the Wilderness, and a mixture of pure relief and abject shame instantly appeared. "Thanks, Sergeant," he said, immediately taking the M16 and slinging it over his formerly bare shoulder.

"Sir, this will never happen again, check?" I said.

"Check, Sergeant, believe me!"

I'll wager that it never did happen again, ever. And I wouldn't be surprised if, at some time in the future, some other newly-minted Second Lieutenant was reminded of the same lesson, courtesy of my older, wiser Lieutenant. The mantle is simply passed on, and on.

Once I had moved back to Pittsburgh, I joined the 405'th Maintenance (several men from the steel company I worked for, Jones & Laughlin Steel, served there) as an Infantry Sergeant responsible for training and small-unit tactics. Fortunately, during my time in Ohio I had taken the Army's MOI (Methods of Instruction) training, a mortar-man's MOS test for Corporal, a full list of Infantry-based Army courses out of Ft. Benning, GA, and graduated from the Non-Commissioned Officer School.

My duties in training with the 405th included re-familiarizing personnel with fundamental Infantry tactics (e.g., setting up a good defensive perimeter, conducting effective ambushes, proper combat patrol techniques and positioning – it's amazing how effective good flank security can be!) and conducting the annual re-qualifications for weapons. Most of these men hadn't done Infantry-type tasks since Basic Combat Training.

During that period, I also took advantage of the U. S. Army Quartermaster School out of Ft. Lee, VA, taking the Basic and Advanced curriculums. It's amazing the number of things I learned at Ft. Lee that I've been able to draw on over the years in my own work career, specifically, how to manage documentation of materials and procedures. This was long before we in Industry realized that someday we might have to actually have proof of what was in cans and other containers, where they were located, and how we knew all of that for sure. The Army was well ahead of OSHA, ISO, and Sarbanes-Oxley!

In 1975 a re-organization in the Pennsylvania ARNG merged the 405th Maintenance with several Infantry outfits to form the 876th Combat Engineer Battalion. Subsequently, I took the Basic and Advanced Combat Engineering courses from the Ft. Belvoir, VA

Combat Engineering curriculum with specialties in Bridge Construction and Demolitions.

Through 1978, I served as a Staff Sergeant in the 876th Battalion. Among my last opportunities for service was the catastrophic Johnstown, PA Flood in the summer of 1977; a diary concerning that event is presented as a final section next.

During 1977 and 1978, the 876th conducted several joint exercises with the 7th Special Forces, a reserve unit made up of former Green Berets, all with at least two tours of duty in Viet Nam. It was here that I really began to develop an appreciation for the skills, courage, and determination of these elite military forces. They were (and are) a special breed. I also found these men to be a wealth of general combat knowledge far beyond the basic Infantry skills and studies that I had been exposed to from the early-'70s.

One particular exercise made a lasting impression on me. Our 876th Company was located on the site of a former Nike missile site which had been tasked in the late-50's with guarding the vital steelmaking areas in Pittsburgh from potential Soviet air attack. Although the actual missiles had been removed long before our arrival, the missile silos remained along with the ancillary support buildings. Being inside of one of the dark, quiet silos was always an eerie experience for me; I could almost feel the "Cold War" tensions seeping out, mixing with the foul, standing water pooled at the base of the concrete bunker. Here, Armageddon had been contemplated and trained for. If these missiles had ever required firing, the whole world was in deep and profound distress.

One chilly October weekend we were tasked with a tactical problem in conjunction with our Special Forces brethren. Specifically, we were given the assignment of providing site-security as part of an enemy force occupying the site. The scenario was the following: the eastern half of the United States had been successfully invaded and placed under complete domination of the victorious Soviet forces. The captured missile site was considered active and fully operational regarding its air-defense capabilities, manned by Soviet Missile Force personnel. In our role as dutiful "comrades", we were told to expect "enemy intruder forces" (whose mission was unknown) at some time within 24 hours.

The "secret mission" was as follows: the 7th Special Forces was given the task of somehow preventing missiles from being fired from the main battery for a minimum of five minutes at a specific time, during which a high-speed, high-altitude photo/reconnaissance plane would be on a spy mission over Pittsburgh. How they were to accomplish this was left to their training and experience. Regardless, a missile launch signal, generated by the mechanical opening of the silo doors, would signal mission failure.

Now let me explain the layout of the base and what the 7th troops were studying via sand-tables. Our missile site was located along the flank of a ridgeline, the northwestern corner sloping downwards across a field of high grass leading abruptly to a tree-line of scrub-pine. A single-lane gravel road led from the main highway fronting the site up to the administration and office building parking lot. The missile silos (for this exercise, only one was considered "active") and support buildings were located to the rear. Uphill from the rear of the building complex was a steep rocky slope leading up to a narrow grass strip abutting a single-strand barb-wire fence. Behind the fence was a long-overgrown field belonging to a neighboring farmer.

Our roughly 110 men were tasked to keep the intruders out. I had been given two rifle squads plus two M-60 machine guns. The general opinion of our CO and his staff was that the most probable area of attack would be across the broad, low field to the northeast where the high grass would provide cover and concealment. In addition, we had been given two "Starlight Scopes" (this was still "gee-whiz" technology for the Reserves) to provide a certain amount of night-vision capability and those were to be under the control of two platoons covering the field. An additional platoon would cover the front approach road and main gate. The remaining troops including my own two squads were assigned security of the building complex.

I've always been a student of history and particularly regarding military tactics. One primary axiom has always been: control the high ground. Not remembering that rule had proven disastrous for soldiers throughout history. The likely fate of the Union had hinged on Confederate General Henry Heth's failure to secure the high ground on the first day of the Battle of Gettysburg. Unfortunately, that same lesson had to be re-learned in every conflict since, including Viet Nam. To me, that narrow strip alongside that barb-wire fence high on the hill behind the buildings looked like a dandy place to situate one or two M-60s. It would provide a commanding view of the entire missile base while being able to give cover fire to either the entry road or the northeast field, albeit at long range. In addition to a commanding field of fire, the building complex would be covered as well.

As a good non-commissioned officer should, I explained my reasoning and volunteered to place a heavy-weapons squad up on the hillside. However, the CO wanted the immediate building complex well-manned, including my men. I argued that besides the questionable advantage of being able to perhaps boast of having an armed guard at each building corner, the manpower would be wasted just standing around. It would be better utilized covering the terrain from the highest point of the missile base.

"Sergeant," the CO had snapped with obvious irritation, "Get your men spread out around here and leave the planning to me and the platoon leaders. I don't need troops free-lancing up on a hill." My Infantryman's pride was wounded and I chafed at both the tone and manner in which I was being addressed.

As an aside, Battalion had dangled the possibility of a "direct commission" to me if I re-signed for an additional year's service – no guarantee, simply "consideration." I felt well-qualified and my military record (including many credits of Combat Engineering School study) was exemplary. Being talked to in such a condescending manner simply rubbed salt into an already festering wound in my ego.

Normally, I would have pushed the point harder, but I reasoned that the time had come to follow lawful orders. If the CO and his staff wanted to run the whole show, fine, let them run it. Strangely, though, I thought I saw a trace of a smile on the "umpire's" face (a Major with Airborne jump wings and the CIB, Combat Infantryman's Badge). Maybe, I thought, he also enjoys watching a non-com being chewed out for no good reason?

At just after dark (and with very little surprise or drama), "the attack" began. Sure enough, the Starlight Scopes could detect movement at the far end of the sloping field. I had to admit that it looked as if the enemy was working to infiltrate the base in a straight-forward manner. I could also sense the CO's self-satisfaction at planning and executing a good site defense.

However, that was just about the time the wheels began to come off of the well-greased plan's little red wagon. The movement at the far end of the field was, it turned out, a clever diversion, as was the presence of a suspicious-looking gray delivery truck lumbering slowly along the main road in front of the missile base.

Instead, the Special Forces guys had infiltrated through the field above the missile base and under the barb-wire fence (AKA, the high ground), set up an M-60 machine gun, and then moved quietly down the slope to the edge of the building complex. At a prearranged time, the M-60 located on the hilltop began to open fire. This brought about a startled re-organization of the building complex guards as they moved to set up a hasty defensive perimeter plus begin to conduct a fire-and-maneuver operation against the M-60 position.

Subsequently, during this period of relative confusion, two Special Forces soldiers had crept undetected over to a 2-1//2 ton truck parked beside the administration building, quickly started the engine, and then proceeded to drive the truck across the back parking lot and, with a surge of the throttle, up over the concrete lip of the door frame and directly on top of the missile silo doors. The doors were horizontally mounted, just off of ground level; still it must have been a wicked jolt to get that truck up and onto the doors. In the meantime, the Green Beret in the passenger seat poured heavy fire into the already wildly confused scene. It was a gutsy move and it took our guys completely by surprise. At least half of the defensive force was caught still assaulting the hillside; in the meantime, that truck was perched on top of the silo doors.

It took almost 4 minutes for the CO and platoon leaders to realize what was happening. In the meantime, the missile silo doors were inoperative. Now, whether the Special Forces guys could have held out for five minutes was probably a matter of debate. Regardless, it was deemed that the Special Forces teams had likely bought enough time for the phantom reconnaissance aircraft to conduct and complete its clandestine photographic mission.

After the exercise was announced as ended we all gathered in our mess hall to receive the comments and critique of the Major. He was pretty blunt: we, the defensive force, had screwed up. We had let ourselves be faked out by the diversionary movement in the lower field; we had no firm consolidation and reorganization plan in the event of a breakthrough. Then, the Major paused. "Your sergeant advised that you should control the high ground," he told the CO while motioning in my direction. "He was correct. That should always be a priority. At the very least, make sure that you have it secured." Then he turned to me again, smiled, and said, "Next time, Sergeant, don't acquiesce so easily." I've never forgotten that admonition – when you know you're right, don't let your ego and feelings of being persecuted divert you from pushing for what you know is the right thing to do. It's easy to give up and simply say, "OK, let them stew in their own juices." Unfortunately, that mentality can lead to serious consequences; and in war, it can mean death to lots of your buddies.

After the post-mortem, the bar was opened, the beer flowed freely, and the conversation loosened up somewhat as we all reminded ourselves that we were all on the same side. Eventually, one of the Green Berets produced a tape-recorder and, after gaining a semblance of silence from the increasingly rowdy group, explained the tape's contents. It was a roughly 20 minute sequence detailing in sound-only a night attack on a South Vietnamese fire base from the late-1960's. As background, the roughly 120 defenders of the fire-base had just returned from a long mission. They were naturally fatigued, hungry, and looking forward to a brief respite from combat. And, although battle-hardened troops, they essentially had screwed up.

Apparently, in hastily setting up their nighttime defensive perimeter to supposedly create effective overlapping fields of fire, one weary platoon had not extended one of their flanks far enough relative to the next platoon. This allowed for a small "uncovered lane" (no overlapping field of fire) to be formed. The experienced Viet Cong troops which had been shadowing the retiring troops began probing the fire-base defenses, quickly located this "safe" fire-free area, and surged through the uncovered gap.

As the fighting intensified and the attackers poured over the defensive barriers, the outnumbered defenders were quickly pushed back into one edge of the pentagon-shaped fire base where they literally fought for their lives. There, a heroic Combat Engineer managed to bulldoze up a low wall of dirt, providing the rapidly decreasing in number defenders at least some meager cover. At that point, the tape contained the sounds of a recoilless rifle being fired from the Combat Engineer vehicle – two rounds. Then there was a muffled "Whump!" The Green Beret casually commented, "That was the Combat Engineer's vehicle being hit. He died instantly."

The sounds of the battle – the shouting, the screaming of the wounded, the automatic weapon fire – were gut-wrenching, somehow both unreal but also intensely riveting. Reportedly, less than 30 men survived the combat-filled night before an armored column arrived at first light to relieve the remnant of the fire base's defenders.

"If you want to get some kind of an idea of what this was like," the Green Beret said, "Watch the John Wayne movie, '*The Green Berets*.' It actually has a very realistic depiction of a Viet Cong night attack on a fire-base." To this day, whenever I watch that part of the movie I close my eyes and just listen to the sounds of battle, mentally matching the mayhem with what we had heard that October night.

We subsequently conducted several additional joint exercises with the 7th Special Forces, sometimes attached to one of their A-Teams. As both an Infantryman as well as a Combat Engineer with a demolitions specialty, I occasionally got pulled into these joint operations with the 7th. After learning of my reluctance to visit high places, they always delighted in exploiting my express fear of heights.

In particular, I usually sat directly in the side-door of the Huey on air-mobile assault operations (for some reason, they wanted my explosives-laden carcass off the chopper quickly in the event of a "hot LZ"). It wasn't really the part where my feet were resting on the thin-tubing of the landing skids that bothered me; rather, it was the thought that the only thing holding me in was that rather thin-looking restraining strap across my body. Usually, though, we were flying low enough that I half-ways convinced myself that if something really bad happened, it wasn't really THAT far to jump, although at about 140 mph (and nothing but forest below) I hadn't entered that forward momentum data into my chance-of-survival equation.

Inevitably, the Special Forces boys would alert the chopper pilots to be sure to bank steeply on my side before flaring into the LZ. That way, I would be clinging to the restraining strap, facing straight down to the ground for what seemed like two-and-one-half lifetimes, while listening to those guys cackle. I wonder if they ever heard me praying out loud?

My lasting impressions: they were all a bit crazy (one or two of them more that a bit); however, they were absolutely first-rate combat soldiers. I will always have the highest regard and respect for the Special Forces and their elite, splendid warriors, all of whom, I'm firmly convinced, have devious, warped senses of humor.

But the lessons learned on this and other joint operations profoundly changed my perception and attitude regarding military training as well as warfare in general. The things that we had been taught – from Basic Training on – had ultimately been given with a purpose. Doing things in a correct, efficient, soldierly manner was more than just "the Army way." It could make the distinct difference between staying alive or perishing along with your comrades. Tasks such as maintaining and assuring good communications between squad members and supporting units, vigilant flank security, quiet and disciplined combat patrol techniques, securing the high ground, effective fire-and-movement techniques, and, yes, insuring overlapping fields of fire, were not simply classical military precepts. In war, they could quickly and easily keep you alive.

Conversely, you ignored them at your own risk. It's easy to let fatigue and pain trick you into taking "shortcuts". Or maybe you just get careless regarding some small details. It doesn't matter; "things" – no matter how minor – can sneak up and kill you just as quickly and easily as an artillery round that happens to land square on top of your head.

Listening to that audio-tape from the embattled fire-base drove home the fact that training simulations could suddenly turn into real-life. That's when you hope that the hours you spent in training will take over and you will do things correctly simply because that's the way you were trained. Eventually, you discover that you can perform the necessary tasks even when you're dog-tired (or scared). That, ultimately, is the goal of the training exercises – you do what you're supposed to do every time because that's what you instinctively have been trained to do.

I remember sitting with everyone after our final joint operation with the 7th, nursing my Miller's, and enjoying the casual beer-lubricated conversation. One of my buddies eventually remarked, "Well, looks like we'll never have to use this stuff anyway. The old Soviet Union doesn't appear to be a threat anymore, we're out of Southeast Asia completely, and no one seems to want to fight regardless. I think we're in for a decade, maybe two, of relative peace and quiet."

The funny thing was – this guy was a History teacher. Apparently, he had not read his own books or at least taken the lessons within to heart. Less than a year later, of course, we began "the Islamic era" – the Iranian revolution, the hostages taken in Tehran, the brutal Iran vs. Iraq war, Saddam Hussein, Kuwait, etc. – along with future albeit brief "brush-wars" in Panama, Granada, Somalia, and the Balkans. Then came 9/11 and the ensuing conflicts in Iraq and Afghanistan. So much for those decades of "relative peace and quiet!" I would suggest that my History buddy was seriously incorrect and/or overly optimistic.

Maybe, however, like many of us, he was just naïve. We haven't become less warlike as a species; we've simply become much more efficient in our weapons. Lasting peace is not on an evolutionary path upward; instead, it appears to me that history rolls on and the War Gods remain infinitely unsatisfied.

I would also venture to say that the same basic Infantry techniques and training that kept soldiers alive in the distant past are probably just as important in protecting and preserving the lives of soldiers of today.

My decision to leave the Service in 1978 was difficult, and I've questioned that choice many times since. As the saying goes, "It seemed like the right thing to do at the time." Family, career, availability of rank (or lack of), and time were all factors. Essentially, it's difficult to be part-time in the Military, regardless of Reserve opportunities. Splitting one's efforts between a full-time civilian job and good, dedicated Military service inevitably leads to some form of second-class status for the former or the latter. I felt that I could not accept that alternative, and that a choice had to be made.

I would never trade my 7 years of Army experience for anything; however, if I had it to do over again, I think I would choose full-time service. In truth, when Jesus stated "You cannot serve two masters…" he could have also been referring to civilian versus Military work. I tried my very best to balance both in my life and to always give each my full measure of devotion and effort. I suppose I'll always wonder how successful I was.

The Reserve commitment was 6 years; I put 7 years in, trying to give it more time and hoping that somehow I could reconcile things personally and professionally. Ultimately, the extra year didn't change my outlook and in March of 1978 I gave and received my final duty salute. I know that my Uncle Jim was disappointed although, in typical Christian kindness, he never said anything unkind to me about it.

To this day, I have never felt so lucky, blessed, and honored than when I served my Country in the United States Army. To my final breath of life I will always and completely remain, an American soldier.

A Soldier's Question – Johnstown, PA 1977

Not every soldier's mission involves meeting the enemy eyeball to eyeball, weapon at the ready. Sometimes the enemy is Mother Nature although her weapons are in no way less fearsome or lethal. My reason for including the following "diary" is that its writing occurred at a kind of crossroads in my own life, a time when I was asking a great deal of personal "Why?"- type questions. The year was 1977, I was 28 years old at the time, had been married less than two years albeit to my "dream girl", but was now facing a new "huge" home mortgage (and the accompanying responsibility of a debt-load of, gasp, $42,000), experiencing a less-than-satisfying job assignment with a very difficult boss, realizing that my dreams of playing professional Baseball were finally just that – dreams, and generally feeling pangs of dread associated with "Is this all there is?" stirring in the pit of my stomach. In short, Life was making its grand introduction to me and its general appearance and future promise were not conforming to what I had originally envisioned.

For the first time in my young life, I was inwardly mouthing the common human lament: "This isn't quite what I had planned for the conduct of my life." A big, threatening World was filling the windshield of my full-speed-ahead "Life Car" and, again for the first time in my life, I found myself questioning my own individual abilities, the apparent unfairness of Life, and even my own personal Faith in God.

Clearly too, I was realizing with an all-too-full understanding that I was definitely not in control of my fate. While I had understood this philosophically (at least I think I had), that reality hadn't yet sunk in to my full-of-youthful-zest thinking. You see, up until that time I had felt that I could make Life play by the rules – my rules, of course – and I was feeling disillusioned to be finding that Life often had absolutely no regard for my puny human designs. As was becoming plainer with each passing month, if it was me versus Life, I was definitely not winning the contest. And, I've always been a very sore loser; it began with tortured games of Checkers with my older brother and never diminished.

But while I was wrestling with my new internal and external adversaries in Life, I continued to serve in the Army Reserve National Guard as a Combat Engineer with special expertise in Bridge-Building (the other was Demolitions; I often told people that I could build 'em and I could also bring 'em down!). I also tell people that the reason I ended up as the "Bridge Specialist" was that I was the only one who could pass – barely, I might add – the seemingly impossible Army Corps of Engineers "Statics and Dynamics" course.

This is not actually true, at least I think it's not, but a harder course of studies I have never encountered, before or since. In fact, when I finally received notification of "Pass" for the course, I wrote back to the School Commandant and said, "I will now burn my class manuals and dance on the ashes!" Thankfully, he had a good sense of humor, personally commended me for my perseverance in completing the Course, and promised me that they would review and revise the Course curriculum to make it less daunting, as apparently the Pass rate was indeed miserably low.

As a result of my new mastery in Bridge construction, earlier that summer I had conducted the "Bailey Bridge Construction Class" during our two-week annual training at Ft. Indiantown Gap, PA, teaching other Combat Engineers the fundamentals of building this structural-steel, built-by-hand "gap-spanner" which combined a number of sound engineering skills along with sheer man-power.

I was a good instructor, so I was told, and each day I had taught a new platoon how to set the support transoms and rollers, carefully guide the assembled heavy cross-supports/transoms and structural panels out over a roughly 10 foot precipice, and accomplish it all in a timely but safe manner. At the end of the two-week period, I had received the "Outstanding Instructor of the Battalion" award. Secretly, though, I had asked myself, "For what? I'll probably never in any way, shape, or form need to know this stuff."

Fortunately for me, both God and Life have always had a lively, if sometimes slightly muted, but also different sense of humor.

In July of 1977, a "once-in-500-years" monster summer storm struck South-Central Pennsylvania and, in particular, Johnstown, PA. The nearly twenty-four inches of rain that fell in roughly 7 hours, from about 10:00PM on July 19, 1977 to 5:00AM on July 20, 1977, quickly took on "perfect storm" status as the mountainous terrain of the Johnstown vicinity provided the gravitational energy to channel and accelerate the overwhelming volumes of raging storm waters into an unstoppable hydraulic force, ultimately inundating the entire City of Johnstown and huge portions of the surrounding area.

The National Weather Service, in an initial statement, described the storm front as "just a steady downpour of rain. The thunderstorm just sat over (the) area." In the early morning light of July 20, Johnstown and the surrounding suburbs were reportedly covered by five-to-seven feet of water. One stream in the southwest part of Cambria County was described by Civil Defense officials as "normally 40 feet wide, now 150 feet wide." They also stated, "It's hard to give an accurate rundown on the situation (because) there are just no utilities at all in Johnstown."

In the town of Seward, further down along the Connemaugh River, roughly 30 house-trailers were reportedly floating downstream. I was to witness the aftermath of this particular happening in great and tragic detail.

Just how bad was the Flood of 1977? Officials reported water levels in parts of the city that were higher than those of the 1889 Johnstown Flood that killed an estimated 2,300 people.

As you can probably see by now, Johnstown was no stranger to devastating floods. In one such disaster back in 1898, the Quemahoming Dam had broken causing death and wide-spread destruction downstream, again the devastation being magnified by the rugged, hilly terrain. Several decades later, in 1936, spring thaws and resulting ice-jams on the Connemaugh River ravaged Johnstown and the surrounding areas once again.

My Dad lived about 25 miles south of the city at that time, and often told me how they watched Stony Creek, the small, meandering rock-strewn stream that wound through his home town of Hooversville, PA, swell and rise ominously, finally breeching the steep creek banks and pouring across the main road, threatening their entire block and the rows of houses thought to be "safe" up on the hill above town. So, flooding in the greater Johnstown area was not completely unknown.

As the decades rolled by after the 1930's, "Floods in Johnstown" eventually became the subject of "old coot stories"; you know, "I used to walk 5 miles to school every day, uphill both ways!" Everyone knew that floods were a part of local history and could conceivably happen again. Then again, everyone would add, "But this is the '70s!"

For some reason, we humans seem to feel that the more technologically savvy we become, the less vulnerable we are to the awesome powers of Nature. I'll wager that the first cave man thought, "Hey, this here cave is pretty neat! Boy, I'm pretty smart!", or something like that, I guess, in Cave man-terms. The Romans living in the shadow of Mt. Vesuvius probably felt that their advanced culture was immune to a few rumbles and ground-shaking from the distant mountain.

In the early part of the 20th Century, we built a ship that the news media pronounced as being so technologically marvelous and absolutely sound "that even God couldn't sink (it)", a towering seagoing monument to our human ingenuity and skill. As everyone knows, this "Triumph of Human Ingenuity", the ill-fated HMS *Titanic,* struck an iceberg on her maiden voyage and subsequently sank in less than 3 hours taking roughly 1400 people to the bottom of the frigid Atlantic Ocean with her.

It's interesting to me that the Bible states "Do not put the Lord thy God to a foolish test." And then, it always makes me wonder why we humans feel the need to tweak the nose of the Creator of the Universe? And, why we're surprised at the results when we do. Perhaps you also remember the "butter" commercial several decades ago with the final line, "It's not nice to fool Mother Nature." Or maybe you remember the Peter, Paul, and Mary ballad line, "When will they ever learn."

In 1977, again with our self-confidence oozing, we seemed to feel that roads, cars, and electricity somehow made us fully immune once again to natural disasters; either that or, as with many things in life, time dulls the memory and lulls us into a sense of our own infallibility. Regardless, in mid-July, again we shook our heads in disbelief as we watched our modern, sophisticated monuments of stone and steel crumble, crush, and wash away like autumn leaves driven by the first heavy, wet snow of winter.

The following story comes from a diary I kept as I was called to Active Duty with the Army Corps of Engineers - Company D, 876th Engineers - to aid the City of Johnstown, PA. Perhaps, as you read this, you can sense the personal questioning, hand-wringing, and ultimately the uneven but gradual growth that I felt during those several weeks of 1977 in a water-logged, mud-covered, thoroughly devastated small city in the mountains of South-Central Pennsylvania.

A Johnstown Diary

July 20, 11:00PM "I happened to turn on TV after an evening stroll on the Boardwalk at Ocean City, NJ. They said, 'there's been a terrible flood at Johnstown; no communication in or out; details sketchy'. I'm wondering if my National Guard Unit has been notified."

Comments - Janet and I had gone on vacation to the Jersey shore along with my Mom and Dad. I was hoping to be able to unwind/relax a bit and also re-consider my job options, as my work-assignment was becoming increasingly stressful. For the first time in my working life I was faced with a difficult, overbearing boss, an old Steel Industry veteran who believed that young metallurgists should be seen and not heard. I didn't know it at the time, but this would not be the last time I would face that situation, although mercifully I would be able to better cope in the future. Also, for the first time in my life, my blood pressure had become elevated and I was having trouble sleeping. Of course, being on-call 24 hours per day with 2:00AM phone calls a matter of routine, was not helping matters at all. Janet and I figured that a week's vacation of sun and surf would be therapeutic for the both of us.

July 21, 10:00AM "Cape May Red Cross has taken my name, rank, and unit but has been unable to tell me if the 876th is active." 4:00PM "The *Philadelphia Inquirer* says that the Pennsylvania National Guard has been called into Johnstown."

Comments - I remember trying to contact my Aunt Pearl and Uncle Bill who lived in Geistown, just outside of Johnstown, but all of the phone lines were down. Dad and Mom were both worried but tried to put on a brave front. Uncle Bill was an old 101st Airborne veteran and tougher than a two-day-old steak; however, he had also been an invalid for several years. It was hard to relax knowing that people you cared for might be in danger.

July 22 "Still no answer available from the Red Cross. Janet and I have decided to go home early. If it's as bad as they're saying, the Guard's Engineers have to be called in."

Comments - Interestingly, a number of people, after the fact, asked me, "Why in the world did you cut short your vacation? If they needed you, they would have contacted you. You should have just stayed put." In retrospect, that's probably true, but all I could think of were people – fellow Pennsylvanians - wet and cold, perhaps including my Aunt and Uncle. I knew that my conscience would accuse me, maybe for the rest of my life, if I stayed lying on a sun-baked beach instead of doing what I could to help immediately. Often in my life, the realization that I would have to deal with my conscience has guided me through the twists and turns of Life and, ultimately, to doing the right thing.

I'm also enough of a realist to recognize that doing the right thing isn't always the same as what a savvy world would consider the smart thing. Or, as my good buddy Rich would often half-jokingly tell me, "What? You're going to do the RIGHT thing?! Haven't I taught you anything?!" I guess I've made the decision to take my chances before my Maker at Judgment Day with a clear, good conscience as opposed to leading the "smart class."

July 23 "I am in Johnstown, Pennsylvania, barracked at the University of Pittsburgh, Johnstown Campus. We can't drink or bathe in the water – all groundwater has been deemed extremely contaminated. I brushed my teeth using a can of carbonated water; like brushing with Alka Seltzer. It's really another world up here. Pulled general clean-up details most of the day."

Comments - Earlier in the day when I had called my Unit outside of Pittsburgh, they immediately said, "Sergeant Lauer, get over here as fast as you can. We've got a chopper heading up to Johnstown in 2 hours." I barely had time to throw some essentials, clean underwear, and my fatigues and spare boots into my duffle bag and speed over to the Armory. As I waited for the next Huey chopper, I began to hear pieces of grim-sounding reports.

Apparently the devastation was appalling; many areas were reported to be totally isolated, most locations continued to be without power, roads had been inundated, severely eroded, and had consequently buckled, even four-lane highways. Later that day I saw an 18" thick section of concrete roadway completely undercut by the water and lying there looking like a roadway piece out of a toy highway construction set. More ominously, the water supply was still classified as unsafe, heightening the fears of disease. Upon arrival, we were immediately given typhoid, cholera, and a number of other inoculations that one would only get if visiting some primitive third-world region. I knew then that this was, indeed, a very serious and probably desperate situation. And it was happening here in my Home State.

We really do take everyday conveniences for granted. Pure drinking water was not available. Canned food and bottled water were okay in themselves; however, if the cans/bottles had been in contact with the floodwaters they were considered contaminated. Routine habits required rational thought: you could take a shower but you had to consciously remember not to get water near your mouth. Even simple things like washing your hands required vigilance and extra attention. Cuts were treated with equal care and first-aid was always linked with an antiseptic alcohol wipe.

Outside of the University complex, power was off. Many times I would enter a building looking for survivors (or worse) and snap on the light switch, immediately being reminded that there was no juice in the lines. It was always amazing how dark the inside of a building could be, even in the day-time and a flashlight lights up only a limited area; that, and the quietness. There was no hum of power, of refrigerators or air-conditioners, just the moldy-silence of water-soaked furnishings and your own "squishing" movements through the endless muck and debris.

July 24, 7:00AM "I took a bulldozer crew out into a field in Riverside to plug a dike which had broken from the force of what was normally a gentle creek, but which this time had smashed through earthen containment walls and completely flooded the community. Our D-7 bulldozer sank twice in the slimy muck within the first hour, but the old Allis-Chalmers pulled itself out each time. A farmer whose field was now completely buried by 4-feet of sand and other assorted muck cleared out his flooded fruit stand and fed us fresh produce he had saved (up in the building rafters), then gave us "pop" out of his undamaged Coke machine and refused to take any money. How do you figure these people? 4:00PM A pretty little house nearby caught fire and burned to the ground by the time the fire departments arrived. The couple who had lived there returned in time to see the little chalet collapse in a charred heap. The woman was nearly hysterical. Somehow, "I'm sorry," just didn't seem to help."

Comments - I remember trying to move dirt in that flooded field with little success. Everything quickly became water-logged goo as soon as weight was on it. The bulldozer's mass was spread out pretty evenly across its heavy tracks but if you weren't careful, you would find yourself quickly sunk up to the top of the track tread. It reminded me of trying to repair a sand castle at the beach once the tide has swirled around it.

The generosity of people in times of trouble astounded me. People who had lost heavily were still quickly willing to help each other and also those of us trying to help the community. This farmer had no ulterior motives in feeding us. He simply was grateful for any help coming to the town and wanted to show his appreciation to us. He was not looking for a future handout or preferential treatment but simply trying to say, "Thanks."

Similarly, my Aunt and Uncle were delighted to see me (their home had escaped the flood waters but they were still without power). Uncle Bill kept asking me, "How about some money. Need some money?" I remember thanking him over and over again but saying, "Uncle Bill, WHERE would I spend it?" Still, I couldn't get away without at least sharing some cold dinner with them and they refused to let me provide some packaged food-stock or C-rations for them – "Give it to people that need it," Uncle Bill had barked. Then he had added, "Let us at least get your fatigues washed." I wanted to remind him that, without power, that was going to be difficult; however, it was the thought that meant the most to me.

I was certainly relieved that they were both okay, particularly my incapacitated Uncle. I wanted to check with them every day but Uncle Bill, having been "Regular Army", would have nothing to do with that. "We're both fine, Barry," he said. "Do your duty and help the people that really need it." I knew better than to argue with him.

Having just recently gone through the mortgage and financing part of home ownership myself, I truly felt badly for the young couple whose house burned down. It was a stark reminder to me that possessions, just like life, can be fragile and fleeting. I didn't know what to say. All I could do was stand by, help move out a few sticks of undamaged furniture, and watch the house burn. The building was situated on a small out-cropping next to the river with a good-sized field surrounding it on three sides. The flood waters had turned the ground into the same gelatinous muck that we had been trying to move most of the day. A fire-truck showed up but couldn't get close enough to even stretch a hose to the house.

We weren't sure exactly what had started the fire, as there was still no electrical power and it seemed very strange to have a blaze surrounded by so much completely unusable water and moisture. For some reason I was particularly saddened as I watched the intricately-carved oak trim around the front door char and turn black before crumbling. Someone had obviously put a lot of time and effort into that woodwork. Again, it was the sheer helplessness I felt that was the most disturbing, along with the continued realization that, for all of our proud technical prowess, we were pretty pathetic in the face of an angry Mother Nature. Looking back on it now, perhaps this was my Scriptural "…did the best he/she could…" effort – simply being there so that that young couple didn't have to stand there all alone.

I think that the worst feeling associated with any disaster is that of feeling alone. Just the fact that we were there – whether or not we could do anything significant – seemed to be a tonic for the local citizenry. Everyone seemed to understand that we weren't going to be able to simply snap our fingers and immediately put everything back the way it had been. For one thing, the ground was just too saturated to let us do too much. I had never experienced such a frustrating task as trying to move mud, even with heavy equipment. Still, one person had told me that just hearing the sound of the bulldozer's diesel engine out in that field had lifted her spirits. However, I know I was thinking, "What earthly good are we doing here?" I didn't even recognize the pun at the time.

July 25, 8:00AM "Back in Riverside, and we continue to try to patch the dike. The ground seems even worse today as the flood waters seem to have permeated down an additional 5 feet making maneuvering even in a small bulldozer hazardous. 11:00AM Rain is falling, getting harder all the time. Once again the bulldozer sinks up to the top of the tracks. We work frantically to free it, but how do you shovel muck? 12:00PM The Lieutenant has just ordered us to abandon the bulldozer and get to high ground due to a flash flood warning. One of the townspeople says Pittsburgh TV has reported that several of the up-stream dams are breaking! Johnstown is in a state of panic as an evacuation report spreads like a prairie wildfire! This can't be real! 1:00PM The rain has suddenly stopped. WJAC TV (Johnstown) interrupts its regular broadcasts to announce that the dams are NOT breaking and that Johnstown will NOT be evacuated. The water rose here at Riverside to within two feet of the top but didn't penetrate our repaired dike. The entire town sighs collectively as the surging river waters sink back down onto the rocky bottom. I think we've made a lot of friends here today."

Comments - At Noon that day, I remember seeing people looking like ants clambering up the sloping hills outside of town. It was like one of those B-horror movies where the town is being fled ahead of the giant-whatever monster/nuclear-radiation-generated mutant who is viciously ready to attack. For the first time in my life, I was watching wild panic unfold in front of my eyes. Oddly, I was as concerned for the mud-bound old D-7 bulldozer as I was for my own safety. Go figure.

I had never seen human panic before. This was akin to watching a disaster movie like "*Earthquake*" except you realized that you were actually participating. I remember seeing a young mother literally dragging two toddlers across a field and up a hill towards a wooded ridge-line. The kids were screaming, terrified because they saw that their mother was panic-stricken. My bulldozer operator and I each grabbed one of the children as we all sprinted uphill. I guess we were all expecting to look back and see a wall of water surging behind us; however, I know I didn't bother to glance back until we had crested the ridge-line.

For some reason, I kept thinking of the old Satchell Page line: "Don't look back; something might be gaining on you." Or perhaps I had been remembering the Old Testament story concerning Lot's wife, a truly "salty" tale. Then, we just stood there, waiting to see if total disaster would play itself out. Very fortunately, the down-stream surge that followed the rainstorm didn't breach our thoroughly waterlogged dike, frankly surprising me, knowing how unstable that dike wall actually was. One other thing I remember: I stared at my muck-covered combat boots and mud-stained fatigues, realizing that despite all of my combat-engineering preparedness, I was still totally at the mercy of natural forces far beyond my mortal level.

July 26 Spent all day hauling contaminated (from flooding) food out of several Johnstown grocery stores. (All foodstuffs have been seized by the Department of Agriculture). I wasn't very hungry tonight."

Comments - This was coincidentally my second Wedding Anniversary, but I was feeling pretty glum. I was half-sick to my stomach from the stench of the day while at the same time it pained me to be throwing out so much "good food". In retrospect, it was an important reminder of all of the little things that come up at a time of a natural disaster. People would say, "Why did you throw canned food away?" Well, anything that had been in contact with the flood waters was potentially a disease carrier. I'm sure that in desperate situations, people could have boiled and then used the canned contents. At that time, however, there was the distinct threat of disease, particularly typhoid. When I talked to Janet that evening by phone, it was a pretty depressing conversation. It was hard to convey what you had seen to someone sitting in an air-conditioned house with lots of good food immediately available.

I was continually amazed at the sheer number of grocery stores that a small town like Johnstown could have. Even further, I was astounded at the number of 5-ton dump trucks it took to clear out a grocery store. Looking back on the whole thing, it would have taken far longer to sterilize the food items and, today, can you imagine the potential legal liability if someone came down with typhoid as a result of incomplete cleaning of a can of tuna? It's always amazing now to me how people simply expect that some giant vacuum cleaner is going to suck up all of the "bad stuff" after a flood or some other natural disaster and all that will need to be done is restock the store shelves. Once again, it was almost as if someone had thrown a gigantic switch and the city was instantly thrown back 150 years or more.

July 27 "Arrived in New Florence, PA, with our five-ton dump trucks. An entire trailer court of 45 mobile homes was washed into a tree line several hundred yards at the far end of a corn field. Rescuers must have a road built back to the tree line capable of supporting heavy equipment to begin the search for victims. All of the rock for the road must come out of a strip mine over past Armagh, PA, about 6 miles away, and I can see that it's going to take a heck of a lot of rock."

Comments - This was a very, very sad time. The floodwaters from the Connemaugh River had quickly surged through and filled the normally sedate stream bed, assaulted and quickly demolished most of the homes on the low-lying side of the one-stoplight town along with the lone one-pier bridge connecting both sides of the village. As the wedge of flotsam and general debris jammed the riverbed, almost within seconds the flood waters backed up and catastrophically breeched the riverbank. A similar scenario had been repeated at multiple locations further upstream, including the town of Seward, where roughly 30 trailers had washed away.

Since all of this had occurred late at night, people living in the New Florence trailer park on the southwest side of the Connemaugh suddenly found their individual units being floated off of their supports, swept across the length of the field, and subsequently slammed into the towering oak trees lining the far end of the field. Some people were crushed and killed as they lay in their beds. Although at the time we knew that there were probably fatalities (and that the only way to untangle the wreckage and get to them was with some very massive mobile cranes), the only question was: how many?

Humans have this urge or need to get into the fight, to roll up their sleeves, pitch in and help. It's commendable and admirable. A huge natural catastrophe, however, tends to stop those immediate reactions in their tracks. At New Florence, the flood-waters had not only swept most everything along with the currents but, in this case, also saturated the ground that had housed the mobile home park. Everyone living in the town had wanted to get in and help and many tried. The problem was simply that the force of the flood had jammed everything back into the tree-line – mobile homes, cars, trees, assorted brush, and anything else not firmly anchored. It wasn't as simple as simply lifting something up to look and see if someone was underneath. There was a massive, mangled mess of twisted debris and shredded sheet metal and all half-submerged in the sticky muck of mud that would barely support a human being let alone a vehicle.

Perhaps the worst part of my experience in Johnstown in 1977 involved having to wait to get in and help. Instead, we had to undertake the task of methodically building a rock-based foundation for a road leading from the remnant of the main road out across a field usually supporting nothing than rows of corn. The only effective way to get into the debris pile and begin to look for trapped victims was to have a firm base to support salvage vehicles.

A five-ton dump truck sounds like it holds a lot of rock and it does; in fact, we were overloaded to better than twice the load limits on the vehicles. Unfortunately, one dump-truck load of rocks provided only a drip in the bucket when it came to actually having a supporting road. The one thing you didn't want to do was rush things, push the limits, and then get a vital piece of equipment stuck. Then, you would have to build more load-bearing surface to work around it plus you had an important vehicle stuck and unusable until it was extricated.

Feeling that someone could still be alive and trapped beneath all of that debris heightened both the urgency and helplessness of the would-be rescuers. Still, mission-focus and hard work were and continue to be hallmarks of the military, and we were driven to get a road built as quickly and as effectively as possible. That meant being disciplined enough to understand that our job was very quickly developing into a "recovery" rather than a "rescue" mission.

July 28 "Life has taken on a dreary routine – out the road four miles to Seward (a small mining town upstream of New Florence), left turn out Route 56, up a steep rock-strewn hill to the town of Armagh (second gear in old D-11, a hulking 5-ton dump-truck), over to the mine entrance, up the steep winding road wide enough for only one truck. Sitting in place (with the brakes set extra-securely), the huge front-end loader would deposit roughly "two scoops" in the dump-back, jouncing the old truck up and down before settling heavy on its springs. Then, back down that narrow, winding road, this time with 12 or 13 tons of rock. It almost felt "good" to be back out on 56 again and over to New Florence, where you would dump your rocky load as far back as the last dumped load of boulders while being extremely careful not to get off into the endless muck on either side. Then, you would pull forward, turn right, and head back yet again. Worked 20 hours today. My left leg feels like it's falling off (from the extra-heavy duty clutch pedal)."

Comments - The old Army dump-trucks we used were very basic. All of the transmissions were manual with no synchronization meaning that when you down-shifted, you had to employ "double-clutching" techniques to synchronize engine and transmission speeds; otherwise, the transmission would grind and complain (and often not go into gear). The clutches were very stiff, requiring brute leg-force to engage. We wore dust masks to try (without any success) to control the all-pervasive clouds of fine grit and silt and, possibly, disease.

Plus, we were very heavily loaded, well beyond the capacities of the 5-ton dumps. This made for excessively-plodding driving mixed with semi-terror on any hills (going down). I guess what kept us all going so hard and so long was the simple realization that people were still possibly trapped and injured back in those trailers and that the only way to get them out was to lay down some sort of rough roadbed and do it as quickly as humanly possible.

We were working as fast as we could, fighting the long hours, the grueling physical stress, and the boredom, all mixed in with the understanding that, with better than twice the rated loads on those military dump-trucks, a few moments of inattention or carelessness could not only jeopardize your life but also further delay the road-building mission. Again, the road up to the rock quarry was single-lane; upset one of the dump-trucks and you would block the way up and down. Knowing that time was slipping away for anyone left alive in the debris really did weigh heavily on all of us drivers. Most of us had never seen civilian deaths before, or any kind of death, for that matter, except perhaps for loved ones dying in their sleep in their own beds.

July 29 "Dust is getting so bad that we wear masks even out on the main roads to keep driving. We're getting closer to the tree line now, and something smells awfully bad back there. We hope it's a wrecked freezer with rotten meat in it."

Comments - For sheer drudgery, I don't know of any job worse than hauling rock. You've got to be paying attention all of the time to avoid any of the huge but not-very-round boulders shifting in your load, you have to watch the road for the occasional fallen debris (and rocks dropped by other trucks), there's constant noise from the straining engine and grinding gears, and the dust seems to permeate every part of your clothing, let alone the feeling of coating your lungs. Regardless, a sense of Duty keeps you going in times like this, even when you're bone-tired.

July 30 "We were wrong. There are indeed fatalities. I'm glad I didn't watch the rescue team bring them out. May God rest their souls."

Comments - This statement was actually intentionally incorrect on my part. Once the heavy mobile-crane could start untangling things, it didn't take long for already-decaying corpses to become visible. I did see some of the victims. One was simply the remains of half of a little girl. I'll never forget the look on her grayish-white little face – peaceful, but empty, and without the lower half of her body. That vision has haunted my dreams occasionally throughout my life and, for the first couple of years, I wouldn't even mention it – not even to Janet. I believe that there were a total of 4 bodies found in the wreckage. There were also several injured people miraculously found amidst the tangled mess of steel, aluminum, and generally jumbled debris; to the best of my knowledge, these few did recover. Suffice it to say that it was a stunned, very silent group of Army dump truck drivers that watched the ambulances slowly pull away from New Florence that evening.

July 31 "Half of the Company was flown home by Chinook (helicopter) for the day. We, as an Engineer unit, will remain active while other National Guard units are being relieved and de-activated. The first thing I did when I got home was get a drink of water from the faucet."

Comments - Although it was just for the day, even a few hours away from the devastation was like a week's vacation at the beach. Going back to Pittsburgh, it was a very hot day and we were packed tightly into the Chinook helicopter. The trip over the mountains was choppy as the summertime thermals tossed even the heavy chopper around like a dried-up autumn leaf; inside, the air was blistering hot. I remember getting my Squad off of the chopper in Pittsburgh and then surreptitiously ducking around a 55-gallon fuel drum to lose my breakfast. At home, I simply showered, put my feet up, sipped cold, clean water, and watched a baseball game on TV with Janet curled up next to me on the couch. I really couldn't talk to her very much about what was going on. It was simply too soon and too painful to recount and I didn't want to waste home-time being any more miserable than I already was.

August 1 "We are to build a 350-foot "Bailey Bridge" over the Connemaugh to connect New Florence with Huff (a small hamlet, actually part of New Florence) and allow emergency equipment to pass. It will be the largest span of its type ever constructed by a National Guard or Reserve Unit. Since I know a bit about the bridge, I am the non-commissioned officer from D-Company assigned to supervise construction. The project seems impossible.

The approaches are too short, the center pillar's condition is unknown, and the wreckage of the old bridge still hangs on the far shore abutment."

Comments - Barely one month before, we had just finished our annual Summer Duty at Ft. Indiantown Gap near Harrisburg, PA – two weeks of active training, required each year. I had conducted the "bridge-building" classes for the entire Battalion which included building a roughly 60-foot bridge over a shallow ravine. The purpose of this exercise was to teach each soldier the rudimentary fundamentals of building this particular Bridge.

The "Bailey Bridge" is a "girder and I-beam" type of bridge structure built in 10-foot sections, all by hand (that is, heavy equipment is not normally necessary in its construction). Up to 10 men were needed on some of the heavier components and watching one's toes was prudent if not essential. The sections were assembled into a steel-framed square grounded on top of a series of rollers and each completed section was subsequently pushed out over the "edge" (ravine, creek, river…) to make room for the next section. Of course, as the bridge grew in length, it would exhibit the tendency to droop; therefore, a good builder would have to calculate and adjust the roller setup and bridge-angle to compensate for the sagging of the lead-section. The worst thing that could happen would be to be too low and not be able to ground the bridge on the far shore rollers. Actually, the worst thing that could happen would be to make a mistake in construction and have the entire structure collapse in a tangled heap on top of a fair-sized group of soldiers.

However, this particular bridge project was far more complex than the simple Bailey we had pieced together months before. Because of the extreme span and load-carrying requirements projected, we would need to construct a "Triple-Triple" Bailey Bridge. There would be three outer frame-panels instead of one meaning construction would be slower, more back-breaking, and much more hazardous, even for Combat Engineers skilled in bridge building.

To make things more difficult, I was now faced with not only an expanse almost six times longer than anything we had ever trained on, but, because of the extreme length, with having to intermediately land the bridge on rollers mounted on the old center pillar standing in the middle of the Connemaugh River. Placement and balance on the center pillar would be critical; otherwise, even a correctly-leveled but slightly off-center bridge could collapse and tumble into the water below. I had never even had to consider such conditions. It seemed to be an impossible situation for a citizen-soldier, engineer or not.

I had asked my Company commander if anyone had ever built a bridge of this size and length before. His response was, "You will be the first."

Fortunately for me, the local Fire Chief took me aside that evening and helped put things in perspective for me; it was a "come to Jesus" moment. He simply explained that having to go roughly 8 miles up-river, across the bridge at that point, and then 8 miles back down-river to end up about 100 yards away would probably, at some point, cost someone in physical distress their life in the intervening 15-20 minutes or so.

Further, the State had no funds to construct a replacement bridge on-site for at least two years. "Sergeant," the old Chief said, "You're essentially 'the Cavalry'; these people need you." That helped to crystallize my thinking. I knew that I had the training, we would soon have the equipment, but more than that I knew there was no other choice –like it or not, it was up to me. Somehow, I began to feel my sagging confidence stiffen.

Later that evening, another experience cemented my resolve and helped further answer my own personal "Why me...?" question. I was taking one last walk around the bridge site collecting my private thoughts regarding the upcoming task. The sun had already set and the late-summer dusk was settling in. I closed my eyes and for a few seconds it seemed like just another quiet country evening with river-crickets beginning their songfest and lightning-bugs decorating the river-bed and nearby fields. I began to sink back into a feeling of insignificance, recognizing that even in the middle of a natural disaster the sun would still rise and set just as it had for many thousands of years. Mother Nature had once more shown herself to be the real master of the planet. I was simply a momentary bit-actor on the cosmic stage.

As I walked down to a small convenience store about a quarter of a mile back towards New Florence, a feeling of gross inadequacy buried deep in my gut, an elderly woman came towards me. She was barely five feet tall, dressed in a blue sweatshirt and slacks, and walked slightly hunched-over. I had barely touched the bill of my cap in a quiet "Hello" when she stopped in front of me, smiled broadly, and then reached up and put her arms around my neck.

"We lost almost everything," she said, tears beginning to well up in her eyes, "But thank you, thank you for being here!" Ever feel like you're really, truly doing something to make a difference? It didn't matter that what I was doing was barely a blip on the massive radar screen of Life; the fact was, I WAS doing something! Call it lighting one candle... or taking "the first step of 1000 miles", I now felt purpose in what I was doing.

A few moments later, she smiled once more, touched my mud-splattered face, and walked on. The whole thing took maybe twenty seconds; I'll remember it for the rest of my life. Renewed purpose, meaning, and making a difference will do that.

August 2 "The old bridge has been cleared away and the center pier scouted and cleared of the remnants of the old bridge. Penn Dot (Pennsylvania Department of Transportation) and Battalion Command have surveyed the entire site and assured me that everything is A-OK. Now I know I'm in trouble."

Comments - Understand, at the time Penn Dot's reputation was terrible. Springtime potholes in Pennsylvania were the stuff of legends as were their "hot-patch" pothole-filling techniques which not only had a tendency to expire within 12 hours but also provided a host of loose stones to chip lower car doors and fenders or launch themselves like 12-gauge buckshot towards an unsuspecting and formerly crack-free windshield. Anyone who has heard that sickening sound somewhere between a "snick" and a "smack" followed by a circular bulls-eye shape directly in front of your eye-level view out the windshield knows EXACTLY what I mean, I'm sure!

Battalion Command was certainly competent, as far as I was concerned; however, I knew that none of them really had any experience in building bridges of this type. And I was sure that, if disaster happened to strike, everyone would likely be diving for cover except for the "non-commissioned officer in charge", at whose trial and subsequent request for mercy would likely precipitate the chant, "Release unto us Barabbas!" In all fairness, it wasn't a military thing, rather, a human nature tendency; after all, who wants to be known as the chief architect of a screw-up? Despite all of this, I was now convinced that everyone officially wanted to give it a try. But most importantly, I knew that I definitely wanted to give it a try. Besides, I had seen enough death; I wanted to do something to fight back.

August 3 "Actual construction began this morning. Parts are still arriving from as far away as Colorado and New Mexico. Some of the components weigh as much as 500-600 pounds each. With only 30 men, the work goes slowly and we had to work right up to darkness."

Comments - The approach to the bridge began to look like some demented scrap-and-salvage yard. As quickly as a truck arrived, the unloading crew would begin to haul materials off, trying to be careful not to set them down where I might need to position some piece of equipment, or the next section of bridge. The approaches on either side were curved, so we didn't have much open space and once off the road berms by even a few feet, the ground was still very soft.

With the weight of the steel parts, it was hard, sheer-muscle work and we had to be increasingly careful as the day went on to not let muscle-fatigue cause a case of the "drop-sies", particularly with the added complication of having to constantly step around other parts and tools. Unfortunately, all of this prevented us from being able to mobilize a large "pre-assemble" area, as the discreet 10 ft. sections weighed several thousand pounds each.

Actually, we developed a rhythm in building the sections, with a select crew (the really big guys) handling the heavy transoms while two other groups man-handled the large girder sections. Another crew would drive the connecting pins while others gathered and assembled ancillary parts. I was amazed at how quickly everyone grasped the construction concepts. Maybe these guys HAD actually absorbed some of my Bridge training at the previous two-week active duty stint. Still, it was heavy, hard, and dangerous work.

August 4 "Word has come down that we are to be deactivated Sunday the 7th. We tried to work past darkness and almost lost a man on the third story. Even with the help of heavy-duty floodlights, dangling steel pieces are downright dangerous. We decided to quit at dusk from now on."

Comments – Understand, we were citizen-soldiers, not Ironworkers. Even with lights, positioning heavy pieces of steel structurals and then pinning them together with sledge-driven pins was not something to be accomplished casually. No "Statics and Dynamics" class I had taken in college could prepare me adequately for this kind of "real-life" work. It wasn't like playing with tinker-toys where you could shove and bend something to make it fit.

By mid-morning that day, we had "landed" the nose of the bridge dead-and-true on the center pier rollers (actually, I was downright amazed at how precisely square we were) and after a quick re-examination of the pier for structural soundness, continued to assemble and push out the finished ten-foot sections.

The near-accident that evening was simply a combination of fatigue, shadows, and inexperience in using the light-crane. Fortunately, a co-worker on the bridge upper-level was able to grab on to his buddy just as balance was being lost, preventing about a 30-foot plunge into the rock-strewn river below. It happened and was over in a second, but it sure put the Fear of the Lord into each of us. After all, the last thing we needed with the Flood was more casualties.

August 5 & 6 "Lay hold, Heave! Oh, my aching back."

Comments - Always looking for efficiency, the Army Corps of Engineers had a simple set of commands for lifting. "Lay hold" meant for everyone to get their grip, set themselves, and prepare for lifting or else call, "Halt." If no one asked for time-out, the command "Heave" was given, and everyone would lift. That cut out the extraneous "on the count of three" civilian stuff. Over the next two days we continued to make slow, steady progress. At the same time, we were also getting worn down physically from the sheer bulk of the bridge construction materials necessary for building several hundred feet of steel bridge. But with each new bridge-section being generated (we did end up using a bulldozer to push the sections out, as we had several hundred tons of steel out there at the time) I was fairly confident that we would eventually and successfully land the bridge. The only question now was if we would run out of time?

August 7, 6:00PM "We aren't finished. The men are exhausted. I've been requested to stay an additional day to help land the bridge on the far shore. 6:30PM D Company stood down from Active Duty."

Comments - I knew that I couldn't leave without getting "my bridge" down on the other side of the Connemaugh. I wanted to get home, sure, but this thing was now my personal "baby". I remember looking at the huge monstrosity hulking over the river in the fading light that evening and thinking, "Darn, I'd never have believed it." It's a good thing it was almost dark, because I'm sure the pride would have shown boldly on my face along with a few tears.

I had been asking "Why?" regarding a number of things in my life. That evening I had one rather large, "Because of this…" sitting there, waiting to be finished. Other questions I would find myself coming to grips with in the years ahead. I would also learn that some problems are not really a big deal in the scheme of things in life, e.g., the job/career. There were other aspects, I would see, that mattered infinitely more.

August 8 "At 4:45PM, 210 tons of bridge was grounded on the Huff side of the Connemaugh. A light crew of volunteers will jack the bridge down on its supports tomorrow and Penn Dot will construct the concrete approaches. 8:00PM I am finally standing down from Active Duty, and I can go home to my Wife and Family. Lord God, comfort those poor people who can do neither."

Comments - I have several pictures of "my bridge", still considered "the largest ever constructed in the USA". It stood for several years allowing single-lane traffic across the Connemaugh River before Penn Dot finally received the funding to build a permanent concrete two-lane bridge.

Roughly 80 people died in the 1977 Johnstown Flood. Bodies continued to be recovered months later, a few having been discovered many miles downstream as far as Blairsville, PA. It took several years to rebuild some of the roads and other portions of the infrastructure, but gradually life returned to near-normal for Johnstown.

About a year later, I received a note from Battalion Headquarters. It said that the Fire Chief in New Florence wanted to pass along a message to me. It seems a woman in Huff wanted to send her thanks to "the bridge soldiers". Her Father, living in Huff, had recently suffered a heart attack. The New Florence Rescue Squad was able to dash across my bridge and respond in less than 5 minutes rather than 15 – 20 minutes if they had been forced to take the circuitous route first up and then down the Connemaugh River. Her message: "Tell them, 'Thanks for helping save my Daddy's life!'"

A "Triple-Triple" Bailey Bridge – New Florence, PA - 1977

NCOIC Barry A. Lauer (right) - 1977

Looking Back...

"Peace is not an absence of war; it is a virtue, a state of mind, a disposition for benevolence, confidence, justice." – Benedict de Spinoza

"The soldier, above all other people, prays for peace, for he must suffer and bear the deepest wounds and scars of war." – Douglas MacArthur

"The principle office of history I take to be this: to prevent virtuous actions from being forgotten, and that evil words and deeds should fear an infamous reputation with posterity." - Tacitus

I didn't begin this work with the idea of gaining personal enlightenment, let alone the intention of offering a definitive, well-reasoned answer to "A Soldier's Question" of "Why me?" And, I'm not concluding with anything resembling a coherent, "Because..." After all, as mentioned in the beginning, I'm an engineer, not a philosopher.

But, too, I was a soldier, as were members of my Family, and all I have tried to do is offer the thoughts of soldiers. None of us were high-level commanders, nor were we responsible for creating and maintaining lofty strategic concepts. My Dad was the first member of his Family to go beyond the 4th Grade, followed by my Uncle Bill. Therefore, the thoughts, questions, and actions presented in the previous pages are from common "grunts", real GI's; however, I am by no means ashamed of those common roots. Any failure to live up to acceptable literary standards lies at my now-wrinkled feet alone.

Still, I know that we Westerners and, particularly Americans, don't like to approach final book chapters with open-ended questions left unanswered; we prefer to see, "And the reason is..." Probably unlike some other cultures, we are not comfortable with an "it is what it is because that's the way it is" way of thinking. For example, the concept of "Karma" is alien to us. We've tried to incorrectly translate that term into something somehow understandable and manageable, kind of like our own concept of "good" or "bad" luck. Then, we've mixed it with the old Casey Stengel view of, "You make your own luck; some people have bad luck all their lives."

After all, we are "cause and effect" people; that is, we assume that if something happens, there must have been a reason for why it happened. And, apparently we are not the only ones. When Jesus' disciples asked Him regarding the reason for a certain man being born blind, they expected a "because" answer; in fact, the Twelve even tried to narrow the options down to two to help Him out: either the man or his parents had sinned. So, it was, "Okay, Lord, choose from Column A or Column B." But apparently God doesn't operate like a take-out Chinese restaurant menu and Christ's response, "Neither", didn't necessarily satisfy His followers. They felt that "something" had to have been the cause of the problem. After all, that's the way everything else in their life worked. In short, though, it's how we humans reason: intuitively, for every action there's a reaction.

We Americans, I believe, try to take it a step further. We tend to feel that, even if we can't offer a logical "Because" answer, there must ultimately be a solution somewhere and someday, even if not in our own individual lifetimes, we'll eventually be smart enough to articulate the answer. Perhaps, as in a cure for cancer, we seem to believe that everything will eventually fall to the power of our human intellects over time.

Carrying this logic one step further, I guess we tend to approach these things expecting our Heavenly Father to act like our earthly dads and say, "Wait ten or twenty years and you'll understand." We don't like the thought of never finding an answer to basic questions, even those that have no answers, such as a soldier's "Why me?", while still in our "earthly tents." We're troubled even more with the additional consideration that no one else will likely have an answer either, ever.

As a species, are we just supremely arrogant? No, I don't think it's as simple as that. Perhaps we just don't like to read a mystery novel only to find that the last page or chapter is missing. We rationalize that life unfolds like a well-organized book and follows the stated table of contents, and reaches a logical, this-sums-up-everything conclusion, even though we instinctively known that it just isn't so.

Somehow, though, I suspect that every generation of mankind has pretty much assumed the same thing. I imagine that it's a thoroughly human trait: that somehow, someday we feel that we will discover the answer to the unanswerable. Maybe it really should be called "eternal arrogance?" At the very least, it seems to be "universal", that impression of eventual attainment of enlightenment.

But I think we make a huge mistake in thinking that, when it comes to fighting and dying, modern man is somehow better able, more mentally capable, certainly compared to soldiers down through history, who we have tacitly, probably at times condescendingly, assumed to be too unintelligent or unsophisticated, to express and understand the "Why me?" question. I know, for example, that Mr. Davidson thought so.

My tenth-grade chemistry teacher espoused the theory that mankind was evolving into "a better, more mentally capable and mature being", sort of a super-homo sapien. Further, he believed that humans today were decidedly superior to those of even 2000 years ago, just as future generations will likely view us as inferior. I remember that he was amused that I didn't necessarily agree, particularly with my scant 16 years on the planet.

Today, in looking at our world over the past 50 years in order to consider how far mankind has improved and evolved, at least in the short term comprised of my life on this earth, to Mr. Davidson's premise I would have to say, "I ain't seein' it yet!" Of course, he would probably say, "Well, you've got to wait at least 100 years, or maybe 200. And who today can prove me wrong?"

But to this perception of a lack of intelligence or sophistication with soldiers throughout history, I would have to say, "Nah, not a chance!" In fact, I'd wager that any number of ancient warriors could and have waxed eloquently on their deep feelings as to "Why me?" And, of course, there are examples.

In the Old Testament, the Book of Esther tells of a young Jewish woman who finds herself improbably in a position of high authority within the Persian Empire. Eventually, though, she and her people are confronted by a deadly enemy who has engineered a sinister plot to exterminate the Jewish race. Esther's uncle, Mordecai, becomes aware of the threat and councils her that she must use her position of influence to intercede with the King of Persia for her people, although doing so (including entering the king's chamber uninvited) could result in her forfeiting her life.

Esther pauses, and then expresses her fears. In response to her very real concerns, Mordecai answers: "Do not think that because you are in the king's house you alone of all the Jews will escape. For if you remain silent at this time, relief and deliverance for the Jews will arrive from another place, but you and your father's family will perish. And who knows but that you have come to royal position for such a time as this?" Esther courageously goes to the king and ultimately saves her people.

Could this be "it?" Perhaps a "real soldier", not one who has joined blindly for greed, power, blood-lust, or slavery-conscription, has always believed that, when all of the patriotic sayings and trappings were stripped away, maybe the "Why me?" question has only one answer – "because you were put in this position for such a time as this and if you do not accept this responsibility, someone else will have to do so."

The "real soldier", and I'll focus particularly on one who has served under the Stars and Stripes, has understood and accepted, I think, that he or she was likely born to the soldier's task for "such a time as this", and the driving force of their willingness to serve has been and is always, as General Douglas MacArthur described -

"Duty, Honor, Country." Somehow too, this devotion to doing one's duty, to acting honorably, and for the sake and love of the Country, never leaves a soldier, even at the close of life.

I think that's why whenever our troops are "in harm's way", American veterans always feel an extra measure of anguish and in some way, even guilt. You see, we feel that somehow we should be "there", somehow making a difference. In 1980, when the American Delta Force tried to execute a very difficult, immensely complicated rescue of the hostages in Iran and met disaster while attempting to coordinate combat helicopters in the choking dust and directionless-waste of the desert at night, I know that I felt the loss personally.

We had conducted many air-mobile assault exercises in Huey attack helicopters, two at night, and I could certainly understand the dangers and confusion that might be experienced when speed, noise, and deadly movement, are mixed with poor visibility. It wasn't a lack of determination, courage, or even planning. What was being attempted was simply extremely hazardous, and when things like that are tried, disaster is always lurking as a real and possible consequence.

When the helmet of one of the F-111F pilots washed up on the Mediterranean shore, downed over Tripoli during the air raid on Libya in 1986, I felt the pain of loss for a gallant comrade. In Desert Shield and then Desert Storm (1990-1991), I agonized knowing the planning, execution, and great danger involved in our soldiers' actions against an unstable, unpredictable, and savage enemy.

When those twenty Rangers were ambushed and died fighting to the last man in Somalia in October of 1993, I grieved. I remembered the promise: "carrying your shield or on it, as long as one Ranger remains alive, you're coming out." It's possible that I trained with the people who trained the people who subsequently trained those Rangers.

When the passenger planes slammed into the World Trade Towers on 9/11/01, I cried as well, not only for the victims in New York, Washington DC, and Shanksville, PA (about six miles from where my Grandfather James R. Kimmel had lived and now lies buried) but also knowing that inevitably our troops would quickly be going into a hot shooting war. I've prayed and "kept the faith" with our troops in Iraq, and now Afghanistan. Strange, isn't it? After World War I everyone felt that they had just fought "the war to end all wars."

Then again, maybe we haven't reached Mr. Davidson's required number of years necessary for mankind to "grow-up."

But most of all, in each of those situations and conflicts, somehow I wished that I could have been there – to do what, I have no clue. It's difficult to describe the feeling to anyone but another soldier. Anytime and anywhere that I have stood at attention saluting The Flag, I've felt that kinship, that fraternal bond, if you will. Particularly for a soldier, I guess, F. L. Stanton's short verse is especially meaningful:

She's up there – OLD GLORY – where lightnings are sped
She dazzles the nations with ripples of red
And she'll wave for us living, or droop o'er us dead –
The Flag of our Country forever.

Someone has stated: "There are no noble wars; only noble warriors." Still, perhaps the American soldier has had the unbelievably good fortune to have fought – at least in almost every circumstance that I can see – for "unique, yet honorable" reasons. In a burst of what I consider God-inspired human genius and triumph, The Declaration of Independence states, **"We hold these truths to be self-evident, that all men are created equal; that they are endowed with certain inalienable rights, that among these are life, liberty, and the pursuit of happiness."**

Considering that this was created when kings, totalitarian despots, and the slavery of abject millions (including a number of the writers of the same Declaration, who were slave-owners) were still the overwhelming rule, not the exception, those words are even more remarkable.

Further defining the startling uniqueness of the Nation, in the middle of the seemingly unending American Civil War, President Abraham Lincoln dared stand at a cemetery in a small Pennsylvania farm town called Gettysburg and claim that the soldiers who gave their lives on the nearby battlefields did so "not in vain" but rather for a just and noble purpose, specifically, in order that "...Government of the People, by the People, and for the People, shall not perish from the earth."

The cynics and critics that first heard those words reportedly were more taken by the brevity of Lincoln's Address; in fact, I often wonder just what the responses would be from the various news analysts and "spin" experts if Lincoln would have uttered those words today?

And yet, those brief words have outlived by far both the speaker and his critics as well. What an astounding affirmation! That government exists for the good and well-being of the citizenry – regardless of status, education, race, creed, or any other human-invented standard of demarcation – and not simply for its own self-edification or even its own existence! The majority of the citizens of the world even today can only dream of living under such noble, profound precepts.

I believe that we Americans fail to understand how profoundly remarkable all of this is. We take all of this "...of the People, by the People, for the People..." very much for granted, and it both amazes and sometimes confuses other nations.

This uniquely American element was perhaps well summed up by the judges at the Nuremburg trials after World War II. I remember one particular statement that essentially proclaimed, for the rest of the world to hear, "...let it now be understood here that we stand for...the sacredness of a single human life."

Ten days after World War II had ended in Europe, Franz Werfel wrote a moving piece in the *Ruhr Zeitung* (19 May 1945) entitled, "*Will Germany Be Able to Save Her Soul?*" In an attempt at "national self-examination", he wrote:

"As a precondition, you will have to take a long look at your past and acknowledge your guilt. German men and women, do you know what they did in your name during the "Great Years of Salvation" (1939-1945) – do you know that it was Germans who killed millions and millions of peaceable, harmless and innocent people with methods that would make even the devil blush with shame? Do you know about the ovens and gas chambers of Maidanek, the dung-heap of rotting corpses in Buchenwald, Belsen and hundreds of other hell camps like these?..."

He continued, "Many of you will pale, turn away and murmur, 'What has all that to do with me?' That is just it: it has to do with you, with every least one of you. If ever the course of history has expressed God's judgment, it has done so here and now. Did you not boast of your 'national communion", in which the individual was no more than a fanatical atom, unconditionally serving the whole? It was not individual criminals, therefore, who committed all these horrors, but your 'communion', in which each stood for all, and all for each. The crimes of National Socialism and the unspeakable denigration of German civilization are but the logical outcomes of the devilish exaltation of the rights of the strongest and the claim that right is merely what serves the nation, or rather a few party bosses and swindlers. Nothing can undo the fact that you not only heeded

these devilish doctrines, but that you embraced
them fervently, defending them with fire, steel, and
blood. Never before has a less heroic generation
boasted a more heroic philosophy. Too late have
your eyes been opened to the revolting behavior of
your leaders, bosses, and generals."

Contrast that Nazi "national communion", where "right is merely
what serves the nation", with "...of...by...for the People". You
can call me naïve, simple-minded, or just plain wrapped in the
Flag. That's okay, I can handle that. But it still sounds to me that
there's something profoundly wonderful about being an American
and, further, an American soldier.

Not too long ago I was watching old videos of the conflict in
Korea (aka "The Forgotten War"). What I saw was an eerie
preview of what the American public would see on the evening
news in the 1960's concerning Viet Nam – savage fighting along
with dead and wounded American soldiers. It struck me that, to
the best of my knowledge, no similar films showing dead Chinese
troops had reached the home-folks in China.

It reminded me of a 2006 business trip to China where, upon
hearing that I had been "an American soldier", one Chinese
individual (fortunately, not a potential customer) asked if I had
possibly served as a "defeated American" in Korea during the
"glorious Chinese victory of 1950?" My first thought was, "Gosh,
do I look THAT old?" My second thought was, "What deranged,
totally lacking-in-fact history book did he pull that out of?" My
third thought was of my Uncle Jim and the wounded and dead GI's
and Marines that had valiantly fought off the Communist human
wave-assaults. My fourth thought was, I confess, both non-
Christian and un-charitable, as well as probably un-printable.

I found myself forcing a polite smile, taking a few deep breaths, all
the while biting my tongue to refrain from replying, "Oh, you
mean the time when the Army Rangers and U.S. Marines,
including my own flesh and blood, kicked the living snot out of

your treacherous PVA at Chosin Reservoir, as is well-documented in any 'free-and-open' historical literature source assuming the meanest intelligence of the reader?" I also suspect that my face was red and, perhaps, smoke was beginning to pour out of my ears. Fortunately, my wise and alert Chinese host took me gently but quickly by the arm and said, "Ah, Mr. Lauer, let us go get another Tsing Tao beer!"

Years earlier I remember U.S. public-service advertisements prior to the general elections in the early 1960's where a cartoon-"Joe Citizen" was shown saying, "I feel, I think, I vote." About that time, my Father hosted a dinner for an engineering colleague from Romania, at the time a country firmly planted behind the Communist "Iron Curtain." Sitting in our living-room before supper, the TV was on and, despite the ongoing conversation, I noticed that Dad's guest was watching the voting-ad. He turned, a genuinely puzzled look on his face and said, "You are encouraged to speak what you think and also vote? Your government will not see this as wise." At the time, I remember thinking how silly that sounded. Today, it strikes me as uniquely wonderful.

Here's what I really find really remarkable, though. According to Time Magazine figures, the conflict in Korea from June of 1950 into 1953 resulted in 900,000 Chinese and 1.8 million Korean deaths, truly staggering mortality numbers. American dead were numbered at 54,000 (the latest total I have seen is 58,267). It's almost beyond belief for me to understand how 900,000 Chinese families – mothers – could not have mourned their dead sons, as I know 54,000-plus American mothers did. It's impossible for me to believe that someone who has been told that their son or daughter has been killed in action could meekly accept the urging to, "Suck it up; he or she died for the State!", in essence a sacrifice for the "national communion." Nor could it be in any way, shape, or form compelling let alone possibly comforting. Somewhere in Asia I have to believe that grief-stricken mothers mourned their sons, even if they had to do so privately, totally alone and in secret.

When I was a boy in the '50s, several times I heard veterans quietly say, "Well, you know, life was always cheap to a Red."

Then, in the '60s I grew accustomed to hearing that this was "typical bourgeois verbiage" from the "industrial-military complex that runs Wall Street America." Time magazine, in their June 14, 1968 issue following the assassination of Robert Kennedy wrote, "For the young people in particular, who had been persuaded by the new politics of Robert Kennedy and Eugene McCarthy to recommit themselves to the American electoral system, the assassination seemed to confirm all their lingering suspicions that society could not be reformed by democratic means."

Viewed through the proverbial microscope of history, this statement and those seemingly-troubled times appear to be almost "quaint." Apparently, the perceived mood was that somehow utopia could be found only through "non-democratic means?" I would simply respond that Communism and their leaders had already explored that concept under the excuse of "the needs of the many outweigh the needs of the few" (thank you, Mr. Spock), and linked it with Werfel's statement regarding "...right is merely what serves the nation..."

The catch, of course, has been, "Oh, and WE (aka, the powers that be) decide who and how many 'the few' is/are!" This may sound just Jim-peachy-dandy, as long as you somehow don't find yourself in the very unfortunate group comprising "the few."

But, as the proverb goes, the devil is indeed in the details, particularly in the exact definition of just how many "the few" are as compared to "the many." Apparently to Joseph Stalin, several million starved and/or executed Russians and Ukrainians qualified as "the few." Similarly, 900,000 Chinese soldiers were apparently "the few" to Mao Tse Tung in Korea.

Again, per Time, the Viet Nam war claimed 57,605 American and 664,357 Vietnamese soldiers' lives. Apparently the 600,000 + dead North Vietnamese and Viet Cong troops met the definition of "the few" to Ho Chi Minh.

Yet for Americans, 54,000 in Korea or 57,000 in Viet Nam were far too many. In fact, for America, one dead GI, Sailor, Marine, or Airman is "too many." There's something that is both unsettling along with glorious about that concept to me. Simply, Americans don't like to decide how many lives to sacrifice, because even one single life matters to us.

In America, we built "The Wall" to remember our fallen Viet Nam soldiers. We've preserved the scenes and battles in hours of video and commentary. Reports and newscasts beamed into American homes in the late-'60s and early-'70s showed a daily record of the horror of armed combat and a litany of dead and dying American soldiers. The horrors of war were shown daily and there was nowhere for anyone to hide the facts.

When the Tet Offensive occurred in January of 1968, Communist leader Ho Chi Minh became despondent as military reports confirmed the horrible slaughter and failed objectives of his troops. He didn't realize at the time that he had, in fact, succeeded beyond his most fervent dreams. Although he had suffered a tactical military disaster in the field in Viet Nam, the shocked Western world had interpreted the mere presence of Communist troops in Saigon and other cities as an inevitable and strategic "Red Victory."

This same American mindset – the value of each and every life – has likely subjected us to the lessons of the last 40 years including the Iranian hostage-taking and suicide bombings on U. S. targets throughout the world, right up to watching the World Trade Towers crash down carrying along with them the innocent passengers of two large commercial airliners.

Obviously, the lives of Americans in those planes and on the ground were of no consequence whatsoever to the Islamic terrorists, any more than were and are the lives of individual Muslim suicide bombers. The both troubling and remarkable thing about this is: Americans continue to be unable to rationally fathom such actions.

In short, I think we take life itself so seriously and hold it as such a precious commodity that we cannot conceive of someone – anyone – who would slaughter humanity on such monstrous scales without an apparent regret or second thought, let alone an apology, at least to their own sacrificed people.

By contrast, America would never, ever have stayed in Korea with 900,000 dead American soldiers, or in Viet Nam with over a half-million dead troops. The Japanese, desperate to try anything at the very end of World War II, probably had precisely the right idea: force the United States to invade the main islands of Japan and inflict such massive, horrific casualties that the American Public would not be able to stomach further conflict. All it would have cost them would have been a couple of million Japanese troops and civilians.

Maybe it's our crowning, eternal glory and most luckless curse at the same time: we Americans treasure human life so dearly and with so much profound respect that we are willing to absorb "the first punch" or tolerate just about anything to avoid having to put our citizens in harm's way through armed combat.

But then, as America has often picked up the pieces and buried the dead, the American soldier has been called upon to "stand in the breach."

As was mentioned in the Introduction and coursing throughout this book, I've been morally guided, if you will, by MacArthur's theme of "Duty, Honor, Country." I was never a MacArthur-worshiper; as I've read various accounts regarding serving under him by other non-commissioned officers, I think that he was probably, as a senior military officer, a royal pain in the a__, along with possessing supreme self-serving and vain character flaws. But I also believe that he was brilliant as a strategic military leader and unquestionably a loyal patriot and American.

Again, in his West Point farewell speech given at the end of his military career on May 12, 1962, *"Duty, Honor, Country"*, he tried to further articulate what it means to be an American soldier. Even though his speech was directed to cadets at the U. S. Military Academy and, although he once more modestly claimed to be "inadequate to do so", I think he did a pretty okay job of speaking to all American soldiers when he said:

"The code which those words (Duty, Honor, Country) perpetuate embrace the highest moral laws and will stand the test of any ethics or philosophies ever promulgated for the uplift of mankind. Its requirements are for the things that are right, and its restraints are from the things that are wrong. The soldier, above all other men, is required to practice the greatest act of religious training – sacrifice.

In battle and in the face of danger and death, he discloses those divine attributes which his Maker gave when he created man in his own image. No physical courage and no brute instinct can take the place of the Divine help which alone can sustain him.

However horrible the incidents of war may be, the soldier who is called upon to offer and to give his life for his country is the noblest development of mankind.

...you are the ones trained to fight. Yours is the profession of arms, the will to win, the sure knowledge that in war there is no substitute for victory; that if you lose, the nation will be destroyed; that the very obsession of your public service must be: Duty, Honor, Country.

Others will debate the controversial issues, national and international, which divide men's minds; but serene, calm, aloof, you stand as the Nation's war-guardian, as its lifeguard from the raging tides of international conflict, as its gladiator in the arena of battle. For a century and a half you have defended, guarded, and protected its hallowed traditions of liberty and freedom, of right and justice.

...You are the leaven which binds together the entire fabric of our national system of defense. From your ranks come the great captains who hold the nations destiny in their hands the moment the war tocsin sounds. The Long Gray Line has never failed us. Were you to do so, a million ghosts in olive drab, in brown khaki, in blue and gray, would rise from their white crosses thundering those magic words: Duty, Honor, Country."

That's why I am unashamedly, unabashedly, and whole-heartedly proud of being part of a line of American soldiers. We've been raised to believe that Life is anything but cheap, whether it be American or not. When we've raised our right hands and taken the oath to "...preserve and defend the Constitution of the United States of America", it's not been just a promise to salute the flag or officiate over a "national communion." It has, instead, entailed preserving the ideas that "all men are created equal" and endowed with rights which cannot be stripped from them, that the Government exists for the benefit of citizens, not the other way around. And we've understood – maybe inherently – that each of our God-given lives is somehow, someway sacred, ironically as is its sacrifice, if necessary.

I believe that this is also the reason why American soldiers approach the question of "Why me?" in such a personal manner throughout their lives. We realize that the only comprehendible answer is: "Because it's the right thing to do for 'Duty, Honor, Country.'"

Sometimes, I think, a person simply decides to stake his or her life on doing the right thing at the right time even though the penalty – the sacrifice of one's life - is the ultimate one. I wonder if, just if, in those circumstances, the sole moment of absolute clarity in regard to the question of "Why me?" might come at that very last second of life when the soldier realizes that he or she is here precisely "for such a time as this ", the course of action is clear, the personal decision has been irrevocably made regarding "Duty, Honor, Country", and the doorstep into eternity simply awaits the soldier's next and final step.

SSG Barry A. Lauer – 7 yrs; Forever